ASEAN
ECONOMIC
COMMUNITY
SCORECARD

The **Institute of Southeast Asian Studies (ISEAS)** was established as an autonomous organization in 1968. It is a regional research centre dedicated to the study of socio-political, security and economic trends and developments in Southeast Asia and its wider geostrategic and economic environment. The Institute's research programmes are the Regional Economic Studies (RES, including ASEAN and APEC), Regional Strategic and Political Studies (RSPS), and Regional Social and Cultural Studies (RSCS).

ISEAS Publishing, an established academic press, has issued more than 2,000 books and journals. It is the largest scholarly publisher of research about Southeast Asia from within the region. ISEAS Publishing works with many other academic and trade publishers and distributors to disseminate important research and analyses from and about Southeast Asia to the rest of the world.

ASEAN ECONOMIC COMMUNITY SCORECARD

PERFORMANCE AND PERCEPTION

EDITED BY

SANCHITA BASU DAS

ISEAS

INSTITUTE OF SOUTHEAST ASIAN STUDIES

Singapore

First published in Singapore in 2013 by ISEAS Publishing
Institute of Southeast Asian Studies
30 Heng Mui Keng Terrace
Pasir Panjang
Singapore 119614

E-mail: publish@iseas.edu.sg
Website: <http://bookshop.iseas.edu.sg>

The responsibility for facts and opinions in this publication rests exclusively with the authors and their interpretations do not necessarily reflect the views or the policy of the publisher or its supporters.

ISEAS Library Cataloguing-in-Publication Data

ASEAN economic community scorecard : performance and perception / edited by Sanchita Basu Das.
1. Southeast Asia—Economic integration.
2. Southeast Asia—Economic conditions.
3. Southeast Asia—Foreign economic relations.
4. Investments—Southeast Asia.
5. ASEAN.
I. Basu Das, Sanchita.
HC441 A851   2013

ISBN 978-981-4414-30-2 (soft cover)
ISBN 978-981-4414-29-6 (E-book PDF)

Typeset by International Typesetters Pte Ltd
Printed in Singapore by Mainland Press Pte Ltd

CONTENTS

FOREWORD

Both this volume and the workshop that led to it were organized and coordinated by Sanchita Basu Das, lead researcher on economic matters in the ASEAN Studies Centre at the Institute of Southeast Asian Studies. On this account alone, and on others as well, we should all be grateful to Sanchita.

As conceived and carried out, the workshop revolved around the concept of a "scorecard" tracking the progress of ASEAN's march towards the ASEAN (Association of Southeast Asian Nations) Economic Community, which ASEAN has proclaimed itself as intending to achieve by 2015, or three years from the time of the workshop.

I am certainly aware that the ASEAN Secretariat maintains its own scorecard and publishes it as an important portion of its website. However, that scorecard seems to be dominated by things like the number of related ASEAN agreements that member-governments have ratified. Moreover, most of the data are supplied by governments, and what can be published, on the website or otherwise, is determined largely by officials.

Clearly, it is extremely important to know what officials think and what their governments' policies are. It is even more important to discern ASEAN countries' aspirations and commitments, which are indicated by the agreements that they conclude, ratify and carry out.

However, building an ASEAN Community, including the ASEAN Economic Community (AEC), involves not just governments and officials but also non-government traders and investors and other people. Furthermore, tracking its progress requires the hard work of sorting out the situation on the ground, of determining how far ASEAN has really gone in accomplishing the many purposes that the drafters of the AEC Blueprint set for the Community.

This is what this volume seeks to do, and we hope succeeds in doing.

Rodolfo C. Severino
Head, ASEAN Studies Centre, ISEAS
Secretary-General of ASEAN (1998–2002)

PREFACE

This book volume is a result of the ASEAN Roundtable 2012 on "Examining the ASEAN Economic Community (AEC) Scorecard" organized by the ASEAN Studies Centre (ASC) at the Institute of Southeast Asian Studies (ISEAS), along with the Konrad Adenauer Stiftung (KAS) on 25 May 2012 at York Hotel, Singapore. The primary objective of the roundtable was to evaluate the current status of and the progress towards the milestones described in the AEC Blueprint. The policy recommendations necessary to meet the end-goals of AEC was expected to help the policy-makers in the future years.

Before elaborating on the progress of implementing the blueprint, let me first give a brief background on AEC. The ASEAN Leaders signed the Declaration of ASEAN Concord II in October 2003 aiming at AEC as an end goal of its economic integration to be achieved by 2020. The Leaders agreed to accelerate AEC establishment to 2015 during the Summit in January 2007 and adopted the AEC Blueprint in the following Summit in November 2007. The end-goal of the AEC is to create a single market and production base where there is free flow of goods, services, investments, capital and skilled labour.

The AEC Blueprint is the first of its kind for ASEAN. The Blueprint is defined by its four main characteristics, namely a single market and production base, a highly competitive economic region, a region of equitable economic development, and a region fully integrated into the global economy. It is further elaborated like a grand plan, consisting of roadmaps to deliver specific outcomes (objectives of the AEC). The Blueprint identified 17 "core elements" to be carried out by 176 "priority actions", all of which are to be undertaken within a "strategic schedule" of four implementation periods (2008–09, 2010–11, 2012–13; and 2014–15). The 17 core elements are listed in Table 1.

TABLE 1
17 Core Elements of the AEC Blueprint

Single Market and Production Base	Competitive Economic Region	Equitable Economic Development	Integration into the Global Economy
1. Free flow of goods 2. Free flow of services 3. Free flow of investment 4. Freer flow of capital 5. Free flow of skilled labour 6. Priority Integration Sectors 7. Food, Agriculture and Forestry	8. Competition Policy 9. Consumer Protection 10. Intellectual Property Rights 11. Infrastructure Development 12. Taxation 13. E-Commerce	14. SME development 15. Initiative for ASEAN Integration (IAI)	16. Coherent Approach towards External Economic Relations 17. Enhanced participation in global supply networks

Source: AEC Blueprint, ASEAN Secretariat, 2008.

The implementation of the Blueprint, as indicated in the AEC Strategic Schedule, is monitored through the AEC Scorecard. The objective of the Scorecard is to follow specific actions that must be undertaken by ASEAN collectively and by its Member States individually to establish AEC by 2015. Till 2012, the ASEAN Secretariat has issued two AEC scorecards, which stipulates that ASEAN has achieved 68.2 per cent of its targets during 2008–11.

This book consists of ten insightful chapters, with seven looking at the core elements of the blueprint — free flow of goods, free flow of services, free flow of investment, free flow of skilled labour, infra-structure development, SME development and Initiative for ASEAN Integration (IAI). The chapters' main focus are to discuss the progress in each of these core elements and hence analyse its effectiveness in meeting the final objective.

This exercise is in parallel to the official AEC scorecard, which gives an aggregate number and is too general to be useful for the understanding of the public. The seven chapters of this publication fill the gap of providing detailed information.

The first introductory chapter links the most important discussions of the later issue-based chapters (chapters 3 to 9). The chapter gives an overall picture of the progress and challenges towards building an AEC and also assesses the usefulness of the AEC Scorecard to meet the said objectives. In addition, the introduction gives concrete policy recommendations that the editor believes would be helpful for the ASEAN policy-makers. The second chapter on "Monitoring the ASEAN Economic Community: Issues and Challenges" gives a brief account of the implementation process as monitored by the official AEC Scorecard. It further discusses the issues and challenges in monitoring the AEC.

The last chapter (chapter 10), a departure from the rest, looks at a country. As an editor for the volume, I felt that it is important to look at Myanmar and its participation in AEC separately. This is because after elections in 2010, Myanmar is now on its way to transform its economy with a slew of political and economic reforms. These reforms will continue as ASEAN prepares to launch its economic community in 2015. A year before that, in 2014, Myanmar will chair ASEAN, which involves hosting the ten-nation group's summits and key political and economic meetings, as well as the wider East Asia Summit that includes the U.S. and Russia. Additionally, Myanmar has not been included in publications looking at ASEAN member countries with respect to

AEC [such as *Achieving the ASEAN Economic Community by 2015: Challenges for Member Countries and Businesses* (2010)]. This volume will address that gap.

I hope this volume will serve as a parallel tool to the official AEC scorecard in order to closely look at the ASEAN economic integration process. The policy-makers, academia and professionals on ASEAN economics can refer to this book to understand the progress and impediments of building an AEC. I hope that the policy-makers will benefit from the recommendations.

Sanchita Basu Das
Editor

ACKNOWLEDGEMENTS

This roundtable discussion was conducted as part of the research activities by the ASEAN Studies Centre (ASC) at the Institute of Southeast Asian Studies (ISEAS), Singapore. Being the coordinator, I sincerely thank Ambassador Tan Chin Tiong, Director of ISEAS and Dr Wilhelm Hofmeister, Director, Konrad Adenauer Stiftung for their kind support in facilitating the project. I am grateful to both Ambassador Tan Chin Tiong and Dr Hosfmeister for delivering the opening remarks at the roundtable, highlighting the fact that ASEAN needs to strengthen its monitoring process in order to effectively track the implementation of ASEAN economic initiatives.

I would like to thank Mr Rodolfo Severino, Head of ASC, for his invaluable advice on the research activity and for writing the foreword for this volume. I acknowledge the chapter writers of this book, who revised their papers to reflect the comments and opinions expressed at the roundtable on 25 May 2012. I thank Ms Moe Thuzar (ASC) who shared her knowledge on Myanmar and ASEAN with us by contributing a chapter in this volume.

Special thanks are also due to Lily Koh and Hnin Wint Nyunt Hman (ASC) who assisted me tirelessly in holding the roundtable at York Hotel, Singapore. I would like to thank Mrs Y.L. Lee and her team at ISEAS for the administrative efforts to make the event a success. Finally, I gratefully acknowledge the dedicated support of Mrs Triena Ong and her staff at the ISEAS Publications Unit for the publication of this book.

Sanchita Basu Das
Editor

THE CONTRIBUTORS

Raymond Atje was ex-Head, Department of Economics of the Centre for Strategic and International Studies (CSIS), Jakarta, Indonesia.

Manu Bhaskaran is a Partner and Member of the Board, Centennial Group Inc., Singapore.

Chia Siow Yue is a Senior Research Fellow at the Singapore Institute of International Affairs (SIIA), Singapore.

Supunnavadee Jitdumrong is currently studying at the London School of Economics. She was a trainee at Thailand Development Research Institute (TDRI), while co-authoring the chapter.

Pratiwi Kartika is a researcher at the Department of Economics, Centre for Strategic and International Studies (CSIS), Jakarta, Indonesia.

Deunden Nikomborirak is the Research Director (Sectoral Economics Programme) at the Thailand Development Research Institute (TDRI), Bangkok, Thailand.

Aladdin D. Rillo is the Director in ASEAN Integration Monitoring Office of ASEAN Secretariat, Jakarta, Indonesia.

Firdaos Rosli is a senior analyst in economics at the Institute of Strategic and International Studies, Malaysia.

Chap Sotharith is the Research Director of the Cambodian Institute for Cooperation and Peace (CICP), Phnom Penh, Cambodia.

Vo Tri Thanh is the Deputy Director General at the Central Institute of Economic Management (CIEM), Vietnam.

Moe Thuzar is an ISEAS Fellow and Lead Researcher (Socio-Cultural affairs) at the ASEAN Studies Centre, Institute of Southeast Asian Studies, Singapore.

Mahani Zainal Abidin is the Chief Executive of the Institute of Strategic and International Studies, Malaysia.

The EDITOR

Sanchita Basu Das is an ISEAS Fellow and Lead Researcher (Economic Affairs) at the ASEAN Studies Centre, Institute of Southeast Asian Studies, Singapore. She has also published the following titles:

Enchancing ASEAN's Connectivity
(editor)

Achieving the ASEAN' Economic Community:
Challenges for Member Countries and Businesses
(editor)

Road to Recovery:
Singapore's Journey through the Global Crisis

1

ASSESSING THE PROGRESS AND IMPEDIMENTS TOWARDS AN ASEAN ECONOMIC COMMUNITY

Sanchita Basu Das

The Association of Southeast Asian Nations (ASEAN) Vision 2020, adopted in December 1997, envisaged "a stable, prosperous and highly competitive ASEAN economic region in which there is a free flow of goods, services, investment and freer flow of capital, equitable economic development and reduced poverty and socioeconomic disparities" by the year 2020. It took a decade for ASEAN to translate its vision into a blueprint. The ASEAN Leaders signed the Declaration of the ASEAN (Bali) Concord II in October 2003 aiming to form an ASEAN Economic Community (AEC) as an end goal of its economic integration. In January 2007, the ASEAN Leaders agreed to accelerate the establishment of the AEC to 2015. They adopted the AEC Blueprint in November 2007.

The AEC Blueprint is a binding declaration and stipulates that "each ASEAN Member Country shall abide by and implement the AEC by 2015." It is organized along the lines of the AEC's four primary objectives: (a) a single market and production base; (b) a highly competitive economic region; (c) a region of equitable economic development; and (d) a region fully integrated into the global economy, with 17 "core elements" and 176 "priority actions", to be undertaken within a Strategic Schedule of four implementation periods (2008–09, 2010–11, 2012–13 and, 2014–15). Ministers concerned from each country and the ASEAN Secretariat were tasked to implement the AEC Blueprint and report regularly on the progress of its implementation to the Council of the AEC.

In the process of its implementation, therefore, ASEAN decided to come up with an AEC scorecard, which is expected to track the implementation of measures and the achievement of milestones committed in the AEC Strategic Schedule. The AEC Scorecard was developed based on similar initiatives such as the EU Internal Market Scorecard.[1] It is aimed at identifying specific actions that must be undertaken by ASEAN collectively and its Member States individually to establish AEC by 2015. It should be noted that currently the AEC Scorecard is only a compliance tool and not a mechanism for impact assessment.

Since the Blueprint was adopted, ASEAN Secretariat came out with two official scorecards, one in 2010 and the other in 2012. According to the scorecard, published in March 2012, ASEAN had achieved 68.2 per cent of its targets for the 2008–11 period. While the first scorecard for 2008–09 reported an implementation rate of around 87.6 per cent of 105 total measures, the second scorecard for 2010–11 reported a lower rate of 56.4 per cent of 172 measures.

But how transparent and efficient is the official AEC Scorecard? A regional economic scorecard is expected to serve as an unbiased assessment tool to measure the extent of integration among its members and the economic health of the region. The scores are expected to create incentives for improvement by highlighting what is working and what is not. Moreover, the AEC scorecard is expected to reflect the true nature of implementation of the measures stipulated in the Blueprint and not just the ratification by all member countries.

Given this, the chapter evaluates the current status of and the progress towards the milestones of the AEC Blueprint and assesses the usefulness of the AEC Scorecard to meet the end-goals. It looks into all the four pillars of AEC Blueprint but focuses more on certain aspects of each pillar. In case of "single market and production base", the chapter looks into four key areas of liberalization — trade in goods, trade in services,

Foreign Direct Investment (FDI), and movement of skilled labour. While for "Competitive Economic Region" the chapter discusses ASEAN's infrastructure connectivity, for "Equitable Economic Development", the discussion is on Small and Medium scale Enterprises (SMEs) and Initiative of ASEAN Integration (IAI). The chapter provides some limitations of the AEC Scorecard and concludes with policy recommendations.

Pillar I: Single Market and Production Base

According to the AEC Scorecard, published by the ASEAN Secretariat in March 2012, the Pillar I — Single Market and Production Base — is said to have implemented 65.9 per cent of the total of 173 targeted measures for the period from 2008–11 (see Table 1.1).

Free Flow of Goods

(i) Tariff and Non-Tariff Barriers (NTBs)[2]

During 2008–11, 57.1 per cent of 56 targeted measures have been implemented under the "free flow of goods". ASEAN-6[3] countries have

TABLE 1.1

Single Market and Production Base Scorecard

Key Areas	Phase I (2008–09)		Phase II (2010–11)		Total Measures	
	FI	NFI	FI	NFI	FI	NFI
Free Flow of Goods	9	0	23	24	32	24
Free Flow of Services	10	3	13	17	23	20
Free Flow of Investment	5	1	5	8	10	9
Free Flow of Capital	1	0	5	0	6	0
Free Flow of Skilled Labour	–	–	1	0	1	0
Priority Integration Sectors	28	0	1	0	29	0
Food, Agriculture and Forestry	8	0	5	6	13	6
Total Number of Measures	61	4	53	55	114	59
Implementation Rate	93.8%		49.1%		65.9%	

Note: FI — fully implemented; NFI — not fully implemented.
Implementation rate is calculated as the ratio of measures that are fully implemented to total number of measures targeted.
(–) depicts no measure targeted for the phase.
Source: ASEAN Economic Community Scorecard, ASEAN Secretariat, 2012.

applied zero tariffs on 99 per cent of goods. The CLMV[4] countries are trading 98.6 per cent of goods at 0–5 per cent of tariff rate. According to Pratiwi Kartika and Raymond Atje (chapter 3), ASEAN-6 countries are also liberalizing ahead of schedule as the number of tariff lines whose tariff is zero is larger than the Inclusion List (IL) products that are scheduled to be duty free by 2010.

ASEAN Trade in Goods Agreement (ATIGA) came into effect in May 2010. This is a comprehensive document that consolidates all commitments related to trade in goods and focuses on tariff liberalization, non-tariff measures, simplification of Rules of Origin and its implementation.

However, removal of non-tariff barriers (NTBs) remains a key issue. The AEC Blueprint clearly states that "the main focus of ASEAN towards 2015 will be placed on the full elimination of NTBs". According to the AEC schedule, ASEAN-5 is expected to have eliminated NTBs by 2010, the Philippines by 2012 and Cambodia, Laos, Myanmar and Vietnam by 2015 with flexibility to 2018 for some sensitive products. Removing the NTBs is very crucial for the region as this reduces the transaction cost of doing business in ASEAN. Moreover, being a key partner of the production network in the region, an increase in the production and administrative costs may deter the investment in the region.

But many ASEAN states are struggling to remove the NTBs. According to a study done by Ando and Obashi in 2010, almost half of all tariff lines in ASEAN were linked to at least one non-tariff measure (NTM). The same study states that while Myanmar, Indonesia and the Philippines were countries applying most of the NTMs, Cambodia and Thailand are the least NTM-restrictive countries.

It is widely accepted that while some trade barriers are necessary — for example, to protect the environment or the health of humans, animals and plants — others unnecessarily distort trade flows and restrict competition. In case of ASEAN, surveys (Eddy and Owen 2007) of business firms operating in the region reveal that facilitating import clearances, license applications and renewals, testing, customs inspections, and work permits are major concerns for businesses. A problem common to several, but not all, ASEAN countries is corruption in the form of bribery. The length of time required for customs refunds and the declaration of goods was cited as a serious impediment to trade.

Moreover, ASEAN faces a constant challenge of demand for protection from its domestic industries. As Nesadurai (2012) points out, a crucial feature of ASEAN's political economy is a close relationship between the

TABLE 1.2

Logistics Performance Index of ASEAN States, 2012

	Rank	Score	% of Highest Performer
Cambodia	101	2.56	50.0
Indonesia	59	2.94	62.2
Laos	109	2.50	48.0
Malaysia	29	3.49	79.8
Myanmar	129	2.37	43.8
Philippines	52	3.02	64.8
Singapore	1	4.13	100.0
Thailand	38	3.18	69.6
Vietnam	53	3.00	64.1

Source: LPI ranking and scores, World Bank, 2012.

ruling elites and the business sector, whether state-owned enterprises, Government-Linked Corporations (GLCs) or private businesses, and this distorts ASEAN's objective of regionalism.

(ii) Logistics

In order to benefit from free flow of goods, ASEAN needs to reduce transportation and logistics costs between and within member countries. According to the Logistics Performance Index (LPI)[5] 2012 (see Table 1.2), there is a wide gap among the ASEAN member states' logistics performance. The gap is so wide that Singapore is ranked 1st and Myanmar is ranked 129th out of 155 countries surveyed.

(iii) Trade Facilitation

As a part of the trade facilitation process, ASEAN plans to form an ASEAN Single Window (ASW), which is a network of the National Single Windows (NSW) of all ASEAN countries. As of 2010, Indonesia, the Philippines, Singapore and Thailand have largely implemented the NSW. But they face several challenges in increasing the effectiveness of their respective NSWs (Pratiwi Kartika and Raymond Atje, chapter 3). These include inefficient coordination among domestic agencies, lack of appropriate human resources for customs matters, and low level of public awareness of NSW efforts and regulations. Cambodia, Laos, Myanmar and Vietnam are still at an early stage and are struggling with their NSWs to be established by 2015.

At the regional level, an ASW pilot project is underway, involving seven states: Brunei, Indonesia, Malaysia, the Philippines, Singapore, Thailand and Vietnam. The project has three components: a study of the establishment of the most feasible network architecture (already completed in February 2011), the setting up of the network infrastructure and conducting evaluations on the outcome of the project, which is at its final phase.

Free Flow of Services

During 2008–11, 53.5 per cent of 43 targeted measures have been "implemented" under free flow of services. Although the services sector makes up a large share of member states' GDPs (52 per cent for Indonesia, 50 per cent in Thailand, 54 per cent in the Philippines) and the employment share in the services industries has been rising, there has been little advancement in the liberalization of the sector, which lags well behind that of trade in goods (Deunden Nikomborirak and Supunnavadee Jitdumrong, chapter 4).

ASEAN has completed seven packages of commitments (at least 65 services sub-sector) to liberalize services trade under the ASEAN Framework Agreement in Services (AFAS). But negotiations for the past fifteen years have resulted only in marginal liberalization of trade in services for ASEAN. AFAS, initially, relied on the WTO's General Agreement on Trade in Services (GATS) form of negotiation. Hence, AFAS did not go much beyond the GATS and did not provide much impetus to liberalize services trade within ASEAN.

It should be noted that service liberalization targets mentioned in the AEC Blueprint are far from those required to support full integration of member economies. First, liberalization in mode 3 (commercial presence) envisions only 70 per cent of ASEAN equity shares. Second, liberalization in mode 4 (movement of natural persons) is confined to movement of professional only; unskilled labour is excluded. There are also many flexibilities and exceptions built into the AEC Blueprint itself, which allow for the possibility of catching up of goals not accomplished in a previous round of liberalization in another AFAS package, substituting targeted sub-sectors for liberalization with those not targeted in the Blueprint, and using the ASEAN minus X formula to meet commitments.

With regard to complying with the AEC Blueprint, in the 7th package, every member country, except for Singapore, has fallen behind liberalization goals in terms of foreign equity participation (mode 3) in 2008 and in 2010. In addition, domestic restrictions with regard to equity holding, land holding, licensing etc. continue to pose significant barriers to intra-regional investment in services. Mode 1 and Mode 2 (removing restrictions on cross-border supply and consumption abroad) have mostly been complied with exceptions for the construction industry.

The financial services sector has delayed its liberalization target to 2020 and member states may choose which part of their financial sectors to liberalize.

Free Flow of Investment

Since the 1997–98 crisis, ASEAN has been struggling to raise the foreign direct investment (FDI) in the region. Also with the opening up of China and India, the region faces serious competition in reclaiming its FDI share of early 1990s. Although ASEAN does provide competitive returns to investors, most investors demand high risk premiums, implying that a risk reduction plan is necessary for member states to increase FDI flows (Manu Bhaskaran, chapter 5).

As an important initiative, the Leaders endorsed the ASEAN Comprehensive Investment Agreement (ACIA) in April 2012. This is a comprehensive agreement covering liberalization, protection, facilitation and promotion and includes new provisions as well as improvements to ASEAN Investment Area (AIA) and ASEAN Investment Guarantee Agreement (AIGA) provisions. But enforceability of the agreement is an issue. According to an ERIA study, 69 complaints were filed for lack of transparency and 121 complaints were for complicated and delayed procedure in 2010. Most of the complaints were in Indonesia, Malaysia, Thailand and Vietnam, suggesting investment facilitation problems.

It should be noted that the regional investment initiatives should be supplemented with proper domestic investment policy. According to the World Bank's annual Ease of Doing Business Index and the World Economic Forum's Global Competitive Index, countries that rank well often attract more FDI (see Table 1.3). In addition, members with better investment climates, i.e. higher incentives and lower country risks, tend to have higher levels of FDI. Singapore, Malaysia and Thailand rank high on the investment scale while Brunei, Cambodia, Indonesia, Laos

TABLE 1.3
Attractiveness of ASEAN Member Countries

	Ease of Doing Business, 2012[1]	Global Competitiveness Index, 2012–13[2]
Brunei	83	28
Cambodia	138	85
Indonesia	129	50
Laos	165	–
Malaysia	18	25
Myanmar	–	
Philippines	136	65
Singapore	1	2
Thailand	17	38
Vietnam	98	75

Note: 1 — out of 183 economies; 2 — out of 144 countries.
Source: Doing Business 2012, World Bank; World Competitiveness Index, 2012–13.

and Philippines rank low in doing business and in competitiveness. Vietnam ranks relatively well, but its competitiveness is low in last few years due to its macroeconomic problems.

On the basis of the AEC Blueprint, the achievement of scorecard goals *vis-à-vis* investment has been sub-par. Phase 1 of the Scorecard had an 83.3 per cent "implementation" rate. However, Phase 2 had a disappointing rate of only 38.5 per cent, getting an average of only 52.6 per cent implementation rate for both phases together. Between 2010 and 2011, countries suffered from the inability to implement most of the measures planned under "free flow of investment".

Main problems with the regional agreements lie with their enforceability (Manu Bhaskaran, chapter 5). The agreements often have underlying clauses (along with temporary exclusion and sensitivity lists) that allow member countries to delay or opt out of implementing measures. Moreover, most regional investment agreements have to be supplemented with effective and well carved-out domestic investment policies. Activities in support of investment promotion and facilitation need to be carried out on schedule and infrastructure development must quicken in order to encourage private investment.

Free Flow of Skilled Labour

The free flow of skilled labour has direct impact on the targeted goals of AFAS Mode 4 on labour movement, the ASEAN Comprehensive Investment Agreement (ACIA), and as a result, AEC integration as a whole. According to the AEC scorecard for 2008–11, the measures under the free flow of skilled labour are "fully implemented". However, implementation in the scorecard means only the signing of agreements at the regional level. There are no reports on the domestic implementation of the MRAs and their effectiveness.

ASEAN countries can be divided into three groups with respect to the mobility of professionals: first, Singapore, Brunei and Thailand (to a certain extent) are cases of net brain gain, where inflows exceed outflows. Second is the case of brain drain in Malaysia and the Philippines, where outflows of skills exceed inflows. Third is the case of Indonesia, Cambodia, Laos and Vietnam, where flows of manpower do not have any particular trend. In these countries, inflows are limited by restrictive regulations, while outflows are less significant because of a small pool of professionals in the country (Chia Siow Yue, chapter 6).

ASEAN governments have allowed flows of skilled professionals (Mode 4) for reasons like facilitating FDI; meeting commitments under GATS; meeting short-term skill shortages etc. For regulatory harmonization, ASEAN provides MRAs, wherein each country may recognize education and experience, licenses and certificates granted in another country. Until now, ASEAN has concluded seven MRAs. Among these, only engineering and architectural services provide standardized recognition of the skills level of registered ASEAN architects and engineers. It should be noted that MRAs do not contain any liberalization commitments but only frameworks or procedures to facilitate the flow of certain professional services between member states. This generates flexibilities and allows member states not to commit to carry out agreements (Deunden Nikomborirak and Supunnavadee Jitdumrong, chapter 4).

Moreover, many countries impose restrictions on foreign nationals or non-residents working as professionals. For example, in Thailand, the Alien Employment Act remains in force. The Act requires a work permit for all foreigners working in the country. Thailand has yet to adopt domestic legislation to implement MRAs. Hence, negotiations of MRAs cannot be equated with market access and effective intra-ASEAN mobility of skilled labour.

A major challenge in the certification of professional qualifications and skills across ASEAN countries is the wide difference in educational systems, training and standards. To address this issue, ASEAN established the ASEAN University Network (AUN), which aimed to promote cooperation among professionals and encourage information dissemination among policy-makers, academic communities and other relevant users.

Pillar II: Competitive Economic Region

The AEC Scorecard states that the second pillar of AEC Blueprint has met 67.9 per cent of its targets of 78 (see Table 1.4).

TABLE 1.4

Competitive Economic Region Scorecard

Key Areas	Phase I (2008–09)		Phase II (2010–11)		Total Measures	
	FI	NFI	FI	NFI	FI	NFI
Competition Policy	2	0	2	0	4	0
Consumer Protection	2	0	5	4	7	4
Intellectual Property Rights	–	–	4	1	4	1
Transport	15	10	6	8	21	18
Energy	0	0	2	1	2	1
Mineral	1	0	7	0	8	0
ICT	2	0	4	0	6	0
Taxation	–	–	0	1	0	1
E-Commerce	–	–	1	0	1	0
Total Number of Measures	22	10	31	15	53	25
Implementation Rate	68.7%		67.4%		67.9%	

Note: FI — fully implemented; NFI — not fully implemented.
Implementation rate is calculated as the ratio of measures that are fully implemented to total number of measures targeted.
(–) depicts no measure targeted for the phase.
Source: ASEAN Economic Community Scorecard, ASEAN Secretariat, 2012.

It should be noted that AEC's objective of a competitive economic region has two aspects: first, there has to be an effective standardized competition policy in the region. However, competition policy is essentially national in application. Malaysia, Philippines and Brunei have yet to enact anti-monopoly laws. Singapore, Indonesia, Thailand and Vietnam have propagated a competition law and have established independent competition authorities. Given the vast differences in ASEAN member states, it looks difficult to have a uniform competition policy regionally. In the long run, what could be achieved is some form of coordination and cooperation across the member states.

Infrastructure Development

The other aspect of the region's competitiveness is with respect to the rest of the world. For this to happen, infrastructure is a key component. The availability of a good infrastructure network in ASEAN is a necessary factor to increase intra-regional trade and investment. In ASEAN, infrastructure development centres mainly on transport, energy, and ICT.

According to the AEC Scorecard, in phase 1, all outstanding measures are in the transport sector. As of April 2012, none of the ASEAN countries have ratified Protocol 2 (designation of frontier posts) and Protocol 7 (customs transit system) of the ASEAN Framework Agreement on the Facilitation of Goods in Transit (AFAFGIT). In addition, three ASEAN countries have yet to ratify Protocol 1 (designation of transit transport routes and facilities) of AFAFGIT.

According to the AEC Scorecard II, transport sector is the biggest laggard with the necessary domestic legislation not enacted for the ASEAN Framework Agreement on Multimodal Transport, ASEAN Framework Agreement on Inter-State Transport, the ASEAN Multilateral Agreement on the Full Liberalization of Passenger Air Services, Protocol 6 of AFAFGIT, the ASEAN Single Shipping Market, and the ASEAN Interconnection Projects. In addition, ASEAN countries find it difficult to reach a common position on implementing soft infrastructure initiatives such as in trade facilitation and customs cooperation (Mahani Zainal Abidin and Firdaos Rosli, chapter 7).

Recognizing the importance of infrastructure, ASEAN adopted the Master Plan on ASEAN Connectivity (MPAC) in 2010. The Plan focuses on improving physical connectivity, people-to-people connectivity and institutional connectivity in ASEAN. It covers all sectors in transport cooperation — land, air, maritime and transport facilitation. According to the Asian Development Bank, ASEAN needs about US$60 billion a year for infrastructure investment for the 2010–20 period. With a well-developed physical infrastructure, ASEAN is envisaged to increase its intra-regional trade to 40 per cent from 24 per cent currently.

Large flows of capital to finance ASEAN infrastructure projects are clearly needed. In May 2012, the ASEAN Infrastructure Fund (AIF) commenced its operation, with a planned start-up capital of US$485.2 million. In addition to the conventional multilateral development banks like the ADB and the World Bank, the role of ASEAN Dialogue Partners is also important in providing financial support to the projects. Finally, the model of public-private partnership is also gaining importance in the light of huge financing needs of ASEAN infrastructure.

Pillar III: Equitable Economic Development

According to the official AEC Scorecard, the third pillar of the AEC Blueprint has achieved 66.7 per cent of its targets (see Table 1.5).

TABLE 1.5

Equitable Economic Development Scorecard

Key Areas	Phase I (2008–09)		Phase II (2010–11)		Total Measures	
	FI	NFI	FI	NFI	FI	NFI
SME Development	1	0	4	3	5	3
Initiative of ASEAN Integration (IAI)	2	0	1	1	3	1
Total Number of Measures	3	0	5	5	8	4
Implementation Rate	100%		55.5%		66.7%	

Note: FI — fully implemented; NFI — not fully implemented.
Implementation rate is calculated as the ratio of measures that are fully implemented to total number of measures targeted.
Source: ASEAN Economic Community Scorecard, ASEAN Secretariat, 2012.

ASEAN faces a serious challenge of development divide among its member states (see Table 1.6). To narrow this gap so that all ASEAN members can reap the benefits of economic integration, the AEC Blueprint looks at two key areas — SME development and Initiative of ASEAN Integration (IAI).

The role of SMEs has become increasingly important for ASEAN as many member countries are challenged by decline in shares of agriculture and industry in total GDP. Moreover, SMEs account for more than 96 per cent of all enterprises and 50–85 per cent of domestic employment. It contributes 30–53 per cent to national GDPs and accounts for 19–31 per cent of a country's exports. As for the IAI programme, it was established in 2000. The first IAI Work Plan, covering the period 2002–08 included infrastructure development, human resources development, ICT development, and capacity building. In 2005, this Work Plan was extended to cover three additional areas — tourism, poverty and quality of life, and general coverage projects. The IAI Work Plan II (2009–15) retains all the seven priority projects. While the first Plan contributed significantly in ICT, the second one currently supports projects in infrastructure development, regional economic development and tourism.

SME Development in ASEAN

Under Pillar III in the AEC scorecard, SME development is said to have "implemented" 62.5 per cent of eight targeted measures for the period 2008–11. With the establishment of its first SME Working Group in 1995, ASEAN continues its efforts on SME development with its ASEAN Policy Blueprint for SME Development (APBSD) 2004–14 and the ASEAN Strategic Action Plan for SME Development (2010–15). The Plan outlines the framework for SME development and covers mandates stipulated in the Blueprint, while the APBSD 2004–14 outlines the framework for SME development in ASEAN and comprises strategic work programmes, policy measures, and indicative outputs.

However, as is evident in the incomplete implementation rate, SME development faces challenges, including limited access to finance and technology, severe competition from MNCs and SMEs of other countries such as China, Japan, and Korea, weak entrepreneurial and management skills, lack of awareness of AEC initiatives and benefits,

TABLE 1.6
State of Development Divide in ASEAN

	Per Capita GDP (PPP, US$)	Trade to GDP Ratio, 2011	HDI Ranking, 2011	Poverty Headcount Ratio (% of population),* Latest Year
Brunei	49,384	99	33	–
Cambodia	2,065	126	139	53.3 (2008)
Indonesia	4,352	44	124	46.1 (2010)
Laos	2,449	64	138	66 (2008)
Malaysia	14,744	148	61	2.3 (2009)
Myanmar	1,254	33	149	–
Philippines	3,920	52	112	41.5 (2009)
Singapore	56,708	298	26	–
Thailand	9,222	132	103	4.6 (2009)
Vietnam	3,143	166	128	43.4 (2008)

Note: *The population living on less than $2.00 a day at 2005 international prices.
Source: World Economic Outlook, IMF; World Trade Organisation; Human Development Report, UNDP, 2011; World Bank.

and difficulties in complying with AEC preferences and market standards (Chap Sotharith, chapter 8).

Initiative for ASEAN Integration

According to the AEC Scorecard II, the IAI programme has achieved 75 per cent of four targeted measures. However, it should be noted that the actions under the IAI programme are very generic like building capacity of government officials to develop/implement economic and social policies.

Despite a high "implementation" rate, there are several challenges with the IAI programme. It was been found that the IAI programme areas may not fully fit the CLMV's key priorities. For instance, Myanmar and Vietnam need to address the issues of agricultural development and climate change, respectively. Yet these areas were not incorporated in the IAI Work Plans. The main reason for the mismatch could be the attempt to adopt a common framework for all CLMV countries, ignoring their heterogeneity and different long-term needs. Many times the areas covered under the IAI are too ambitious given the resource and time constraint. The countries also lack the necessary institutions to implement trade and investment reforms, hence slowing down the process of integration (Vo Tri Thanh, chapter 9).

In several instances, the IAI may not follow closely the new issues or challenges. These include the emergence of bilateral and regional FTAs, the urgency of meeting the targets of AEC 2015 or the rising BRICS[6] economies in the aftermath of the global financial crisis. Lastly, IAI lacks adequate consultation with all relevant stakeholders in the CLMV, which can help identify their needs and give support to other modalities (technical assistance, cooperation, training etc.) of project delivery.

Pillar IV: Integration into the Global Economy

This is one of the most successful pillars of the AEC Blueprint with 85.7 per cent of the total targets met, as per the official ASEAN scorecard (see Table 1.7).

ASEAN continued to support the creation of ASEAN Plus One Free Trade Agreements (FTAs). The region saw the realization of the ASEAN-

TABLE 1.7

Integration into the Global Economy Scorecard

Key Areas	Phase I (2008–09)		Phase II (2010–11)		Total Measures	
	FI	NFI	FI	NFI	FI	NFI
External Economic Relations	5	0	7	2	12	2
Total Number of Measures	5	0	7	2	12	2
Implementation Rate	100%		77.8%		85.7%	

Note: FI — fully implemented; NFI — not fully implemented.
Implementation rate is calculated as the ratio of measures that are fully implemented to total number of measures targeted.
Source: ASEAN Economic Community Scorecard, ASEAN Secretariat, 2012.

China and ASEAN-Korea FTA, commencement of ASEAN-CER FTA and the ASEAN-India trade in goods agreement. ASEAN also played a role of "bridge builder" among countries in the greater scope of Asia. It drove the process of ASEAN+3, East Asia Summit and the latest Regional Comprehensive Economic Partnership (RCEP). The addition of the U.S. and Russia in EAS affirms the importance of ASEAN and the value of ASEAN centrality in the regional and global arena.

Official AEC Scorecard

As mentioned earlier in the chapter, ASEAN developed an AEC scorecard, which is expected to track the implementation of measures and the achievement of milestones committed in the AEC Strategic Schedule. It is aimed at identifying specific actions that must be undertaken by ASEAN collectively and its Member States individually to establish AEC by 2015. According to the scorecard, published in March 2012, ASEAN had achieved 68.2 per cent of its targets for the 2008–11 period.

But the AEC scorecard, in its current form, is not very useful. Although it specifies that the shortfall is mainly caused by delays in the ratification of signed ASEAN-wide agreements, their integration into national laws, and in the implementation of specific initiatives, the aggregate scores fail to reveal the true rates of implementation for individual countries. It is too brief and omits too much detail to be informative to various ASEAN stakeholders. The aggregate scores fail to reveal the reasons for delays.

The scorecard does not give a country-specific breakdown, and is too general to be useful for the ASEAN citizens. It also defies the understanding of the private sector as it does not assess the benefits for the policy implemented in terms of lower transaction cost, reduced prices and expanded consumer choices.

Policy Recommendations

It could be inferred from the above, that it is highly unlikely that ASEAN would be able to meet all its integration goals by the year 2015. On the other hand, one needs to see the ASEAN economic integration as an on-going process for which the leaders (not sure) have laid down the initial foundation by 2015. Rest of the process would follow beyond 2015.

From now on, what is important for ASEAN is to deliver on its promises as stipulated in the AEC Blueprint in the shortest possible time. This is to raise its profile and maintain centrality in the international community. Few points that ASEAN must keep in mind are as follows:

1. Achieving the milestones set in the AEC Blueprint requires cooperation and coordination among different sectors of the economy. Each member country has to align its national policies to their regional initiatives.

2. ASEAN has to work towards bridging the development gaps among its member states. In fact, it is not necessary for the CLMV countries to catch up with the ASEAN-6 but they should reach a level of development which will allow them to effectively participate in the AEC process.

3. The most important task is to raise awareness of the benefits of AEC to business people. Importance must be given to public-private sector partnerships and regular consultations. Written material on ASEAN and AEC should be readily available to businesses in English and local languages. Industry associations have to play a significant role in this regard and have to arrange workshops and involve mass media in disseminating information about ASEAN and the AEC.

4. To achieve the AEC 2015, measures for trade facilitation should be given priority. Focus should be on smoother customs and logistics integration. It is also advisable to review the progress and effectiveness of ASEAN's central NTBs database system and its implementation.

5. ASEAN should unlock the potential of SMEs. They are also more vulnerable to economic integration than the larger firms. The SMEs lack financial and technical know-how and thus need support and knowledge of markets to venture into ASEAN countries. Government agencies need to increase their assistance in providing the support and information needed. They should educate and energize the sector so that SMEs are aware of how to take advantage of regional economic integration. They should also know who to talk to when undertaking cross-border business in ASEAN. There should be proper investment and trade development networks, which can provide assistance in setting up an office, simplifying the forms or providing some guarantees that improve investor's confidence.

6. The current form of the scorecard, though a good initiative, needs to be strengthened significantly if ASEAN wants to develop a tool for encouraging its member states to achieve the goals stipulated under the AEC Blueprint. The scorecard needs to be enriched with information on member states' implementation process so as to increase transparency and make the ASEAN businesses and citizens understand the ASEAN economic processes.

NOTES

1. The EU Internal Market Scoreboard is one of the tools used to track how national authorities transpose EU internal market rules.
2. The chapter uses NTBs and NTMs interchangeably.
3. Brunei, Indonesia, Malaysia, the Philippines, Singapore and Thailand.
4. Cambodia, Laos, Myanmar and Vietnam.
5. LPI constitutes border control efficiency (customs), infrastructure quality, ease of arranging competitively priced shipments, competence of its logistics services, ability to track and trace consignment, timeliness in shipments of reaching destinations.
6. BRICS — Brazil, Russia, India, China and South Africa.

REFERENCES

Ando, M. and A. Obashi. "The pervasiveness of non-tariff measures in ASEAN — evidences from the inventory approach". In *Rising Non-Tariff Protectionism and Crisis Recovery: A Study by Asia-Pacific Research and Training Network on Trade* (ARTNeT), edited by M. Mikic and M. Wermelinger. Bangkok: United Nations, 2010.

Eddy, Catherine and Rowena Owen. "An Investigation into the Measures Affecting the Integration of ASEAN's Priority Sectors (Phase 2): Region-wide Business Survey". REPSF Project No. 06/001e (May 2007).

Nesadurai, Helen E.S. "Trade Policy in Southeast Asia: Politics, Domestic Interests and the Forging of New Accommodations in the Regional and Global Economy". In *Routledge Handbook of Southeast Asian Politics*, edited by Richard Robison. London and New York: Routledge, 2012.

Shujiro U. and A. Mitsuyo. "Investment Climate Study on ASEAN Member Countries". Economic Research Institute for ASEAN and East Asia (ERIA) publication.

2

MONITORING THE ASEAN ECONOMIC COMMUNITY:
Issues and Challenges

Aladdin D. Rillo

Regional economic integration is a complex process. It requires not only the ability to implement initiatives to support the markets, but also a high level of commitment by countries to ensure that policies are supportive of integration. Effective and sustainable regional integration process can only be reached with sufficient levels of participation by relevant stakeholders and systematic monitoring of the various initiatives and measures.

It is within this context that the monitoring of the ASEAN Economic Community (AEC) should be viewed. Ever since ASEAN has envisioned building an integrated region by 2015, efforts have been strengthened to ensure that this objective can be achieved. Obviously, building an economic community is not easy, given the diversity of the region and the challenges facing the countries in the implementation of various measures. Hence, monitoring the progress of AEC implementation is crucial.

I. Monitoring the AEC: Some Fundamentals

One approach towards monitoring ASEAN economic integration is the AEC Scorecard.[1] Developed in 2008 to support the AEC Blueprint, the Scorecard is designed to measure the implementation of the various measures under the AEC Blueprint, as well as to track the extent to which countries comply with their commitments in the Blueprint. It covers the four elements under the AEC Blueprint, namely: a single market and production base; a highly competitive economic region; a region of equitable economic development; and a region fully integrated into the global economy.[2]

The AEC Scorecard at this juncture is only a compliance tool to ensure ASEAN and its member states are on track with the implementation of their commitments. It is not a tool to evaluate the impact of these measures. Nonetheless, the AEC Scorecard should be an evolving document that could be improved or revised and could be used in tandem with other instruments for evaluation purposes.

As designed the AEC Scorecard has three major components. These include the provision of qualitative and quantitative indications of the ratification, adoption, and transposition into domestic laws, regulations, and administrative procedures of agreed obligations and commitments within the prescribed timeframes as specified in the AEC Blueprint. Another component is tracking the implementation of agreements and commitments and achievements of milestones in the AEC Strategic Schedule. Finally, the Scorecard itself shall provide statistical indicators on the AEC.

In terms of process, monitoring[3] is done through a simple reporting and updating of measures by the various working bodies that are responsible for implementing the measures in their respective areas (e.g., for measures under trade in goods, reporting is coursed through the Coordinating Committee on ASEAN Trade in Goods Agreement). In calculating the implementation rate, a measure is considered as implemented only when all ASEAN member states have implemented the said measure, and all activities under the said measure are fully implemented. Measures to be implemented by individual ASEAN member states are not counted as measures for ASEAN. These measures will be counted for the country scorecards. Thus, measures by individual ASEAN member states will be more than or equal to the measures for ASEAN. To ensure that the timelines and targets of AEC are met, it was agreed that the AEC will be monitored in four phases: 2008–09; 2010–11; 2012–13; and 2014–15. To date, ASEAN has completed Phase I (2000–09) and Phase II (2010–11) of AEC implementation and is scheduled to implement Phase III (2012–13).

II. Tracking the AEC: What has been Achieved So Far?

Since the actual monitoring exercise began in 2008, two scorecards have been reported, covering the measures due to be implemented under Phase I and Phase II, respectively.

Under Phase I (1 January 2008–31 December 2009), 105 measures have been targeted to be implemented, of which 92 have already been completed, resulting in implementation rate of 87.6 per cent.[4] Among the key deliverables under Phase I include the signing/ratification/entry into force of 16 regional agreements/protocols on: trade in goods (ASEAN Agreement on Trade in Goods), services (4th Package of Commitments on Financial Services under the ASEAN Framework Agreement on Services), investment (ASEAN Comprehensive Investment Agreement), transport[5] (goods in transit, air services, and inter-states transport), and free trade arrangements with China, Japan, India, South Korea, and Australia and New Zealand. During this period the National Single Windows on customs was also operationalized in the ASEAN-5 and Brunei Darussalam, while standards and conformance were further enhanced with the implementation of key initiatives.

Efforts are now focused on completing the remaining 16 measures, which include three services liberalization measures, and 13 measures on ratification of transport protocols and agreements. Among the important measures that require immediate implementation include the pending commitments under the 7th Package of AFAS Commitments and ratification of the pending protocols under the three transport agreements: ASEAN Framework Agreement on the Facilitation of Goods in Transit (AFAFGIT), ASEAN Multilateral Agreement on Full

Liberalization of Air Freight Services (MAAFS), and ASEAN Multilateral Agreement on the Air Services (MAAS).

For Phase II (2010–11), a total of 172 measures have been targeted but only 97 measures were completed, which translates to an implementation rate of 56.4 per cent. Among the key deliverables come from initiatives under trade in goods and services, with specific accomplishments in tariff and non-tariff reduction (e.g., entry into force of the ASEAN Trade in Goods Agreement on 17 May 2010), implementation of mutual recognition arrangements for medical, dental and nursing services, and conclusion of 5th round of negotiations for financial services.

However, more efforts are still needed to implement the 75 remaining measures. Critical here are measures on customs integration, services, investment, standards and conformance, consumer protection, agriculture, and transport. In the case of customs, for example, areas that need particular attention are the establishment of pre-clearance arrival for customs clearance and cargo release, development of advance ruling systems for tariff classification and value assessment, implementation of ASEAN Customs Declaration Document, implementation of cargo processing model, finalization of customs Protocols 2 (designation of frontier posts) and 7 (customs transit system), and development of legal framework to implement the ASEAN Single Windows in the region. For standard and conformance assessment, measures pertaining to development and implementation of standard MRAs as well as harmonized regulatory regimes for certain products are priorities this year. In the area of consumer protection, there is a need to prioritize the development of notification and information mechanism particularly to address consumer redress. For services, priority is to complete the measures under the 8th AFAS package. Finally, for transport, finalizing the pending protocols and agreements under ASEAN Multilateral Agreement on the Full Liberalization of Passenger Air Services (MAFLPAS), AFAFGIT, and MAAS remains a priority.

III. Issues and Challenges of Monitoring the AEC

While progress has been made, the road to the ASEAN Economic Community by 2015 is still a long one. Although various initiatives have been carried out, more efforts are still needed to deepen the region's economic integration. The truth is that economic integration is a very complex agenda with many challenges, requiring greater scope of critical actions. By the end of 2011, only 68.2 per cent of all measures due to be implemented under the AEC Blueprint have been realized (see Table 2.1). This means that still a number of measures remain pending and require immediate action by member states.

Despite this progress, some measures have not been fully implemented, particularly those under trade facilitation (customs modernization and standard and conformance), services liberalization, investment, agriculture, consumer protection, and ratification of transport agreements. One reason for this shortfall is the delay in the ratification of the signed ASEAN agreements and its protocols and completion of countries' specific commitments in the Blueprint. Meanwhile, ASEAN has started to identify the prioritized measures scheduled under Phase III (2012–13). However, to ensure a higher implementation rate as well as to avoid backlogs of unimplemented commitments, a number of challenges remain.

First, to ensure that AEC is realized by 2015, ASEAN should strengthen the implementation of programmes at the national level. ASEAN member states have been urged to ensure that regional commitments are transposed into national commitments through appropriate domestic processes. At the same time, capacity building, particularly for less developed ASEAN economies, should be given particular emphasis to enable policy-makers in those countries to follow through with their commitments.

Second, it is imperative that a stronger monitoring be put in place both at the country and regional levels. This should be the priority. In the absence of an effective and well-functioning mechanism to monitor the outcomes, identify issues and address implementation gaps, the risks of the AEC falling short of achieving its targets by 2015 are high. Strengthening the monitoring mechanism also requires improving coordination among national agencies at a country level.

Third, given the difficult and complex process of building a single market, it is only logical that regional institutions be developed over time to enforce rules and monitor progress of implementation. ASEAN has taken steps to develop its institutional support to integration, such as the development of enhanced dispute settlement mechanism. But more steps are needed. One critical institutional support is the strengthening of mechanism for private sector consultation. Formal

TABLE 2.1
AEC Scorecard (1 January 2008–31 December 2011)

AEC Pillar	Key Initiatives	Implementation Rate*	Key Achievements
Single Market	ATIGA, AFAS, ACIA, AMNP, RIA-Fin**; Priority Integration Sectors (PIS), agriculture and food security	66.5%	Completion of tariff elimination schedules; operationalization of National Single Window in ASEAN-6; completion of 7th AFAS package; entry into force of ACIA; development of Capital Market Implementation Plan.
Competitive Economic Region	Transport, infrastructure, intellectual property rights, consumer protection, energy and mineral cooperation.	69.2%	Completion of Regional Guidelines and Handbook on Competition Policy in ASEAN; establishment of Coordinating Committee on Consumer Protection; completion of various transport roadmaps.***
Equitable Economic Development	Initiative for ASEAN Integration (IAI), SME development	66.7%	Development of IAI Strategic Framework and Work Plan; development of SME Strategic Action Plan.
Integration into the Global Economy	Free Trade Agreements (FTAs)	85.7%	Realization of ASEAN Plus One FTAs (Australia and New Zealand, China, India, Japan, and Republic of Korea).
AEC (2008–11)		**68.2%**	

Notes: * Measured as the ratio of the number of measures implemented to the total number of measures due to be implemented. The implementation rate for each pillar and for overall AEC reported here covers the period 1 January 2008–31 December 2011; monitored as of end-April 2012.

** ATIGA = ASEAN Trade in Goods Agreement; AFAS = ASEAN Framework Agreement on Services; ACIA = ASEAN Comprehensive Agreement; AMNP = Agreement on Movement of Natural Person; RIA-Fin = Roadmap on Monetary and Financial Integration of ASEAN.

*** These include the Strategic Plan for ASEAN Single Shipping Market and ASEAN ICT Master Plan 2015.

consultations with private sector and regional authorities may still be used, but new strategies to involve the private sector in the integration process should be explored. Moreover, there is a need to enhance the monitoring mechanism of the AEC. The establishment of the ASEAN Integration Monitoring Office within the ASEAN Secretariat is a step in the right direction, but this has to be complemented by well-developed mechanisms at a country level to ensure that monitoring is effectively carried out both at the country and regional levels.

Finally, since regional economic integration is not an end in itself, but a policy instrument designed to achieve development goals, greater macroeconomic and policy coordination is needed. In particular, the coordination of trade and financial policies is crucial to ensure that both policies support each other. It goes without saying that both financial and trade integration should go hand in hand. To facilitate trade, financial instruments are needed to hedge the risks of trade and investment flows. In the same manner, financial integration is needed to facilitate specialization and exploitation of economies of scale, which are related to trade. Without significant integration of financial systems, deeper integration of trade and investment is unlikely to happen.

NOTES

1. The decision to establish an ASEAN Economic Community (AEC) as an end-goal of regional economic integration was made in Bali, Indonesia during the 16th ASEAN Summit in 2003. In early 2007, the Leaders agreed to develop "a single and coherent blueprint" to implement the AEC, and consequently, the AEC Blueprint was signed in November that same year. To ensure that this Blueprint is implemented on time, the AEC Scorecard was developed in 2008 to track countries' compliance of their commitments to the AEC Blueprint, as well as to measure the implementation rate of the Blueprint.

2. Under each of these pillars various measures and targets have been identified. For example, to achieve a single market and production base, specific measures on free flow of goods, services, investment, skilled labour, and freer flow of capital have been targeted.

3. Monitoring is undertaken by the ASEAN Secretariat through its ASEAN Integration Monitoring Office (AIMO) established in 2010. In developing the Scorecard, AIMO compiles all measures as earlier identified by the various sector bodies in the AEC Scorecard Master Plan. The list is then circulated

to all working bodies for validation and approval. The approved list of measures becomes the basis for the scorecard for that particular phase of monitoring.

4. The implementation rate reported in this chapter refers to the outcome of the monitoring exercise undertaken by the ASEAN Secretariat as of end-April 2012. This means that the progress of implementation was monitored based on available information to the Secretariat as of that cut-off date.

5. To provide for a harmonized and integrated transport facilitation environment, ASEAN has signed seven transport agreements and their corresponding protocols to support the AEC. These include, among others, the ASEAN Framework Agreement of Goods in Transit (AFAFGIT), ASEAN Multilateral Agreement on Air Services (MAAS), and ASEAN Framework Agreement of the Facilitation of Inter-States Transport (AFAIST).

3

TOWARDS AEC 2015:
Free Flow of Goods within ASEAN

Pratiwi Kartika and Raymond Atje

I. Introduction

ASEAN is embarking on an ambitious endeavour to — among other goals — create an ASEAN Economic Community (AEC) by 2015. To achieve this objective ASEAN has adopted the AEC Blueprint, which describes the main features of the AEC and outlines the measures that ASEAN member countries must undertake.

AEC has four pillars, and one of them is to turn ASEAN into a single market and production base. One characteristic of this pillar is free flow of goods within the region. In this context "free flow of goods" implies that "properly defined goods produced in one member country can enter other members' markets without being subjected to import duties or other non-tariff restrictions". This requires the ASEAN member countries to remove all tariff and non-tariff barriers.

Note, however, that the removal of all tariff and non-tariff barriers is not an end in itself. There is also a need to expedite the transfer of goods across borders between ASEAN countries. It should be noted that since ASEAN is not a custom union, border inspections remain necessary. There is therefore also a need to minimize the transit costs, i.e., costs resulting from border control/inspection. ASEAN countries have agreed to implement trade facilitation measures that aim at simplifying, harmonizing, and standardizing the trade and customs process, procedures, and related information flows. One of the related activities is to install an ASEAN Single Window (ASW).

The ultimate goal of AEC is to improve the well-being of every ASEAN "citizen". Again, to appreciate this view, consider the following. In a fully integrated market, the price difference between any two places within ASEAN depends solely on transportation costs and other logistic costs to transfer goods between the two places. Without efficient transportation and logistics services, these costs can be significantly high. This is, perhaps, one reason why ASEAN members have agreed to include logistics services as a priority sector.

This chapter aims to review the AEC Scorecard II report issued by the ASEAN Secretariat in March 2012. It is a report about the implementation of measures listed in the AEC Blueprint for the period 2008–11. That the report needs a review may sound rather odd. After all, a scorecard report is supposed to provide all information about the progress made in the implementation of the AEC Blueprint, i.e., whether the listed measures have been properly implemented as scheduled or whether there have been deficiencies in the implementation process and if so, why. This information is not, however, to be found in the AEC Scorecard II report. For instance, according to Rillo (2012) there are 47 measures associated with the free flow of goods that have to be implemented during the period under consideration. Furthermore, only 23 of them have been fully implemented. The report does not, however, provide these numbers, let alone information about what those measures are and the reason or reasons for the shortcomings in the implementation. This deficiency in the report may be traced to the unwillingness of the AEC Scorecard to put the blame on any party.

This chapter consists of seven sections including the introduction. Section II offers some comments on the AEC Scorecard. Section III provides a short review of the removal of tariffs. Section IV concerns the removal of non-tariff barriers, while Section V pertains to trade facilitation and Section VI surveys other beyond border issues. Section VII gives concluding remarks. It should be noted that in its attempt to elucidate the Scorecard report, the chapter complements the report with relevant information that the authors have obtained from various sources.

II. Some Notes on the AEC Scorecard II

To keep track of the progress in the implementation of the AEC Blueprint, the ASEAN Secretariat has designed and periodically published an AEC Scorecard. The Scorecard is supposed to provide all the necessary information regarding the implementation of the Blueprint during the period under consideration. That is, it is meant to inform readers as to whether measures, as stipulated in the Blueprint have been implemented on schedule by all member states, thus identifing any non-compliance, and explaining the reasons behind it.

So far, the ASEAN Secretariat has published two scorecard reports, one for the 2008–09 period (Phase I) and another for the 2010–11 period (Phase II). Overall, the reports are too brief and omit too much detail to be informative and useful to various ASEAN stakeholders. For instance, anyone who wants to find information in the report about the progress in the implementation of the Single Regulatory Scheme for Cosmetics (among many other measures) will be disappointed. The reports do not provide such information.

To be more specific, according to the Scorecard II report, between 2008 and 2011, 67.5 per cent of AEC measures have been implemented. With regard to the establishment of a single market and production base, only 66 per cent of the measures scheduled for the period under consideration have been implemented. In addition, the implementation rate during Phase II has been much lower than it was during Phase I. In particular, during Phase I, all measures under the free flow of goods category were fully implemented, but during Phase II only 49 per cent of measures in the same category have been implemented. However, the report fails to provide further information regarding the reasons for this shortcoming, let alone manage to propose remedial actions.

Another example of the limitation of the report is as the following. The Scorecard reports that during Phase II each country has implemented more than half of the measures scheduled in the agenda to achieve the free flow of goods. Nevertheless, the Scorecard also reports that ASEAN as a whole has implemented less than half of the measures in the free flow of goods category. The report does not explain the reason for this discrepancy, nor does it identify any of the measures in question, whether they have been fully implemented or not.

Annex I of the Scorecard II lists the outstanding measures at the end of Phase II, some of them carried over from Phase I. One of the outstanding measures from Phase I concern some protocols of the ASEAN Framework Agreement on the Facilitation of Goods in Transit (AFAFGIT) that are yet to be finalized and ratified. Meanwhile, some outstanding measures in Phase II include trade facilitation, customs facilitation and integration, and standards and conformance. The report does not provide any explanation behind the deferments in the implementation of these measures, or any hint as to when they will eventually be implemented.

III. Removal of Tariff Barriers

In principle, the free trade area covers all manufactured and agriculture products, although timetables for reducing tariffs and removing quantitative restrictions and other non-tariff barriers differ. Products in the Inclusion List (IL) must undergo immediate liberalization through tariff reduction or elimination. Items on the Sensitive List (SL) and Highly Sensitive List (HSL), which include unprocessed agricultural products (SL) and rice (HSL) among other products, are given a longer time-frame before they are subjected to liberalization through gradually being phased into the IL for subsequent tariff reduction and removal.[1]

Based on time schedule in the AEC Blueprint, during Phase II, Brunei, Indonesia, Malaysia, the Philippines, Singapore, and Thailand (ASEAN-6), should have eliminated import duties on all products in the original IL — except for those products phased in from the SL and HSL — by 2010. In addition, they should have also completed the process of phasing the remaining products in the SL into the IL and reduced their tariffs to 0–5 per cent by 1 January 2010. During the same period, Cambodia should have applied 0–5 per cent tariffs for all products in its IL in 2010 and at least 60 per cent of them should have zero tariffs. Meanwhile, Vietnam should have eliminated import duties on 80 per cent of all products in its IL.

For each of the ASEAN countries, Table 3.1 compares the percentage of products in the original IL with the percentage of products that have zero tariffs in 2010. ASEAN member states have been quite successful in reducing and eliminating import duties as scheduled in the AEC Blueprint. For the ASEAN-6, the number of tariff lines whose tariff is zero is larger than the IL products that are scheduled to be duty free by 2010, implying that they have not only complied with the tariff reduction schedules outlined in the Blueprint but are liberalizing ahead of schedule. The same is true with Laos and Myanmar, which have successfully reduced import duties on all products in the IL to between 0–5 per cent. Cambodia and Vietnam are exceptions. Cambodia needs to reduce the tariffs of almost 20 per cent of its products to between 0–5 per cent to meet the target of 98.3 per cent of its products having between 0–5 per cent tariffs by 2010. Meanwhile, Vietnam was expected to have reduced the tariffs on 80 per cent of its IL products to zero in 2010. However, it has only succeeded in eliminating tariffs on 55.6 per cent of its IL products by 2011 (not shown in Table 3.1).

While the failure of some ASEAN member states to comply with the Blueprint's tariff reduction and elimination timetable is regrettable, this shortcoming is a relatively minor problem. Firstly, the removal of tariffs is a fairly simple task. In most countries, tariffs are administered under a single government's institution, usually the ministry of finance. All that is required is a government declaration proclaiming their removal. Secondly, ASEAN has complete information regarding all the tariffs lines that each member state continues to apply. Moreover, it is relatively easy

TABLE 3.1
Tariff Schedule of Member States, 2010

Country	0% Tariff	IL	Country	0–5% Tariff	IL
Brunei	99.03	92.89	Cambodia	78.45	98.30
Indonesia	98.66	78.39	Laos	95.18	95.20
Malaysia	98.68	87.39	Myanmar	99.28	99.30
Philippines	98.63	79.61	Vietnam*	96.68	96.60
Singapore	100.00	97.95			
Thailand	99.84	94.00			

Note: *Data of IL 96.60 refers to the year 2011 while data of 0–5 per cent tariff 96.68 refers to the year 2010.
Source: Okabe and Urata (2012).

for anyone to find out the progress of tariff removal in each member state. On the other hand, the member states' failure to accomplish this relatively easy task may erode the confidence of ASEAN's stakeholders about their ability to accomplish the AEC by 2015.

IV. Removal of Non-Tariff Barriers

According to the AEC Blueprint, Brunei, Indonesia, Malaysia, Singapore, and Thailand should have eliminated their non-tariff barriers (NTBs) by 2010. The Philippines should do the same by 2012, and Cambodia, Lao PDR, Myanmar, and Vietnam (CLMV) by 2015 (with flexibility stretching to 2018 for some sensitive products). It seems, however, that member states are still struggling to remove the NTBs according to schedule. Unlike the removal of tariffs, the elimination of NTBs is likely to be a much more difficult endeavour for a number of reasons.

Firstly, data immediately preceding the implementation of the AEC Blueprint suggest that the use of non-tariff measures (NTMs) was pervasive. Ando and Obashi (2010) used NTM data from 2007 and found the pervasiveness of the overall NTMs in ASEAN to be around 49. This means that almost half of all tariff lines in ASEAN were linked to at least one NTM. However, not all the NTMs applied were the core ones, i.e., NTMs that potentially act as NTBs. Core NTMs include financial control measures (e.g., multiple exchange rates) and quantity control measures (e.g., non-automatic licensing, quotas, prohibitions, and enterprise-specific restrictions). These core NTMs were applied to well above a quarter of all tariff lines in the region. Among the member states, Myanmar, Indonesia, and the Philippines were applying NTMs the most. All the NTMs applied by Myanmar might be classified as core NTMs. Indonesia was the second most NTMs-restrictive country after Myanmar. Almost half of Indonesia's tariff lines were linked to core NTMs, but overall Indonesia applied more non-core NTMs than core ones. In contrast, although 100 per cent of the Philippines' tariff lines were linked to NTMs, merely 5 per cent of its tariff lines were linked to core NTMs. At the other end of the spectrum, Cambodia and Thailand were the least NTMs-restrictive countries in ASEAN. Cambodia applied core NTMs to only 4 per cent of its tariff lines and overall NTMs to 6 per cent of its tariff lines, while Thailand also applied core

TABLE 3.2
Frequency Ratio of NTMs, 2007

	Overall NTMs	Core NTMs
ASEAN-10	49	27
Brunei	46	29
Cambodia	64	4
Indonesia	100	45
Laos	20	–
Malaysia	43	36
Myanmar	100	100
Philippines	100	5
Singapore	27	21
Thailand	11	4
Vietnam	34	22
By industry		
Foods	63	29
Chemicals	59	39
Light mfg.	39	18
Metals	37	15
Machineries	48	30
Others	48	24

Source: Ando and Obashi (2010).

NTMs to 4 per cent of its tariff lines and overall NTMs to 11 per cent of its tariff lines.

Ando and Obashi also explored the tendency to use NTM restriction among industries in the region. They found that the differences in restrictiveness among industries were not as large as those among AMSs themselves. On one hand, food and chemicals industries seemed to be the most restrictive. Sixty-three per cent of all tariff lines in the food industry were linked to at least one NTM and around half of them were linked to core NTMs. As for the chemicals industry, 59 per cent of the industry's tariff lines were subjected to NTMs and almost 40 per cent were subjected to core NTMs. On the other hand, metals and light manufacturing industries were among the least restrictive. In the metals industry overall NTMs and core NTMs were applied to 37 per cent and 15 per cent of all tariff lines, respectively. The overall NTMs and core NTMs in the light manufacturing industry were 39 per cent and 18 per cent of all tariff lines, respectively.

The study also investigates the pervasiveness of NTMs in certain industries for each country. Brunei applied high NTMs restrictions on its food, chemicals, and machineries industries but not its metals and light manufacturing industries. As the least NTMs-restrictive country in the region, Cambodia applied relatively high NTMs restrictions on its food industry only. Meanwhile, Indonesia imposed the highest NTMs restrictions on chemicals industry, followed by its machineries and food industries. Laos put relatively low NTMs restrictions on all its industries. The data, however, do not provide any information on the country's core NTMs. Malaysia also seemed to protect its chemicals and food industries the most. In addition, it put higher NTMs restriction on its metals industry compared to its machineries industry. As mentioned above, Myanmar put core NTMs to all of its industries. The Philippines put relatively high restrictions on its food industry but low restrictions on its machineries and light manufacturing industries. However, there is not much information on NTMs in the country's chemicals, metals, and other industries. The performance of Singapore was also relatively different. It applied high NTMs restrictions on chemicals, machineries, and other industries but, unsurprisingly, low restrictions on its food industry; Singapore imports most of its food products. Thailand, as aforementioned, placed low NTMs restrictions on all of its industries and a slightly high restriction only on its food industry. Data from Vietnam also exhibits a relatively different pattern compared to those of the other ASEAN countries. It put relatively high NTM restrictions on its light manufacturing industry but low restrictions on its food, chemicals, and metals industries.

Secondly, with regard to NTBs, ASEAN seems to have abandoned the standstill and rollback principle stated in the AEC Blueprint. Paragraph 14 of the AEC Blueprint calls on member states to abide by the commitment of a standstill and rollback on NTBs, to be effective immediately after the implementation of the Blueprint. However, the ASEAN Trade in Goods Agreement (ATIGA) does not reaffirm this principle. Instead, the ATIGA adopts a more ambiguous approach to NTMs.[2] Article 40(1) of the ATIGA states:

Each Member State shall not adopt or maintain any non-tariff measure on the importation of any good of any other Member State or on the exportation of any good destined for the territory of any other Member State, except in accordance with its WTO rights and obligations or in accordance with this Agreement.

This change in attitude might be due to ASEAN's realization that it could not enforce the standstill and rollback principle. ASEAN did not and, as will be elaborated below, still does not have sufficient information about the extent of the utilization of NTBs in the region. Without such information it simply could not monitor the implementation of the principle.

Thirdly, although the Scorecard report provides a positive description of the progress in the removal of NTBs, the actual outcome seems rather disappointing. Under the ATIGA, Brunei, Indonesia, Malaysia, Singapore, and Thailand (ASEAN-5) have to remove their NTBs in three tranches — in 2008, 2009, and 2010 — while the Philippines has to do the same in 2010, 2011, and 2012. Accordingly, the ASEAN-5 should have eliminated all their NTMs by 2010 and the Philippines should have completed the removal of the second tranche by 2011. The Scorecard, however, only states that the elimination of NTBs under the three tranches has continued and gained momentum. It also reports that Malaysia and Thailand have eliminated the third tranche of their NTBs in 2011. The report does not give information about the other four countries, however. One possible explanation is that Brunei, Indonesia, Singapore, and the Philippines failed to meet their respective commitments and that only Malaysia and Thailand have done so, albeit one year late.

Another possible explanation is that the four countries, i.e., Brunei, Indonesia, Singapore, and the Philippines, claimed that they removed all their NTBs but that ASEAN could neither challenge nor verify their claims. Accordingly, the Scorecard report could not provide information about the status of NTMs in these countries. This may sound strange, especially in light of the pervasiveness of NTBs in ASEAN as reported by Ando and Obashi. Yet, as the Scorecard report implicitly admits, ASEAN does not have sufficient information about the extent of NTB-utilization in the region. On the one hand ASEAN relies on the voluntary submission of a list of NTMs in general and NTBs in particular from its member countries. On the other hand, ASEAN is still in the process of stocktaking and updating its NTMs database. Without effective monitoring, verification, and enforcement, bluffing can be a powerful tool at the disposal of member states that, for one reason or another, want to postpone implementing their commitments.[3] And, unless it has severe repercussions on their economies, members might be unwilling to contest another member's bluffing, for they themselves might have committed or considered doing the same.

Note further that ASEAN does not provide a clear cut distinction between NTBs and NTMs. As it is, each member state is free to determine whether a particular measure constitutes an NTB or an NTM. Under such a condition, as stated above, a member state may decide not to report every NTB until other member states point it out. In addition, as also noted above, the member states are not yet required to notify ASEAN regarding NTBs, which clearly violates the ATIGA injunction on this matter. Article 11 (1) of the ATIGA provides:

> Unless otherwise provided in this Agreement, Member States shall notify any action or measure that they intend to take:
>
> (a) which may nullify or impair any benefit to other Member States, directly or indirectly under this Agreement; or
> (b) when the action or measure may impede the attainment of any objective of this Agreement.

This particular article requires every member state to report all measures that may negatively affect other member states. Furthermore, concerning a new NTM, Article 40(3) provides:

> Any new measure or modification to the existing measure shall be duly notified in accordance with Article 11.

Pursuant to the ATIGA, ASEAN should have insisted that every member state submit the list of all the NTMs that it utilizes. However, as the Scorecard report admits, this has not been the case. Unless Article 11 of the ATIGA is rigorously enforced, one wonders how ASEAN would be able to monitor and verify its members' compliance to the NTMs elimination measure.

One implication of ASEAN's indecisiveness is an increase in the utilization of NTMs among the ASEAN member states in recent years. A study by Evenett (2012) found that countries including AMSs have lately tended to use more NTBs. The study revealed that, as a result of the recent global financial crisis, countries around the world have tended to adopt protectionist policies. It notes that as many as 226 new protectionist measures were being introduced during 2010–11. The report also provides statistics of protectionist measures adopted by Indonesia. There are 47 measures that have been implemented by Indonesia that almost certainly discriminate against foreign commercial interests. Trade defence such as the use of safeguards is the most common, accounting for 32 per cent of Indonesia's protectionist measures. Meanwhile, export taxes or restriction are the second-most-common type of measures that harm foreign interest. One export restriction, newly enforced in 2012, affects 65 mining commodities. The measure includes a 20 per cent export tax on mining products. In addition, exporters must register themselves to the Ministry of Trade and Ministry of Energy and Natural Resource prior to the transaction. Finally, the products must be verified by surveyors. On the other hand, the report also revealed 16 measures applied by other member states that negatively affect the Indonesian economy.[4]

V. Trade Facilitation

Broadly defined, trade facilitation refers to all measures that aim at smoothing cross-border trades. In the ASEAN context it comprises, among other measures, customs integration, the establishment of an ASEAN Single Window (ASW), and standard and conformance. ASEAN as a whole is expected to greatly benefit from these endeavours, as the following two studies suggest.

The first study by Otsuki (2011) attempted to identify benefits that would be derived from improving trade facilitation. Trade facilitation in this sense refers to port efficiency, customs environment, regulatory environment, and service sector infrastructure. Using a gravity model, he regressed bilateral trade flow on each of those trade facilitation indicators and several macroeconomic indicators. The regression results showed positive signs of the estimated coefficients for all of the trade facilitation indicators. Then, he conducted simulations to calculate the gains more precisely. First, a 5 per cent improvement of trade facilitation in the whole world apparently resulted in an increase in the world's trade value by around 16 per cent. Second, he conducted simulation with two scenarios: trade facilitation reform only in ASEAN countries, and the same reform only in the rest of the world (RoW). He found that ASEAN's trade gain from reform in the RoW is only half of that which would be gained from reform in the ASEAN countries (see Figure 3.1). Reform in the ASEAN countries would generate substantial trade gains, with one-fourth coming from intra-regional trade and three-fourths coming from ASEAN's trade with the RoW (see Figure 3.2). Therefore, the study concluded that ASEAN's trade facilitation reform would very beneficial in boosting trade volume both among the member states and with the RoW, even if the RoW does not improve their trade facilitation.

Another study by Shepherd and Wilson (2008) investigated the effect of several trade facilitation components on trade. The study's main purpose was to identify which particular trade facilitation components would have substantial impacts on Southeast Asia's trade values. Using a gravity model, the study regressed import value on the quality of port facilities and inland waterways, the quality of passenger air transport, internet service provider (ISP) sector competition index, irregular payments in import/export, simple average tariff, and several gravity variables. The results suggested that trade facilitation would be significant in expanding trade volume, particularly air-transport infrastructure and

FIGURE 3.1

Comparison of ASEAN's Trade Gains

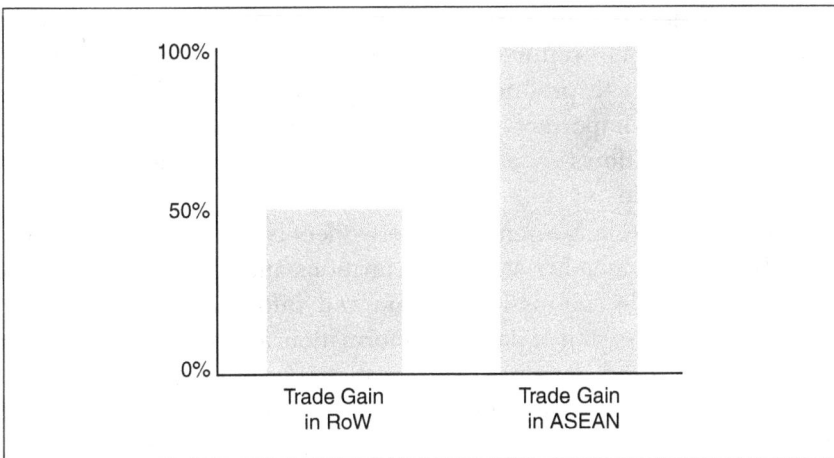

Source: Otsuki (2011).

FIGURE 3.2

Sources of ASEAN's Trade Gains from Its Trade Facilitation Reform

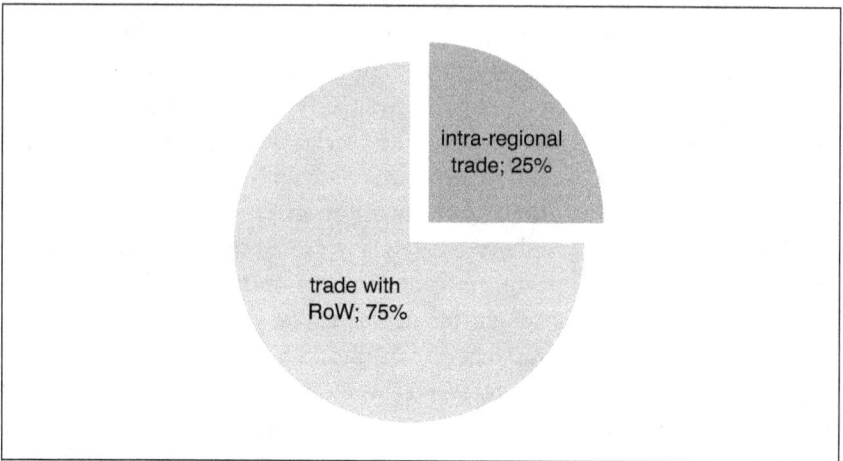

intra-regional
trade; 25%

trade with
RoW; 75%

Source: Otsuki (2011).

the level of competition in the ISP sector. A 1 per cent improvement
in the quality of air-transport infrastructure led to a 5 per cent trade
expansion. Moreover, a 1 per cent increase in the ISP sector competition
index resulted in well above a 1 per cent expansion in ASEAN's
trade. This finding may be in line with the occurrence of a regional
production network in East Asia. Such a network requires intense
communication, as producers in various countries need to cooperate
closely to be able to produce a shared product. In brief, both studies
pointed out the importance of trade facilitation reform in enhancing
ASEAN's trade flows in accordance with its role in smoothing the
cross-border trade.

As for the ASW, it is essentially a network of National Single Windows
(NSWs) of every member state. The functions and roles of an NSW are
based on a single submission of data and information, a single and
synchronous processing of data and information, and a single decision for
customs release and clearance. At the national level, the implementation
level of an NSW in each country has been assessed by the Economic
Research Institute for ASEAN and East Asia (ERIA) (P. Intal et al.
2011). The scoring used in the ERIA study considers three particular

aspects: preparatory measures, the implementation of the single window business processes and technical components, and its live implementation. The result shows that Indonesia, the Philippines, Singapore, and Thailand (ASEAN-4) have largely implemented the NSWs with scores of 87.7. Meanwhile, the implementation of NSWs in CLMV is still at the early stage, with a score of merely 20. According to the study, CLMV needs a huge effort to complete their NSWs by 2015. However, the ASEAN-4 also face challenges. Thailand has a coordination problem among agencies involved in its NSW. The Philippines has problems of data standardization and business process simplification. Indonesia needs to improve in several aspects, such as coordination among offices involved in the NSW, human resources capacity in its customs office and related agencies, and public awareness regarding this new initiative and the new regulations surrounding the implementation of the NSW. Furthermore, an initial assessment cast some doubts on the effectiveness of using an NSW to reduce transit cost. Some private sector representatives claim that following the implementation of the NSWs, there has been very little, if any, improvement in the customs clearance process. Needless to say, ASEAN countries are still in a learning process with regard to utilizing their NSWs. The customs clearance process is expected to improve along with the proficiency of the customs staff to utilize the NSWs.

At the regional level, ASEAN has committed to an ASW Pilot Project. The project consists of three components. Firstly, there is a study regarding the most feasible network architecture through which to conduct the ASW Pilot Project. The idea is to use a Federated approach, which does not involve a central server. Secondly, the project includes a design to set up a network infrastructure necessary for the implementation of the ASW Pilot Project. Thirdly, a study will be done to evaluate outcomes of the Pilot Project, and based on the evaluation formulate recommendations for the eventual ASW. The first component has been completed and endorsed by the member states in February 2011. The second component was conducted from November 2011 until October 2012. As part of the project, the ASW's legal framework agreement is currently being discussed. The pilot project is being conducted in seven AMSs: Brunei, Indonesia, Malaysia, the Philippines, Singapore, Thailand, and Vietnam.

TABLE 3.3

Logistics Performance Index (LPI) of ASEAN Member States, 2012

Rank	Country	LPI	Customs	Infrastructure	International Shipments	Logistics Competence	Tracking and Tracing	Timeliness
1	Singapore	4.13	4.10	4.15	3.99	4.07	4.07	4.39
29	Malaysia	3.49	3.28	3.43	3.40	3.45	3.54	3.86
38	Thailand	3.18	2.96	3.08	3.21	2.98	3.18	3.63
52	Philippines	3.02	2.62	2.80	2.97	3.14	3.30	3.30
53	Vietnam	3.00	2.65	2.68	3.14	2.68	3.16	3.64
59	Indonesia	2.94	2.53	2.54	2.97	2.85	3.12	3.61
101	Cambodia	2.56	2.30	2.20	2.61	2.50	2.77	2.95
109	Lao PDR	2.50	2.38	2.40	2.40	2.49	2.49	2.82
129	Myanmar	2.37	2.24	2.10	2.47	2.42	2.34	2.59

Source: World Bank (2012).

VI. Other Beyond the Border Measures

The removal of all tariff and non-tariff barriers and the full implementation of all trade facilitation measures are necessary but not sufficient to ensure that ASEAN "citizens" receive the maximum benefit from the free flow of goods within ASEAN. To achieve that objective, ASEAN also needs to reduce transportation and logistics costs between member countries as well as within each country. Logistics are important since a better logistics performance ensures a freer flow of goods. According to the Logistics Performance Index (LPI) 2012, there is a wide gap among the member states' logistics performance. The gap is so wide that Singapore is ranked 1st and Myanmar is ranked 129th out of the 155 countries surveyed. Among the nine member states observed in the study, three countries are among the top or the best logistics performance group: Singapore, Malaysia, and Thailand. Three other countries — namely the Philippines, Vietnam, and Indonesia — are in the second ranked group. The last three countries are in the fourth (or lowest) ranked group. They are Lao PDR, Cambodia, and Myanmar. Among LPI components, the lowest score for Malaysia, Thailand, the Philippines, Vietnam, and Indonesia is in customs, i.e. the efficiency of the clearance process. Infrastructure is also a challenge for Vietnam and Indonesia. Cambodia, Lao PDR, and Myanmar seem to have problems in all components of the LPI: border control efficiency, infrastructure quality, ease of arranging competitively priced shipments, competence of logistics services, ability to track and trace consignment, timeliness in shipments of reaching destinations.

Despite the hurdles in the logistics sector, all member states except Thailand and the Philippines have experienced an improvement in their LPI compared to the previous LPI that was released in 2010. It seems that there is a catching-up process going on, since countries with a relatively poor performance in the past have experienced greater improvements than countries that had a relatively good performance in 2010. According to this survey, although all better-off countries have enhanced the efficiency of their clearance process, this issue continues to be the most problematic.

VII. Conclusion

Part I of the AEC Scorecard II report states:

> To ensure a timely implementation of the AEC initiatives, ASEAN has
> established a monitoring mechanism called the AEC Scorecard. As a
> compliance tool, the AEC Scorecard reports the progress of implementing
> the various AEC measures, identifies implementation gaps and challenges,
> and tracks the realization of the AEC by 2015 (p. 1).

Upon reading the AEC Scorecard report, one cannot help but marvel
at the discrepancy between the expectations generated by the above
sentences and the contents of the report. The report is anything but
clear and informative. Details are omitted and sentences are often too
vague to be able to provide useful information. For instance, on the
subject of the removal of NTBs, which this chapter has discussed at
length, the report provides only three rather vague sentences.

As noted above, these authors believe that this shortcoming may
be traced to the unwillingness of the AEC Scorecard to place blame on
any party. But there are many ways to write a clear and informative
report without offending any party. For example, Rillo (2012) finds that
with regard to the free flow of goods, member states were supposed to
implement 47 measures during the Phase II period. Of these measures,
23 have been fully implemented and the remaining 24 have not. In
ASEAN parlance, a measure is considered fully implemented only if
it has been implemented by all member states. The Scorecard report
could easily incorporate this information but it does not. It could do
even better by providing a list of these measures, the status of their
implementation, and further comments about the gaps and challenges in
their implementation. Instead, Annex 2 of the Scorecard report provides
a table on the implementation of the Scorecard by country under Phase
II. The table is too general and vague to be informative.

One of the main challenges in preparing this chapter is the lack of
recent data. The most recent data is necessary if one wants to follow the
progress of the AEC closely. ASEAN Secretariat should make available
the most recent data in its possession on issues such as products in the
exclusion list of each member state, tariffs, and non-tariff barriers. In
addition to that, future scorecard reports should also provide information
on the enforcement of legal instruments such as Mutual Recognition
Arrangements (MRAs) by each country. It is also important that a

scorecard report evaluate the effectiveness of the AEC measures that have already been implemented by the ASEAN countries, similar to the studies by Wignaraja et al. (2010*a*, 2010*b*). The first study investigates the impact of FTAs on the Philippines' transport, food and electronics firms, and the second investigates the impact of FTAs on Thailand's exporting firms. It seems that so far, ASEAN has given only scant attention to the ex-post evaluation of the impact that the implementation of these measures has had on the real economy.

NOTES

1. There are also products that are permanently excluded from the free trade area for reasons of protection of national security, public morals, human, animal or plant life, and health and articles of artistic, historic, and archaeological value.
2. ASEAN makes a distinction between non-tariff measures and non-tariff barriers. Measures that are allowed under the WTO are classified as NTMs. Otherwise they are NTBs.
3. ASEAN officials who did not wish to be identified confirmed that occasionally this indeed was the case.
4. The report does not provide detailed information about the NTMs that other member states introduced during the period under consideration.

REFERENCES

Ando, M. and A. Obashi. "The pervasiveness of non-tariff measures in ASEAN: evidences from the inventory approach". In *Rising Non-Tariff Protectionism and Crisis Recovery*, edited by M. Mikic and M. Wermelinger. A Study by Asia-Pacific Research and Training Network on Trade (ARTNeT), United Nations, Bangkok, 2010.

ASEAN Trade in Goods (accessed 26 February 2009).

Association of Southeast Asian Nations. "ASEAN Economic Community Blueprint". In *Roadmap for An ASEAN Community 2009–2015*. Jakarta: ASEAN Secretariat, 2009.

Evenett, S.J. *Debacle: The 11th Global Trade Alert Report on Protectionism*. London: Centre for Economic Policy Research (CEPR), 2012.

Intal, P., D. Narjoko, H.H. Lim, and M. Simorangkir. "ERIA Study to Further Improve AEC Scorecard and Trade Facilitation". Powerpoint presentation at ASEAN Trade Facilitation Forum, Manado, Indonesia (accessed 13 August 2011).

Okabe, M. and S. Urata. "The Impact of Trade Liberalization in ASEAN on Intra-ASEAN Trade Flows". Paper presented in ERIA ASEAN Economic Community Blueprint Mid Term Review (MTR) Project 2nd (Second) Technical Meeting, Jakarta, Indonesia (accessed 9 February 2012).

Otsuki, T. *Quantifying the Benefits of Trade Facilitation in ASEAN.* OSIPP Discussion Paper: DP-2011-E-006. Osaka: The Osaka School of International Public Policy, Osaka University, 2011. <http://www.osipp.osaka-u.ac.jp/archives/DP/2011/DP2011E006.pdf> (accessed 27 June 2012).

Rillo, A.D. "Monitoring the AEC: Update and Challenges ASEAN Economic Performance and Outlook". Powerpoint presentation at ASEAN Roundtable 2012, Singapore (accessed 25 May 2012).

Shepherd, B. and J.S. Wilson. "Trade Facilitation in ASEAN Member Countries: Measuring Progress and Assessing Priorities". The World Bank Policy Research Working Paper 4615. Washington, D.C.: The World Bank Development Research Group, 2008.

The ASEAN Secretariat. *ASEAN Economic Community Scorecard, Charting Progress Toward Regional Economic Integration Phase I (2008–2009) and Phase II (2010–2011).* Jakarta, 2012.

Wignaraja, G., D. Lazaro, and G. DeGuzman. "FTAs and Philippine Business: Evidence from Transport, Food, and Electronics Firms". ADBI Working Paper 185. Tokyo: Asian Development Bank Institute, 2010*a*.

———. "How Do FTAs Affect Exporting Firms in Thailand?". ADBI Working Paper 190. Tokyo: Asian Development Bank Institute, 2010*b*.

World Bank. "Global Rankings, Logistics Performance Index". <http://www.lpisurvey.worldbank.org/> (accessed 27 June 2012).

4

AN ASSESSMENT OF SERVICES SECTOR LIBERALIZATION IN ASEAN[1]

Deunden Nikomborirak and
Supunnavadee Jitdumrong

I. Introduction

ASEAN has made a remarkable achievement in liberalizing trade in goods through the ASEAN Free Trade Agreement (AFTA), where tariffs on virtually all imports have been reduced to zero within ASEAN 6 since 2010, bar a few sensitive items for six original members. The progress made in liberalizing trade in services, however, has not been as impressive. Liberalization efforts in services in the past have been focused on two areas: the promotion of trade services by using the GATS approach of request and offer of liberalization by services sector and the promotion of flows of skilled labour through the establishment of Mutual Recognition Arrangements (MRAs) of professional services. After several rounds of negotiations and eight commitment packages since the ASEAN Framework Agreement on Trade in Services (AFAS) was established in 1995, the region has failed to liberalize services trade between member economies. Commitments made thus far are marginal to those already made in the WTO. As for MRAs, although several have been signed since 2005, their actual impact on promoting greater flows of professional services within the region is at best negligible.

At its 9th Summit in October 2003, ASEAN announced its intention to create an ASEAN Community based upon three pillars: ASEAN Political-Security Community, ASEAN Economic Community, and an ASEAN Socio-Cultural Community. The ASEAN Economic Community (AEC) envisions regional economic integration by 2015. In 2007, at the 13th ASEAN Summit, the ASEAN Economic Community Blueprint (AEC Blueprint), a coherent master plan guiding the establishment of the ASEAN Economic Community 2015, was adopted. The AEC Blueprint will establish ASEAN not only as a single market, but also a single production base which requires free flow factors of production, namely capital and skilled labour.

This chapter seeks to assess the progress ASEAN has made thus far in liberalizing services trade within the region according to the milestones and targets stipulated in the AEC Blueprint. The first section provides an overview of the relative importance of the service sector to ASEAN economies. The second section describes service trade negotiation modality and liberalization commitments made thus far under the AFAS as well as those prescribed in the AEC Blueprint. Section three examines the extent to which member countries have met the liberalization milestones prescribed in the AEC blueprint. The fourth and final section will provide recommendations on how ASEAN may move forward to prompt member countries to open up their service sectors in order to be able to achieve the regional economic integration goal of the ASEAN Community.

II. Importance of Services Sector in ASEAN Economies

Share of Services Sector in Total GDP

The size of the services trade share of a country's Gross Domestic Product (GDP) varies according to the stage of economic development and the structure of the particular economy. However, in general, contribution of the services trade to GDP tends to be higher in developed economies than in developing countries due to changes in both the production and consumption pattern. Wages in developed countries tend to be high such that industries need to shift from labour-intensive production of manufacturing goods to skill-intensive provision of services. At the same time, higher income leads to greater expenditure on personal services such as health, education, and tourism. This general observation seems to hold in the case of ASEAN as well.

As can be seen in Figure 4.1, Singapore, a member country with, by far, the highest GDP per capita, also shows the highest ratio

FIGURE 4.1

Share of Services Sector in Total GDP (%), 2001–10

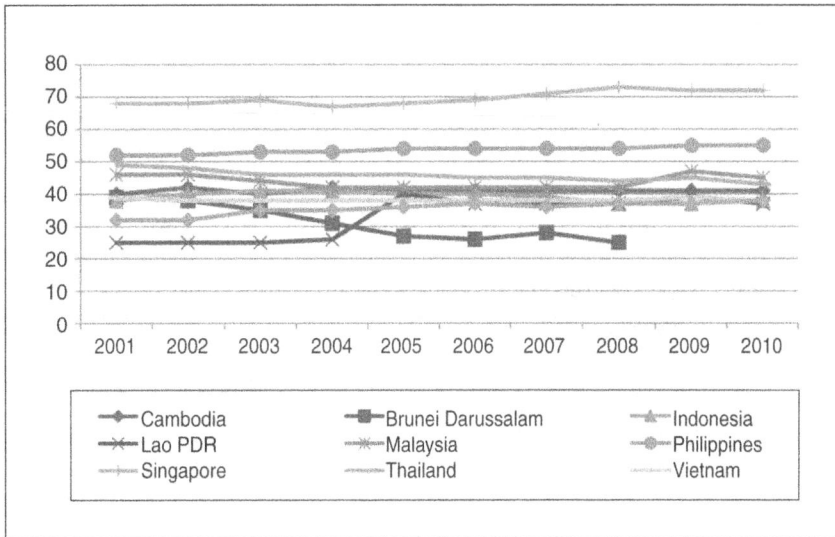

Source: Author's estimate.

of services value added to GDP, which is in the seventies. The figure for the Philippines, the second ranked, is in the distant mid fifties. The remaining member countries show ratios in the thirties and forties, bar Brunei. As an oil rich country, services trade remains rather insignificant for the economy despite the high per capita GDP.

ASEAN countries as a whole showed an increasing trend of the percentage of services value added to GDP over the past decade, especially for Singapore and the Philippines. For manufacturing-based member countries such as Indonesia, Thailand, and Malaysia, the services sector GDP is either stagnant or in decline. Nevertheless, service sector contributes to roughly 40 per cent of the GDP in these countries, a share which is comparable to the manufacturing sector (see Figure 4.1).

Share of Services Sector in Total Employment

As an emerging market, the overall structure of the ASEAN economies has been shifting from agriculture to industry and to services. As a result, employment in the services sector has been on a rising trend since the 2000s. Data from International Labour Organization (ILO) report in 2008 shows that, bar Lao PDR, the employment share of the services sector for all ASEAN countries increased from 2000 to 2006, as shown in Figure 4.2.

It is worth noting that barring Lao PDR, lower-middle income countries such as Vietnam, Cambodia, Philippines, and Indonesia, all experienced rising services sector employment shares. This illustrates the importance of the services sector to all ASEAN member countries regardless of the level of economic development. Moreover, the ILO's Annual Report, which addresses the Labour and Social Trends in ASEAN in 2008, shows that from 2006 to 2007, the services sector trumps the agriculture and manufacturing sectors in terms of the absolute number of additional workers employed as shown in Table 4.1. In terms of percentage growth, however, the industrial sector still trumps the service sector, indicating that economic expansion in the ASEAN region as a whole is still driven by manufacturing industries. Nevertheless, the service sector, which tends to be labour intensive, has significant implications on the region's

FIGURE 4.2

**Sectoral Employment Share of ASEAN and Its Member Countries,
1996–2009**

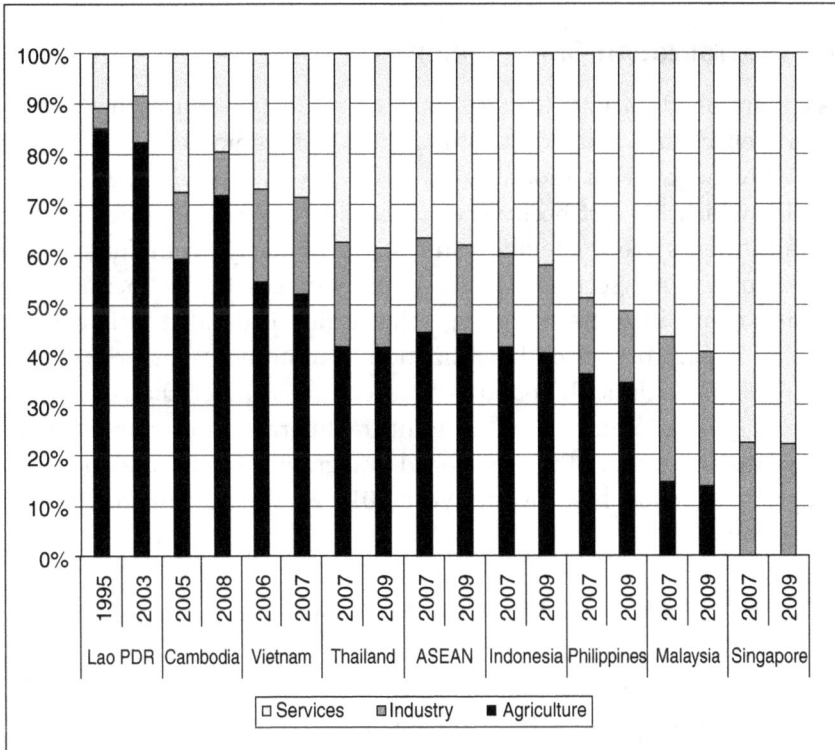

Source: International Labour Organization's Annual Report: *Labour and Social Trends in ASEAN 2008.*

TABLE 4.1

Sectoral Employment in ASEAN, 2006–07

	Agriculture	Industry	Services
Employment growth ('000s)	2,235	2,484	3,163
Employment growth (%)	1.9	5.1	3.3
Share in total employment	44.5	19.0	36.5

Source: International Labour Organization's Annual Report: *Labour and Social Trends in ASEAN 2008.*

employment. Thus, higher growth in the services sector can make non-trivial contribution to member countries' employment and hence, income.

III. Liberalization Commitments

As mentioned earlier, liberalization of trade in services in ASEAN lags well behind that of trade in goods. This is not surprising given that the negotiation modality is based on that established by the GATS, which has not been very successful on garnering liberalization commitments from member states, particularly from developing economies. This section describes the services trade liberalization commitments in ASEAN thus far. The section is divided in two parts. The first part describes liberalization commitments in opening up services trade through rounds of negotiations under the AFAS. The second part examines past and future liberalization commitments designed to support the envisioned integration of the region into a single production base by the year 2015 as spelled out in the AEC Blueprint.

ASEAN Framework Agreement in Services

ASEAN has completed several rounds of negotiation under AFAS, which is based on the request and offer approach as in the GATS. Under such an approach, WTO members choose in which sectors to offer binding commitments in response to requests from other WTO members. Commitments are made in schedules opening up only the sectors included — this is known as the "positive list" or "bottom-up" approach. The agreement is not reached until all members are satisfied with the totality of the package being offered. This does not prevent any country from making commitments unilaterally or liberalizing autonomously at any time. This approach, which lacks clear liberalization targets, has not been successful in fostering "offers" to liberalize from member countries that do not wish to open up their services sector to foreign competition in the WTO. The same goes for AFAS.

As can be seen in Table 4.2, ASEAN has completed seven packages of commitments to liberalize services trade thus far. But negotiations

TABLE 4.2

ASEAN Achievements in Services Trade Negotiation, 1995–2011

Package of Services Commitments	Signed	Modality
1st Package (Round 1)	December 1997	Request and offer approach
2nd Package (Round 1)	December 1998	Request and offer approach
3rd Package (Round 2)	December 2001	Common sub-sectors (if minimum 4 countries => multi-lateralize)
4th Package (Round 3)	September 2004	Modified common sub-sectors/ (If minimum 3 countries => multilateralize but ASEAN minus X)
5th Package (Round 4)	December 2006	same as above
6th Package (Round 4)	November 2007	same as above
7th Package (Round 5)	February 2009	Negotiation according to AEC Blueprint
8th Package (Round 5)	Due to be completed in August 2011	same as above
9th Package	2013	same as above
10th Package	2015	Attainment of the AEC liberalization targets

Source: Author's compilation.

for the past fifteen years have resulted only in marginal liberalization of trade in services in ASEAN. Corbett (2008)[2] noted that:

> The broad conclusion here is that AFAS is not particularly liberalizing compared with GATS commitments (Stephenson and Nikomborirak, 2002; Vo and Bartlett, 2006; Roy et al., 2006; Fink and Molinuevo, 2007) and that most regional Preferential Trade Agreements (PTAs) do not add significant new liberalizing elements over GATS (Ochiai et al., 2007). Since AFAS does not go much beyond the GATS, it is not providing much impetus to liberalize services trade within ASEAN.

Lim (2008) quantified commitments made in AFAS compared to those made in the GATS. Table 4.3 illustrates the Sectoral Coverage Ratio (SCR) of AFAS commitments. SCR is defined as the ratio of GATS + AFAS sectoral coverage in the numerator and the GATS sectoral coverage in the denominator. That is, the larger the ratio, the more advanced are commitments made in the AFAS as compared with those made in the GATS. The minimum ratio, which is one, indicates that concessions made in the regional forum under the AFAS are not any more advanced than those made in the multilateral forum under the GATS.

As can be seen, except for Brunei, Myanmar and the Philippines, the SCR figures for member countries are marginally greater than one. The low SCR scores for Cambodia and Vietnam, however, can be explained by their already advanced liberalization commitments made in WTO (due to their relatively late accession) rather than their unwillingness to open up their services sector at the regional level. Table 4.3 shows quantitative indicators of individual ASEAN country's GATS commitments index.[3] As mentioned earlier, Cambodia and Vietnam obtain the highest scores of 49.08 and 30.15, respectively. Brunei and Myanmar made very little concession in the GATS, while larger ASEAN economies such as Indonesia, the Philippines, Thailand, Malaysia, and Singapore, receive scores that range from the lowest at 9.52 for Indonesia to highest at 25.4 for Malaysia. For these countries, barring the Philippines, AFAS commitments are only marginal to those made in the WTO as the SCR figures are between 1.09 for Singapore and 1.56 for Indonesia. ASEAN's average SCR score is only 1.58. Although Brunei and Myanmar made marked concessions in the AFAS over those made in the GATS, their

TABLE 4.3

**Liberalization Commitment in Services Trade under AFAS
Compared with those made in the WTO**

	(1) GATS Commitment	(2) SCR ((WTO + AFAS)/AFAS)	(3) (1) * (2)
Brunei Darussalam	4.35	3.38	14.70
Cambodia	49.08	1.21	59.38
Indonesia	9.52	1.56	14.85
Lao PDR		–	
Malaysia	25.40	1.26	32.00
Myanmar	4.94	3.00	14.82
Philippines	14.08	3.03	42.66
Singapore	22.66	1.09	24.69
Thailand	19.73	1.35	26.63
Vietnam	30.15	1.09	32.86
ASEAN average	13.0	1.58	20.53

Source: GATS commitment index compiled from the World Trade Indicator, the World Bank (2008) and SCR scores from Lim (2008).

commitments in the GATS were negligible to begin with such that commitments in the AFAS, too, were marginal. As a result, the net liberalization indicators (shown in column 3) for these two countries remain rather low compared with those of other member countries. Only the Philippines made a meaningful progress in liberalizing her services trade under AFAS.

Mutual Recognition Arrangements (MRAs)

The AEC addresses the importance of MRAs by enabling the qualifications of professional services suppliers to be mutually recognized by signatory member states; hence, facilitating easier movement of professional services providers in the ASEAN region. It should be noted that MRAs do not warrant unrestricted flow of foreign professionals as domestic rules and regulations would still apply.

As of July 2011, ASEAN has concluded seven MRAs as shown in Table 4.4. However, each MRA is different, as follows:

TABLE 4.4

ASEAN MRAs, 2005–11

MRA on Sector	Detail
Engineering services	signed on 9 December 2005 in Kuala Lumpur, Malaysia
Nursing services	signed on 8 December 2006 in Cebu, the Philippines
Architectural services, surveying qualification	Both signed on 19 November 2007 in Singapore.
Medical Practitioners, Dental Practitioners, and Accountancy Services	All signed on 26 February 2009 in Cha-am Hua Hin, Thailand.

Source: Compilation by the author; ASEAN Secretariat, <http://www.asean.org/>.

1. MRAs on engineering and architecture provide recognition for registered ASEAN professionals by providing harmonized standards and qualifications. Member states that would like to participate must notify the ASEAN Secretary-General;
2. The MRA on nursing was designed to strengthen professional capabilities by promoting the exchange of expertise, experience, and best practices;
3. MRAs on Accountancy and Surveying services lay down the broad principles and framework for the negotiating bilateral and multilateral MRAs; and
4. MRAs on medical and dental professions are based on bilateral registration processes. Member states that wish to defer the implementation must notify the ASEAN Secretary-General.

In sum, ASEAN MRAs provide the "tools" for ASEAN member countries to promote mobility of professionals within the region on a voluntary basis, rather than prescribing binding commitments. The extent to which these MRAs impact the ASEAN economy will depend on member countries' willingness to liberalize professional services.

The AEC Blueprint

As mentioned earlier, the AEC envisions ASEAN as a single production base which requires the free flow of goods, services, investment, capital, and skilled labour. To promote the free flow of services, liberalization will be achieved through five consecutive more rounds of negotiations, where remaining restrictions on trade in services are to be removed progressively until 2015, when substantially all restrictions shall be removed. The minimum number of new sub-sectors[4] for each round has been spelled out and priority sectors targeted for earlier liberalization have been identified.

According to the AEC Blueprint, the following actions need to be taken by the member countries to achieve the free flow of services by 2015:

1. Remove substantially all restrictions on trade in services for four priority services sectors, air transport, e-ASEAN, healthcare, and tourism by 2010, and for all other sectors by 2015;
2. Schedule packages of commitments according to the following parameters:
   i. No restrictions for mode 1 (cross border supply) and mode 2 (consumption abroad), with exceptions due to bona fide regulatory reasons;
   ii. Allow for foreign (ASEAN) equity participation[6] of not less than 51 per cent for the four priority sectors in 2008, 70 per cent in 2010; for other sectors, 49 per cent in 2008, 51 per cent in 2010 and 70 per cent in 2015, except for logistics services the target year is 2013;
   iii. Remove other mode 3 (commercial presence) market access limitations by 2015.

These liberalization targets can be summed up in Table 4.5.

3. Complete mutual recognition arrangements (MRAs) in architectural services, accountancy services, surveying qualifications, medical practitioners by 2008, and dental practitioners by 2009. Implement MRAs expeditiously according to the provisions of each respective MRA and identify MRAs for other professional services by 2012, to be completed by 2015.

It should be noted that the liberalization milestones stipulated in the AEC are to be implemented by rounds of negotiations in the AFAS. As shown in Table 4.2, AEC service liberalization targets are to be implemented through four consecutive rounds of negotiations in the

TABLE 4.5
Service Sector Liberalization Targets

Sectors	Targets
Priority Sectors:	51% — 2008
e-ASEAN, Healthcare and tourism services	70% — 2010
Logistics	51% — 2010
	70% — 2013
Others	51% — 2010
	70% — 2015
Construction	51% — 2008
	70% — 2015

Source: AEC Blueprint.

AFAS (eighth to eleventh packages) that are expected to be completed every two years until the year 2015.

Table 4.3 reveals that service liberalization targets established in the AEC are far from those that are required to support full integration of member economies. First, liberalization in Mode 3 (commercial presence) envisions only 70 per cent of ASEAN equity share, i.e., wholly owned foreign (ASEAN) companies are still not allowed.

Second, liberalization of Mode 4 (movement of natural persons) is confined to movement of professionals only, while unskilled labour is excluded. And even then, the goal established to promote the movement of professional services does not prescribe any liberalization obligations, but rather an agreement framework to facilitate liberalization, as will be discussed later in this chapter in greater detail. In short, the AEC services liberalization target is far from ambitious. Nevertheless, these liberalization targets are binding on member countries.[6] However, the AEC allows for flexibility in complying with these commitments. Section 3 of the Blueprint states that in meeting clear targets and timelines, there should be "pre-agreed flexibilities to accommodate the interests of all ASEAN Member Countries". This has translated into section 21(ix) under the free flow of services section, which stipulates as follows:

> Allow for overall flexibilities,[8] which cover the sub-sectors totally excluded from liberalization and the sub-sectors in which not all the

agreed parameters of liberalization of the modes of supply are met, in scheduling liberalization commitments. The scheduling of liberalization commitments in each round shall be accorded with the following flexibilities:

- Possibility of catching up in the next round if a Member Country is not able to meet the parameters of commitments set for the previous round;
- Allowing for substituting sub-sectors that have been agreed to be liberalized in a round but for which a Member Country is not able to make commitments with sub-sectors outside the agreed sub-sectors; and
- Liberalization through the ASEAN Minus X formula.

This flexibility provision is nothing but vague. First, it is not clear how the 15 per cent flexibility will be measured and quantified in practice. Second, while the inventory of restrictions to trade in services have been compiled and continuously updated, there has been no disclosure and assessment of this very important database on which the design of the flexibility conditionality is based. Third, while section 20 of the AEC stipulates that there shall not be "back-loading" of commitments, allowing catching up of commitments will no doubt lead to such a problem. Fourth, it is not clear how a member country can switch out of a prescribed liberalization commitment by substituting with other sub-sectors not subject to liberalization. Can, say, a member switch out of commitments to open up a priority sector such as tele-communications (e-ASEAN) by making compensatory commitment in a less economically significant service sub-sector such as leasing or advertisement? If so, what would be the use of specifying "priority sectors"? Finally, the option of *"Liberalization through the ASEAN Minus X formula"* appears to be saying that if a member country cannot comply with the liberalization thresholds and the deadlines established, then it can always opt out. What if X equals 10 and no country fulfils the prescribed commitments? The flexibility clause seems to dilute what is supposed to be "binding" commitments into nothing more than those based on "best effort".

Financial services sector liberalization is dealt with separately in the AEC Blueprint because the economic sensitivity of the financial sector as well as the diverse stage of development of the particular service sector in various member countries. The sector is also negotiated by

Finance Ministers rather than Trade and Industry Ministers as is the case for other services.

The distinctive feature of the financial sector liberalization under the AEC is that: (1) the liberalization target is extended to the year 2020 instead of 2015 and, (2) there is no pre-specified scope of liberalization in terms of both the breadth and the depth of the commitment to be made as member countries are allowed to carve out sub-sectors they do not wish to open up under the "pre-agreed flexibilities", much like the sensitive list in trade in goods liberalization. However, in this case, the list indicated by member states turns out to be a positive rather than a negative one as shown in the Table 4.6. This implies that the scope of liberalization would likely be very limited.

Moreover, there is no minimum commitment required of all member states. For example, none of the original ASEAN-5 member states are willing to open up their banking sectors. Interestingly, only CLV (Cambodia, Laos and Vietnam) countries committed to do so. Perhaps this was because banking sector liberalization was required as part of the liberalization package for Cambodia's, Vietnam's and Laos' relatively late accession to the WTO (years 2005, 2007 and 2012, respectively). For Laos, it has also signed a bilateral trade agreement

TABLE 4.6

Financial Services Sub-Sectors Identified for Liberalization by 2015

	Sub-sectors	Member Countries
Insurance	Direct Life Insurance	Indonesia, Philippines
	Direct Non-life Insurance	Brunei, Cambodia, Indonesia, Malaysia, Philippines, Singapore and Vietnam
	Reinsurance and Retrocession	Brunei, Cambodia, Indonesia, Malaysia, Philippines, Singapore and Vietnam
	Insurance Intermediation	Cambodia, Indonesia, Malaysia, Philippines, Singapore and Vietnam
	Services Auxiliary to Insurance	Brunei, Cambodia, Indonesia, Malaysia, Philippines, Singapore and Vietnam

Banking	Acceptance of Deposits and Other Repayable Funds from the Public	Cambodia, Laos and Vietnam
	Lending of All Types	Cambodia, Laos and Vietnam
	Financial Leasing	Cambodia, Laos and Vietnam
	All Payment and Money Transmission Services	Cambodia, Laos and Vietnam
	Guarantee and Commitments	Cambodia, Laos, Myanmar and Vietnam
Capital Market	Trading for Own Account or for Account of Customers	Brunei, Indonesia, Malaysia, Philippines, Singapore and Thailand
	Participation in Issues of All Kinds of Securities	Indonesia, Philippines (subject to constitutional and legislative limitations)
	Participation in Issues of All Kinds of Securities	Indonesia, Philippines (subject to constitutional and legislative limitations)
	Participation in Issues of All Kinds of Securities	Indonesia, Philippines (subject to constitutional and legislative limitations)
Others	Provision and Transfer of Financial Information, Financial Data Processing and Related Software by Suppliers of Other Financial Services	Philippines and Myanmar
	Advisory, Intermediation and Other Auxiliary Financial Services	Philippines, Singapore, Thailand and Vietnam

Source: 2007 ASEAN Economic Community Blueprint available online at <http://www.aseansec.org/21161.pdf>.

with the U.S. in 2005, which entails liberalization of major service sectors, such as banking and telecommunications. Undoubtedly, the bilateral liberalization can easily extend into a multilateral one. Vietnam also signed a similar agreement in 2001.

On the other hand, incumbent members with large domestic market and businesses to protect are less willing to open up. For example, Thailand, probably the least progressive member country when it comes to services sector liberalization, made commitments only in the capital market and none in the banking and insurance sectors.

IV. Compliance with the AEC Blueprint

ASEAN's decision to abandon the request and offer approach to negotiating services trade liberalization agreement in favour of an approach that provides for clear quantitative liberalization targets and milestones as prescribed in the AEC Blueprint is laudable. However, the built-in flexibility which is both vague and broad undermines the attainment of free flow of services by 2015, as envisioned in the AEC Blueprint.

According to the AEC Scorecard released in March 2012, the region has fallen behind in the liberalization goals required for free flow of services during Phase II (2010–11) of the implementation, as only 13 out of 30 measures have been fully implemented.

The AEC Blueprint indicates that the service liberalization goals are to be achieved through five consecutive rounds of negotiations until the year 2015. As of today, ASEAN has concluded on only one round of negotiations which produced the 7th service liberalization package in February. The conclusion of the 8th package has been delayed several times.

Comparing commitments made in the 7th package with the milestones as prescribed in the AEC Blueprint (see Table 4.7), it is clear that every member country, barring Singapore, has fallen behind the liberalization goals in terms of foreign equity participation (Mode 3) in 2008 and in 2010. As for Mode 1 and Mode 2, the AEC envisioned no restrictions except for bona fide regulatory reasons. Here, as can be seen from Tables 4.8 and 4.9, with very few exceptions, members have largely complied with this commitment. The only problematic area is construction where cross-border services remain unbound for many member states. On the contrary, all member countries, barring Singapore, fail to raise the

TABLE 4.7

The 7th Services Liberalization Package and AEC Goals (Mode 3)

Subsectors		AEC		AFAS 7					
		Targets	Year	Thailand (18 May 2009)	Malaysia (16 Oct 2009)	Singapore (1 Oct 2009)	Philippines (17 Aug 2010)	Indonesia (9 May 2009)	Brunei (23 Oct 2009)
E-ASEAN	Mobile telephone service	51% 70%	2008 2010	49%	51%	73.99%*	40%	49%	*********
	Online information and database retrieval	51% 70%	2008 2010	49%	51%	**	***	51%	100%
	Consultancy services related to the installation of computer hardware	51% 70%	2008 2010	100%	100%	100%	40%****	Joint operation through a representative office in Indonesia	–
Healthcare	Hospital services	51% 70%	2008 2010	49%	51%	51%	40%*****	49%	100%
	Medical and dental services	51% 70%	2008 2010	49%	51%	100%	–	49%	100%
	Dental Services	51% 70%	2008 2010	49%	51%	100%	–	49%	–
Tourism	Hotel lodging services	51% 70%	2008 2010	49%	51%	100%	100%	100% in Eastern Part of Indonesia and 51% for other areas	It must be a joint venture with local company subject to local regulation.
	Meal serving services	51% 70%	2008 2010	49%	51%	100%	100%******	51% in Eastern Part of Indonesia only	

TABLE 4.7 (continued)

Subsectors		AEC		AFAS 7					
		Targets	Year	Thailand (18 May 2009)	Malaysia (16 Oct 2009)	Singapore (1 Oct 2009)	Philippines (17 Aug 2010)	Indonesia (9 May 2009)	Brunei (23 Oct 2009)
	Travel agency and tour operator services	51% 70%	2008 2010	49%	51%	100%	60%	49%	–
Construction		49% 51% 70%	2008 2010 2015	49%	51%	100%	40%********	55%	55%
Logistics	Maritime freight forwarding	49% 51% 70%	2008 2010 2013	49%	49%	100%	40%*******	49%	49%
	Storage and warehouse services for maritime transport	49% 51% 70%	2008 2010 2013	49%	49%	100%	100%	49%	49%
Others	Maritime cargo handling services	49% 51% 70%	2008 2010 2015	49%	49%	100%	100%	60%	49%
	Freight transportation	49% 51% 70%	2008 2010 2015	49%	49%	100%	40%	49%	–

Note: * A cumulative total of 73.99% foreign shareholding, based on 49% direct investment and 24.99% indirect investment is allowed.
  ** Foreign companies are required to either set up a local branch of their company duly registered with the Registry of Companies and Businesses in Singapore, or grant a power of attorney to a local agent for the provision of their VAN services in Singapore.
  *** Operation subject to securing of:
  (a) Franchise from Congress of the Philippines, and
  (b) Certificate of Public Convenience and Necessity (CPCN) from the National Telecommunications Commissions.

**** 100% foreign equity participation is allowed in the following cases:

(a) paid-in equity capital is not less than US$200,000 for domestic market enterprises;

(b) paid-in equity capital is not less than US$100,000 for domestic market enterprises employing at least 50 direct employees;

(c) paid-in equity capital is not less than US$100,000 for domestic market enterprises involving advanced technology as determined by the DOST; or

(d) the service provider exports 60% or more of its output.

***** Up to 100% foreign equity participation is allowed provided:

(a) paid-in equity capital is at least US$200,000; or

(b) paid-in equity must not be less than US$100,000 for domestic market enterprises employing at least 50 direct employees.

****** Enterprises with paid-up capital of US$2.5 million or more may be wholly owned by foreigners.

******* Up to 100% foreign equity participation is allowed, provided that paid-in equity capital is not less than $200,000, otherwise up to 40% foreign equity participation is allowed.

******** 40% foreign equity for construction of locally funded private projects and 100% foreign equity for foreign-funded/assisted internationally-bid construction projects.

********* Subject to license by the appropriate regulatory authority and Brunei Darussalam Companies' Act.

Source: Author's compilation.

TABLE 4.8

The 7th Services Liberalization Package and AEC Goals (Mode 1)

Subsectors		AEC		AFAS 7					
		Targets	Year	Thailand (18 May 2009)	Malaysia (16 Oct 2009)	Singapore (1 Oct 2009)	Philippines (17 Aug 2010)	Indonesia (9 May 2009)	Brunei (23 Oct 2009)
E-ASEAN	Mobile telephone service	No restrictions for mode 1 and mode 2, with exceptions due to bona fide regulatory reasons	2015	None, other than — traffic shall be routed through gateways in Thailand operated by suppliers duly licensed; — the provision of concerned services shall be agreed by the supplier duly licensed on both ends.	None	Subject to commercial arrangements with licensed operator(s)	Subject to commercial arrangement with licensed operators	None	Subject to commercial arrangements with licensed operator(s)
	Online information and database retrieval				None	*	Only through duly enfranchised and certificated domestic public telecommunications carriers	None	None

Sector	Service						
	Consultancy services related to the installation of computer hardware	None	None	None	None	None	None
Healthcare	Hospital services	Unbound due to lack of technical feasibility	None	Unbound	Unbound	None	None
	Medical and dental services	None	None	–	Unbound	None	None
	Dental Services	–	None	–	None	None	None
Tourism	Hotel lodging services	None	None	None	Unbound	None	None
	Meal serving services	–	None	None	None	None	None
	Travel agency and tour operator services	–	None	None	None	None	Unbound
Logistics	Maritime freight forwarding	None	None	None	None	None	Unbound
	Storage and warehouse services for maritime transport	None	None	Unbound	None	None	None

TABLE 4.8 *(continued)*

AEC			AFAS 7					
Subsectors	Targets	Year	Thailand (18 May 2009)	Malaysia (16 Oct 2009)	Singapore (1 Oct 2009)	Philippines (17 Aug 2010)	Indonesia (9 May 2009)	Brunei (23 Oct 2009)
Others	Maritime cargo handling services		None	None	None	Unbound	Unbound*	None
	Freight transportation		None	None	None	None	None	-
Construction			Unbound	Unbound due to lack of technical feasibility	None	Unbound due to lack of technical feasibility	Unbound*	Unbound due to lack of technical feasibility

Note: * Provision of VAN services is subjected to licence from the Infocomm Development Authority of Singapore (IDA).
      The basic requirements for VAN licence are:
    – Foreign companies are required to either set up a local branch of their company duly registered with the Registry of Companies and
      Businesses in Singapore, or grant a power of attorney to a local agent for the provision of their VAN services in Singapore;
    – VAN does not carry traffic which resembles any of the basic telecommunication services.
Source: Author's compilation.

TABLE 4.9

The 7th Service Liberalization Package and AEC Goals (Mode 2)

Subsectors	AEC Targets	AEC Year	Thailand (18 May 2009)	Malaysia (16 Oct 2009)	AFAS 7 Singapore (1 Oct 2009)	Philippines (17 Aug 2010)	Indonesia (9 May 2009)	Brunei (23 Oct 2009)
E-ASEAN								
Mobile telephone service	No restrictions for mode 1 and mode 2, with exceptions due to bona fide regulatory reasons	2015	None, other than — traffic shall be routed through gateways in Thailand operated by suppliers duly licensed; — the provision of concerned services shall be agreed by the supplier duly licensed of both ends.	None	None	None	None	Subject to commercial arrangements with licensed operator(s)
Online information and database retrieval				None	None	None	None	None
Consultancy services related to the installation of computer hardware			None	None	None	None	None	None

TABLE 4.9 (continued)

Subsectors		AEC		AFAS 7					
		Targets	Year	Thailand (18 May 2009)	Malaysia (16 Oct 2009)	Singapore (1 Oct 2009)	Philippines (17 Aug 2010)	Indonesia (9 May 2009)	Brunei (23 Oct 2009)
Healthcare	Hospital services			None	None	None	None	None	None
	Medical and dental services			None	None	None	–	None	None
	Dental services			None	None	None	–	None	
Tourism	Hotel lodging services			None	None	None	None	None	None
	Meal serving services			None	None	None	None	None	
	Travel agency and tour operator services			None	None	None	None	None	
Logistics	Maritime freight forwarding			None	None	None	None	None	None
	Storage and warehouse services for maritime transport			None	None	None	None	None	None

	None	None	None	None	None	None
Others						
Maritime cargo handling services	None	None	None	None	None	–
Freight transportation						
Construction	None	None	None	None	None	None

Note: * Mode 1 "None, except…" due to bona fide regulatory reasons:
Health and Safety reasons: foreign professionals who intend to practise in Brunei Darussalam should submit plans of the proposed developments through licensed practicing companies/partnerships/architects in Brunei Darussalam to provide for an entity or a body that will be liable for the development.
Source: Author's compilation.

foreign equity level in keeping with the schedule established in the AEC Blueprint. If there is no marked improvement in commitments in the 8th package, then it would be highly unlikely that the region will be able to meet its service investment liberalization goals by the year 2015.

V. Exploitation of Trade Privileges

Although negotiations under the AFAS have produced several packages of commitments to liberalize services trade within ASEAN, the margin of liberalization thus far has been minimal. Besides, the ASEAN Secretariat does not have a database on the exploitation of services trade privileges, particularly in investment (Mode 3). This lack of enthusiasm to track down intra-regional equity investment in the service sector perhaps can be attributed to both the lack of data at the national level as well as the insignificance of the privileges accorded by the regional agreement. In addition, domestic restrictions with regard to equity holding, land holding, licensing, etc., continue to pose significant barriers to intra-regional investment in services. Since the AEC does not reach into the behind-the-border issues, it is likely that these barriers will persist in the foreseeable future, making the relaxation of equity holding as prescribed in the AEC futile in attracting regional investment.

As for the promotion of the movement of skilled professionals, seven MRAs have been concluded and signed by ASEAN Economic Ministers (AEM). Among these, only engineering and architectural services provide standardized recognition of skills level of registered ASEAN architects and engineers.

The ASEAN engineering MRA brought about the ASEAN Chartered Professional Engineers Coordinating Committee (ACPECC), a regional engineering committee that controls a standardized registration of engineers recognized by the ASEAN member countries. Engineer graduates in ASEAN have to pass the domestic exams on engineering and obtain domestic licenses of an engineering career before applying through ASEAN Chartered Professional Engineers (ACPEs) to work as Registered Foreign Professional Engineers (RFPEs) under the Professional Regulatory Authority (PRA) of each participating ASEAN

Member Country. Table 4.10 shows the data on a number of domestic engineers in ASEAN countries who have been registered as ACPEs.

As can be seen from Table 4.10, out of ten, only four member states have registered ACPEs. This is because certain members such as Brunei, Lao, Cambodia, and Vietnam, did not have a proper Professional Regulatory Authority that can register ACPEs. Vietnam and more recently, Brunei, have passed the law establishing such an authority. In the case of Thailand, there has been much delay in passing internal rules and procedures governing the registration and the licensing of ACPE due partly to legal complications and partly to the Council's reluctance to open up the engineering professional services to foreign nationals.

It should also be noted that the number of ACPEs shown above by no means describes the extent of the flow of professional services across the borders within the ASEAN region. What is required would be the number of ACPEs that actually work in another member country. It is likely that ACPEs will face multiple barriers in obtaining permission to work overseas because the MRA merely states that ACPEs shall be "eligible" to apply to the Professional Regulatory Authority (PRA) of a host country to be registered as a "Registered Foreign Professional Engineer (RFPE)" as mentioned early and shall be permitted to work as RFPE subject to domestic laws and regulations. Indeed, most countries impose restrictions on foreign nationals or non-residents working as professional engineers.

TABLE 4.10

Number of ASEAN Chartered Professional Engineers (ACPEs) in ASEAN Countries

Country	Numbers of ACPEs
Malaysia	149
Singapore	183
Indonesia	99
Vietnam	9
Total	440

Source: <www.acpecc.org/modules/acpes.php> (accessed May 2012).

For example, the Thai Engineer Act 1999 does not explicitly impose a nationality requirement for the granting of a professional engineer license. However, the law prescribes that applicants for such a license must be a "regular" or "irregular" member of the Council of Engineers. And, in a separate section of the law, it is stipulated that regular members need to hold Thai citizenship. Hence, foreign registered engineers qualify only as "irregular" members whose scope and conditionality of work will be subject to the rules and regulations set by the Council. In Malaysia, foreign engineers may be licensed by the Board of Engineers for specific projects and must be sponsored by the Malaysian company carrying out the project. Normally, the Malaysian company must demonstrate to the Board of Engineers that they cannot find a local engineer for the job. In general, a foreign engineer must be registered engineer in his or her home country, have a minimum of ten years' experience and have a physical presence in Malaysia of at least 180 days in a calendar year.

Similarly, in architecture, the ASEAN Architect Council (AAC) has been founded as an organization that controls a standardized registration of architects in ASEAN. That is, after an architect graduates from a university, obtains a domestic license from the Professional Regulatory Authority (PRA) of the Country with relevant work experience, he is then eligible to apply to the ASEAN Architect Council (AAC) to be registered as an ASEAN Architect (AA) under the ASEAN Architect Register (AAR). But again, the permission to work as a foreign registered architect will depend on the domestic laws and regulations of each member country. And, as in the case of engineers, most countries impose certain restrictions on residency or nationality to become fully licensed architects. Foreign architects are often allowed to work only on a project basis and even then, in some countries, employers have to submit proof that a suitable national professional is not available for the role. Currently, there is no registered ASEAN Architect since the AAC has begun to function in May 2011.

For other MRAs, the harvesting of the benefits from the agreements has also been very limited. For example, in the case of nursing, although the MRA provides a great opportunity for nurses in the region to acquire experiences in other member countries, they still need to comply with domestic rules and regulations governing the registration of nurses imposed by the national nursing regulatory body. For example, in order for a Filipino nurse to practise in Thailand, the candidate must pass the national licensure exam in Thai language.[7] Since the MRAs do not address domestic rules and regulations that may pose barriers to the mobility of foreign nurses, the MRA may prove futile.

As for the surveying profession, the MRA merely provides the enabling framework of broad principles for further bilateral and multilateral negotiations among ASEAN member states. Currently, the Asean Federation of Land Survey and Geomatics (AFlag) is attempting to design a model MRA that can be used for bilateral and plurilateral agreements. However, unlike the legal, accounting and other professions, the definition of the surveying profession services and scope of responsibilities is not yet determined and the service is not yet codified according to the UN's Central Product Classification Code (CPC Code). These factors make an MRA in Surveying most challenging to implement.

To conclude, the halting progress in liberalizing trade in services in ASEAN due to member countries' lack of willingness to open up their service markets may impede ASEAN's goal of regional economic integration. But even if member states were able to meet all the milestones set in the AEC Blueprint, it remains uncertain whether full integration of the region's economies can be achieved. The next section addresses the key behind-the-border restrictions that may pose significant barriers to the free flows of services in the region.

VI. Conclusion and Policy Recommendations

This chapter makes four important discoveries. First, the service sector liberalization goals established in the AEC are far from ambitious with the partial liberalization of foreign equity share in Mode 3. Second, the implementation process remains vague with multiple flexibilities, some of which are opaque. This serves to undermine the realization of the liberalization goals in 2015. Third, actual implementation is already far behind the milestones established in the AEC, perhaps because of the flexibility clause that permits back-loading of liberalization commitments. Fourth, foreign equity limitation, which is the only factor being negotiated in services liberalization thus far, is not the only major barrier to services trade. The right to hold land, hire foreign professionals, and obtain a business permit, is just as crucial for the decision to establish commercial presence overseas.

With these discoveries, the AEC is unlikely to make any meaningful difference to ASEAN services trade in the foreseeable future. However, very few people recognize this fact and still anticipate a massive tide of cross border investment and movement of labour in 2015. Perhaps the myths surrounding the AEC will help shake up the dormant and well-protected services sector to face greater competition from outside.

The author is of the opinion that the rather unambitious liberalization goals and lax implementation in services trade established in the AEC, reflect the unwillingness of ASEAN member countries to open up their cosseted and at times, lucrative, service sectors. In the absence of political will, it will be difficult to envision an integrated ASEAN service market in the foreseeable future. Many studies have revealed that almost all past services sector liberalization in ASEAN can be attributed to unilateral policy moves rather than regional commitments.

Perhaps to push the service liberalization agenda forward the ASEAN Secretariat would need to build an effective coalition supporting the liberalization agenda by demonstrating the inherent inefficiency of the existing service sector in various ASEAN countries. For example, the cost and quality of certain services, such as banking or telecommunications, in highly protected service sectors in certain ASEAN countries can be benchmarked against those in countries where such services have been liberalized and exposed to competition. The comparison would be most effective if the benchmark case is an ASEAN member country, say, Singapore, that has unilaterally liberalized the services market. This inefficiency would then need to be translated into foregone economic growth in order for the lay person to appreciate its significance. Consumers and small businesses are not the only likely advocates, the media and academics will also need to come on board to effectively push the liberalization agenda.

At the same time, it would also be important to identify the proponents of liberalization — i.e., those who benefit from the current protection in order to understand the political economy of the liberalization of services trade. For example, in many member countries, state enterprises operating in various vital service sectors such as telecommunications, energy, and even banking, enjoy the exclusivity and the monopoly profits afforded from protection. As less developed economies tend to rely heavily on revenues generated from SOEs engaged in lucrative businesses to fill their fiscal coffers, they are thus reluctant to liberalize. Hence, one cannot discuss the issue of liberalization without first addressing monopolization and the role of state-owned enterprises. It may be necessary for ASEAN to first consider more elementary steps before jumping to the liberalization of cross border investment. This task can be easily be handled by academics but the ASEAN Secretariat may provide the necessary funding to launch these studies.

Indeed, the legal, institutional, political, or economic rationale for protection is likely to be diverse across different service sectors. Perhaps it would be more effective if ASEAN concentrates on sector specific liberalization, much like what took place in the WTO with the specific services annexes. The sector specific negotiation can be done in parallel with the existing broad-based request and offer modality based on the GATS. However, the commitments to be made in the specific service sector would be carefully tailored in keeping with the unique legal, political context and are more stringent (similar to the WTO Agreement on Basic Telecommunications which includes a Reference Paper on Telecommunications addressing the regulatory aspect of the liberalization). There should also be no built-in flexibilities that serve to "water down" the commitments in order to ensure the effective liberalization. However, the implementation time-frame may be made more accommodating by allowing certain member countries to postpone implementation to a pre-specified date. Given the highly sensitive nature of service sector liberalization, dealing with a single — or a few — sectors (s) may be more palatable to liberalization-averse policy-makers.

NOTES

1. This chapter is drawn from a longer paper on "ASEAN Trade in Services", which is a part of the ISEAS-ADB Project on "Assessment of Impediments & Actions Required for Achieving AEC by 2015". The papers of the project is a forthcoming publication (*The ASEAN Economic Community: A Work in Progress*) by Institute of Southeast Asian Studies.

2. Jenny Corbett, "Services Trade Liberalization in the ASEAN Economic Community and Beyond", Australian National University and the Productivity Commission of Australia Research Council, Canberra, 2008.

3. The GATS commitments index ranges from 0 (unbound or no commitments) to 100 (completely liberalized) for 155 service subsectors as classified by GATS in the four modes of trade in service. A simple average of the sub-sectoral scores was used to generate aggregate sectoral scores.

4. There are in total 128 services subsectors based on the WTO GATS W/120 classification.

5. Note that according to Article 6 in AFAS, the definition of "ASEAN investors" includes legal person owned or controlled by non-ASEAN persons which are "engaged in substantive business operations" in an ASEAN country. Therefore, a company registered under the laws of an ASEAN is also entitled to the privileges offered under the AFAS. This concept is consistent with that used in the GATS. However, The GATS does not provide for a clear definition of a substantive business operation. ASEAN has yet to codify the key word "substantive", without which the scope of investment liberalization in the region cannot be properly assessed.

6. Article 24 of the Charter of the Association of Southeast Asian Nations stipulates that "disputes concern the interpretation or the application of ASEAN economic agreements shall be settled in accordance with the ASEAN Protocol on Enhanced Dispute Settlement Mechanism". The latter is based on the WTO dispute settlement mechanism.

7. The 15 per cent figure for overall flexibility will be reviewed upon the completion of the inventory of limitations in 2008.

REFERENCES

Corbett, Jenny. "Services Trade Liberalization in the ASEAN Economic Community and Beyond". Australian National University and the Productivity Commission of Australia Research Council, Canberra, 2008.

Lim, H. "Policy Recommendation to Facilitate Implementation". In *Deepening Economic Integration in East Asia: ASEAN Economic Community and Beyond*, edited by Hadi Soesastro. ERIA, 2008. Accessed at <http://www.eria.org/research/images/pdf/PDF%20No.1-2/No.1-2-part2-3.pdf>.

5

THE INVESTMENT DIMENSION OF ASEAN[1]

Manu Bhaskaran

I. Introduction

This chapter focuses on the investment dimension of the ASEAN Economic Community (AEC). The first section studies recent patterns and trends in foreign and domestic investment in the region. The key finding is that these trends have been largely disappointing. The second section examines the underlying factors that might explain the disappointing performance. There appears to be a disjuncture between the relatively good fundamentals for investment in the region and the actual outcome, a disjuncture mainly related to country-specific weaknesses in the investment climate. The third section assesses the progress in implementation of the AEC and finds that despite progress, implementation leaves much to be achieved before the 2015 target. The final section presents some recommendations as to what could be done to improve the situation. I believe that a key thrust must be to create economies of scale so as to boost ASEAN's competitiveness in attracting investment relative to the large dynamic economies of China and India.

II. Weakening FDI and Domestic Investment in ASEAN

Attracting foreign investment has been an important component of the growth strategies of most ASEAN countries. In assessing the overall investment climate in ASEAN, we begin with an analysis of FDI trends before studying domestic investment.

FIGURE 5.1	FIGURE 5.2
ASEAN has a good share of global stock.	**But its share of flows has been declining.**

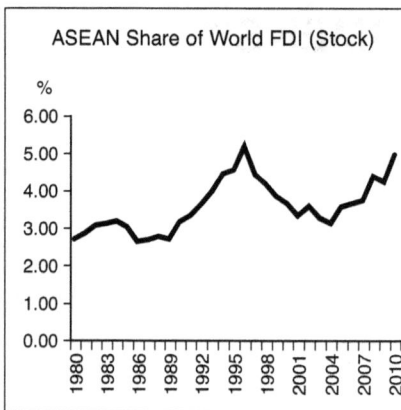

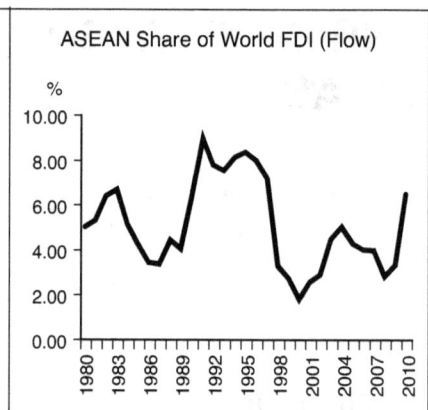

Source: Calculated by Centennial Asian Advisors using UNCTAD data.

ASEAN's Share of FDI Flows has Declined

Despite numerous attempts and initiatives to foster the appropriate investment climate for foreign investors, ASEAN as a whole continues to struggle in raising inward FDI beyond levels achieved prior to the Asian financial crisis of 1997–98. Figure 5.1 shows ASEAN's share of the stock of global FDI over the past three decades; this share rose to a peak of more than 5 per cent just before the financial crisis of 1997, and although it has been rising over the past few years, ASEAN's stock of world FDI has not reached its 1996 level. In terms of the annual flow of FDI, ASEAN's share has ebbed significantly in the 2000s from an average of 8 per cent in the mid-1990s before recovering to about 6 per cent in 2010.

An area of concern is ASEAN's declining proportion of both stock and flow of FDI within developing countries. Figure 5.3 indicates that ASEAN accounts for around 15 per cent of developing countries' total stock FDI for the last decade — lower than its peak of 20 per cent before the financial crisis. Its share of annual FDI flows has experienced a dramatic decline, languishing at around 14 per cent in 2010 as compared to 37 per cent in 1990.

FIGURE 5.3	FIGURE 5.4
ASEAN losing market share ...	**... to other developing economies**

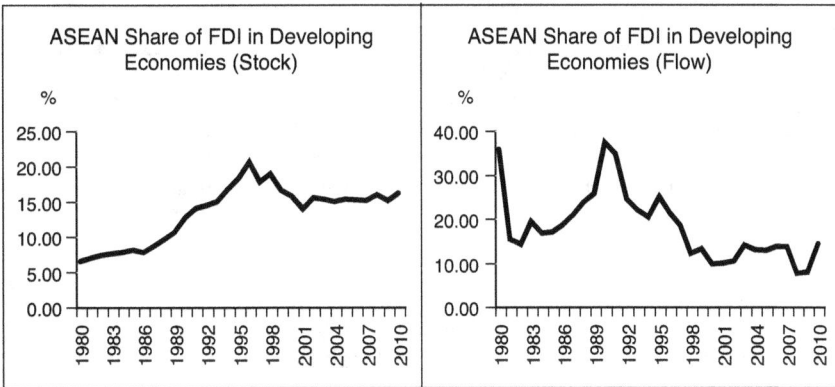

Source: Calculated by Centennial Asian Advisors using UNCTAD data.

The Opening of China and India Coincided with the Growing Challenge for Global FDI

Increased competition for FDI is clearly an issue for ASEAN. ASEAN countries' share of rising FDI until mid-1990s seems to be due to the fact that they were among the first to pursue export-led growth policies. Subsequently, China followed by India started to open up and provided stiff competition to ASEAN in claiming the FDI share. The economic rise of China and India has attracted the attention of investors eager to take advantage of the massive economies of scale offered by the huge and rapidly growing consumer markets in these giants whose middle classes, in particular, are enjoying substantial growth in spending.

FIGURE 5.5

China is a big competitor for FDI.

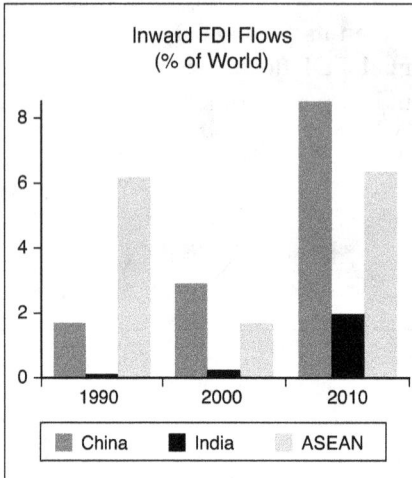

FIGURE 5.6

India is building momentum too.

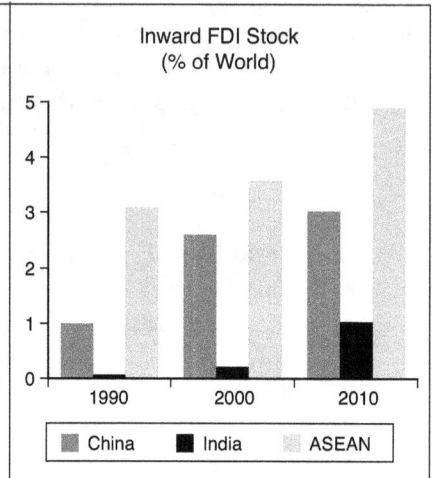

Source: Calculated by Centennial Asian Advisors using UNCTAD data.

Figures 5.5 and 5.6 show that China has overtaken ASEAN in FDI received in 2010, while its stock of total FDI is also rising quickly. On the other hand, India still lags behind ASEAN but is picking up momentum and could soon pose a much bigger threat to the region's share of world FDI.

Domestic Investment has Fallen

Total domestic investment within core ASEAN economies has remained below the levels achieved in the 1990s. Table 5.1 tabulates gross fixed capital formation (GFCF) as a percentage of GDP for economies with available data. It shows that Singapore, Thailand, and Malaysia's domestic investment rates have fallen considerably while domestic investment has become a much greater growth driver (36 per cent of GDP) in Vietnam. On the contrary, China and India's domestic investment have grown significantly with respect to their GDPs. In essence, the disappointing numbers for both foreign and domestic investment cast questions on the investment climates in ASEAN economies.

TABLE 5.1
Domestic investment rates have fallen since 1990s.

	1990	1991	1992	2007	2008	2009	2010
Brunei	–	–	–	13.0	13.7	17.5	15.9
Philippines	24.2	20.0	20.9	19.9	19.7	19.0	20.5
Singapore	31.1	32.5	34.3	23.6	28.3	28.6	25.0
Thailand	40.4	41.6	39.3	26.4	27.4	24.1	24.7
Vietnam	13.1	13.7	16.7	38.3	34.6	34.5	35.6
Indonesia	30.7	28.1	27.3	24.9	27.7	31.1	32.2
Malaysia	33.9	37.8	38.6	23.1	22.3	21.4	21.9
Cambodia	8.3	11.8	14.4	21.4	20.8	16.6	–
China	34.9	34.8	36.6	41.7	43.9	47.5	48.6
India	25.5	24.3	24.8	35.8	33.9	32.9	31.8

Source: Calculated by Centennial Asian Advisors using CEIC database.

Clearly, the 1997 Asian financial crisis marked a major break in the overall investment trend: the political, economic, and financial shocks of that period do not appear to have been fully offset in the years that followed.

III. Factors Contributing to Unsatisfactory Investment Levels

ASEAN does not perform all that badly in terms of the determinants of investment flows. Private investment is largely driven by a quest to maximize returns. The capacity to generate globally competitive rates of return on capital employed should, therefore, be an important consideration in determining gainers and losers in the share of global investment.

There is a clear disjuncture between the capacity to deliver high returns in some key ASEAN economies and the low investment rates that they actually achieve. Returns on investment have been quite good, yet ASEAN is unable to break out of a downward trend in overall investment. Table 5.2 provides data on comparable rates of return on investments by U.S. corporations across the world. Figure 5.7 shows that the ASEAN's return on capital has indeed declined below the levels in the early 1990s but is still not lower relative to the world average

TABLE 5.2
Return on Capital Employed (ROCE) in Asia for U.S. Corporations

(in %)	2000	2005	2010
All countries	10.2	12.1	10.5
ASEAN Average	16.8	18.6	19.0
Average Developing Asia	14.3	16.2	14.6
China	10.9	19.8	16.9
Hong Kong	18.8	13.9	10.9
India	9.2	16.5	12.2
Indonesia	18.6	–	23.6
Japan	10.5	13.3	9.7
Korea, Republic of	14.8	13.1	13.1
Malaysia	19.6	24.5	22.9
New Zealand	6.0	12.3	7.2
Philippines	12.7	10.8	13.5
Singapore	16.8	20.7	15.8
Taiwan	17.5	14.8	9.9
Thailand	16.2	18.3	19.4

Source: Centennial Asia Advisors using U.S. Bureau of Economic Analysis, Dept of Commerce data.

despite a sharp fall in the returns premium after the global crisis of 2008. Figure 5.8 plots the return performance for U.S. multinational companies (MNCs) in Asia. ASEAN has held up well even as China and India have improved.

Figures 5.7 and 5.8 indicate the following:

- First, return on capital is not the sole determinant of investment decisions;
- Second, ASEAN's fortunes are highly tied to the global economy. A big decline in world economic health affects the profits of firms in ASEAN more negatively than in other economies such as China and India; and
- Third, investors demand risk premiums for investing in ASEAN countries as, theoretically, there should not be an outflow of

FIGURE 5.7	FIGURE 5.8
Return on capital above world average	**Also comparable to China and India**

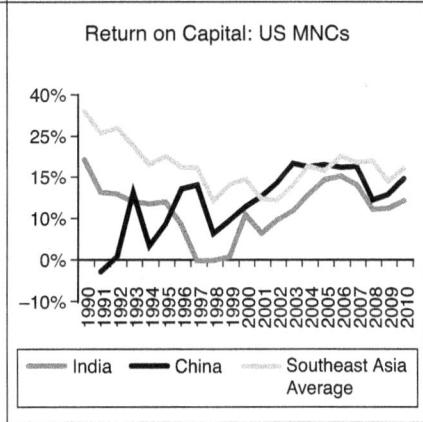

ASEAN Return on Capital Relative to World Return on Capital

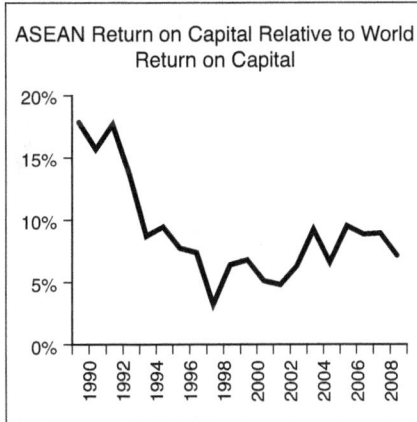

Return on Capital: US MNCs

India — China — Southeast Asia Average

Source: Calculated by Centennial Asian Advisors using CEIC database.

investments if returns are higher than or matches other economies outside the region.

These observations suggest that efforts to enhance the investment climates of the region should focus on reducing country risks for firms in ASEAN economies in order to attract and retain investment. Country studies such as the World Bank's annual Ease of Doing Business Index and the World Economic Forum's Global Competitiveness Index (GCI) consistently show that countries that rank well often attract more FDI. Figures 5.9 and 5.10 show the recent Ease of Doing Business rankings and The Heritage Foundation's ranking of economic freedom, respectively, while Figures 5.11 and 5.12 show the GCI and the Economic Research Institute for ASEAN and East Asia's (ERIA) FDI Restriction Score.

The following findings are observed:

- Singapore is in a league of its own, topping all the metrics we look at in Figures 5.9 to 5.12. It has maintained its number one position in the Doing Business Index for the past three years,

FIGURE 5.9

Singapore, Malaysia, Thailand rank high

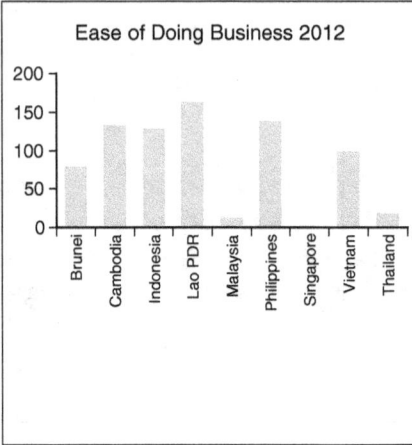

FIGURE 5.10

Other members are below average

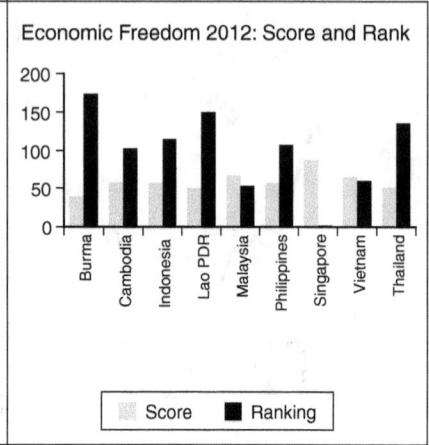

Ease of Doing Business 2012

Economic Freedom 2012: Score and Rank

Source: World Bank and The Heritage Foundation.

FIGURE 5.11

Competitiveness is comparable to China and India.

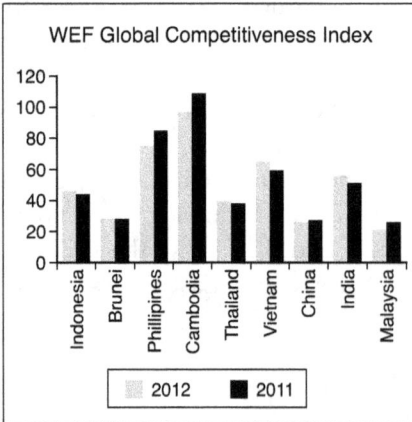

FIGURE 5.12

But Malaysia and Indonesia have stringent FDI rules.

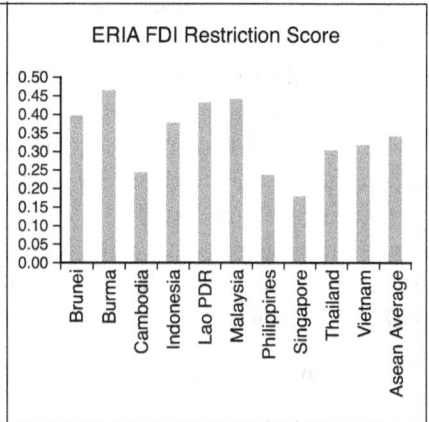

WEF Global Competitiveness Index

ERIA FDI Restriction Score

Source: World Economic Forum, Economic Research Institute for ASEAN and East Asia (ERIA).

placed second on the index of economic freedom, and jumped one place to second in the newest GCI for 2012. The ERIA measure is designed such that the lower the score, the more open the economy's FDI regime and Singapore clearly outperforms its ASEAN counterparts;

- Thailand and Malaysia seem to rank next according to most but not all metrics. Apart from Singapore, these economies rank far higher than the remaining ones in terms of the ease of conducting business and economic freedom. However, Malaysia has above average restrictions on FDI, probably due to its law that forces foreign investors to have partnerships with indigenous firms in some industries instead of having full ownership of the business;

- Vietnam appears to come next, performing relatively well and improving over time although competitiveness has declined in the past year because of macroeconomic instability such as high levels of inflation and a volatile currency;

- Brunei, Cambodia, Indonesia, Laos, and the Philippines make up the next group whose performance is indifferent. These economies rank in the lower echelons of the Doing Business rankings and are generally considered to fare poorly in terms of competitiveness of their industries. Although Brunei is ranked respectably on the GCI, its FDI restriction score is the highest in ASEAN — reflective of the economy's inward and protectionist nature. Myanmar (Burma) is not covered in most surveys due of its lack of available and reliable data but it performs particularly badly where it is covered.

Respective Country Conditions Still Most Critical FDI Factor

These findings corroborate with Figures 5.13 and 5.14 which show the wide disparities of FDI levels among ASEAN countries. It is clear from the figures that member states with better investment climates — higher incentives and lower country risks — tend to have higher levels of FDI. Accordingly, Singapore dominates other member economies by attracting almost half of total FDI stock and 40 per cent of total FDI inflows in ASEAN followed by Thailand and Indonesia. Peripheral economies, such as Myanmar, Cambodia, Brunei, and Laos account for less than 5 per cent of ASEAN's FDI.

Figure 5.13

FDI flow in ASEAN

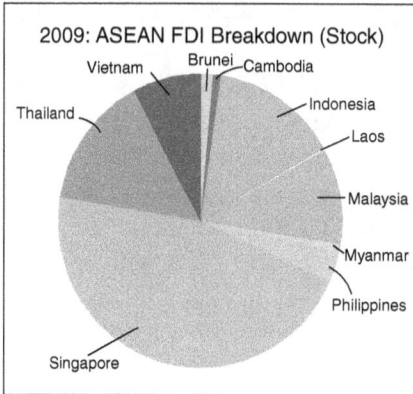

Figure 5.14

Singapore dominates both FDI stock...

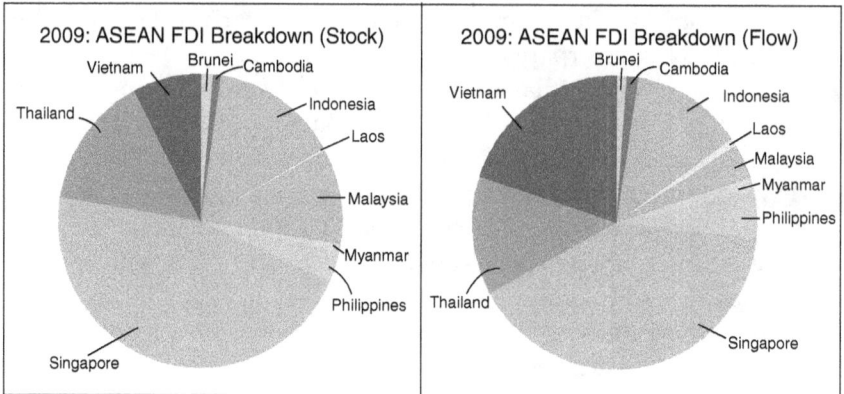

Source: Calculated by Centennial Asian Advisors using UNCTAD data.

ERIA Study also Validates Need to Improve Country Factors Even for Major ASEAN Economies

ERIA conducted two separate surveys involving Japanese firms and non-Japanese foreign firms in ASEAN countries. Essentially, the surveys confirm that impediments to FDI exist not only in the policies, but also in their implementation. Overall, the studies suggest that ASEAN have improved the explicit investment climate but many direct barriers to FDI still exist. The results yield the following observations:

- Complaints with FDI facilitation are overwhelmingly greater than FDI liberalization, suggesting that the more serious problem in ASEAN lies with implementation (country factors) and not the lack of policies drawn up to attract FDI. For instance, 86 complaints were filed in 2010 seeking improved transparency and institutional policies and regulations concerning investment. Of these, 69 complaints (nearly 80 per cent) were in Indonesia, Thailand, Malaysia, and Vietnam. Similarly 91 out of 121 complaints that were filed again, on complicated and delayed procedures, were in Indonesia, Thailand, Malaysia and Vietnam. This shows that even major ASEAN economies which attract the bulk of FDI in the region, excluding Singapore, have major facilitation problems which, if addressed effectively by their respective governments, would likely increase the level of FDI they attract; and

- The above trend persisted from 2008 through 2010, suggesting that the AEC has thus far failed to address and reduce country-specific flaws that have led to complaints by investors. The hardware and software constraints at the country level need to be addressed. ERIA's study clearly indicates the areas that the ASEAN countries need to improve at individual country level. After all ERIA findings are based on the interviews with the business people who are supposed to bring FDI.

IV. Challenges that Impede the AEC

The AEC Blueprint has a greater likelihood of producing a positive effect compared to previous initiatives because of its comprehensiveness and the disciplines it contains to encourage member states to show progress in key areas. However, the deadline of 2015 may not be realistic.

FDI figures in the last two years showed that the prospect of the AEC has failed to inspire a significant rebound in FDI in ASEAN countries. In fact, similar to previous investment agreements, there appears to be a great deal of scepticism over what the AEC will eventually achieve. More significantly, a business survey assessment carried out by the Institute of Southeast Asian Studies and the Asian Development Bank shows that there is a distinct lack of awareness of the AEC among the business community in the first place. In our opinion, the 2015 is not realistic because there are too many obstacles that will prevent the full realization of the AEC.

Many of these challenges are political, such as vested interests and fear of competition, as seen by the inability for region-wide ratification of important agreements. This is not helped by the fact that ASEAN member states come from very diverse bases, both culturally and economically, which make cooperation more difficult. Historical legacies, territorial disputes, and misunderstandings lead to mutual suspicion and increase the difficulty of close cooperation. Furthermore, it was not too long ago that most of these ASEAN members were victims of colonization which has raised the level of nationalism and love for sovereignty that has resulted in resistance against an accelerated level of investment liberalization. Some consequences of these differences are the high levels of red tape in areas such as customs and migration and the immobility of labour and capital throughout the region.

Results of the Second AEC Scorecard

According to the results of the first two AEC scorecards, the region has achieved 67.5 per cent of the targets for the periods 2008–09 and 2010–11. Table 5.3 categorizes the progress of each main component of the AEC Blueprint in these periods. This is a potential source of concern as it marks an overall deterioration from the first period's assessment where 73.6 per cent of targets were met.

We take a closer look at Pillar 1: Single Market and Production Base, as our focus is on one of its key areas, "Free flow of Investments". In the scorecard, the second phase reflected a poor performance as just 38.5 per cent of targeted measures to liberalize investment flows were successfully implemented. This contrasts to the first period when all targeted measures were implemented. Most countries only managed to implement over half of the planned measures under "free investment flow" between 2010 and 2011, but Thailand's dismal implementation rate dragged the entire bloc's average rate down to 38.5 per cent for

TABLE 5.3
Implementation of the Targets under the AEC's Four Pillars

Component	Target Achievement Rate after Phase 1 (%)	Target Achievement Rate after Phases 1 and 2 (%)
Single Market and Production Base	82	65.9
Competitive Economic Region	50	67.9
Equitable Economic Development	100	66.7
Integration with the Global Economy	100	85.7
Overall	**73.6**	**67.5**

Source: AEC Scorecards I and II.

phase II. Presently, just 52.6 per cent of all measures relating to "free investment flows" have entered into force. The scorecard's findings on key areas under Pillar 1 and individual country's performance in the area of "free flow of investments" are summarized in Tables 5.4 and 5.5, respectively.

The Scorecard reported that there are two main outstanding measures requiring further action for investment liberalization. First, all measures under the ASEAN Investment Agreement (AIA) Temporary Exclusion Lists and Sensitive Lists under the ASEAN Comprehensive Investment Agreement (ACIA) need to be subsumed upon entry into force of the AIA. Second, activities support of investment promotion and facilitation need to be conducted as scheduled.

Currently, there are 184 signed legal instruments under AEC, of which 137 (74.5 per cent) have already been entered into force and the remaining are still awaiting ratification by member states. Most of the legal instruments signed and entered into force are concentrated under Pillar 1. Overall, this does not reflect marked progress from the 73 per cent of the total of 124 legal instruments reported in the first scorecard. This backlog of initiatives will persistently hinder targets. Consequently, higher scores will prove to be out of reach in the past evaluation as unmet targets in the first and second phase remain unfulfilled.

TABLE 5.4
Country Progress on Free Flow of Investment

Country	Implementation rate, Phase 1	Implementation rate, Phase 2	Overall Implementation rate
Brunei	100%	>50%	>50%
Cambodia	100%	>50%	>50%
Indonesia	100%	>50%	>50%
Laos	100%	>50%	>50%
Malaysia	100%	>50%	>50%
Myanmar	100%	>50%	>50%
Philippines	100%	>50%	>50%
Singapore	100%	>50%	>50%
Thailand	100%	**<50%**	>50%
Vietnam	100%	>50%	>50%
ASEAN	100%	**<50%**	>50%

Source: AEC Scorecard II.

TABLE 5.5

Implementation of Targeted Measures under Pillar 1 — Single Market and Production Base

Key Areas	Phase 1 (2008–09)		Phase 2 (2010–11)		Total Measures	
	Fully Implemented	Not Fully Implemented	Fully Implemented	Not Fully Implemented	Fully Implemented	Not Fully Implemented
Free flow of Goods	9	0	23	24	32	24
Free flow of Services	10	3	13	17	23	20
Free flow of Investment	**5 (83.3%)**	**1**	**5 (38.5%)**	**8**	**10 (52.6%)**	**9**
Free flow of Capital	1	0	5	0	6	0
Free flow of Skilled Labour	–	–	1	0	1	0
Priority integration sectors	28	0	1	0	29	0
Food, forestry and agriculture	8	0	5	6	13	6
Total number of measures	61	4	53	55	114	59
Implementation rate	93.8%		49.1%		65.9%	

Source: AEC Scorecard II.

The Truth about Regional Agreements

A lengthy list of investment agreements have failed to stem and subsequently reverse the declining FDI trend in ASEAN after the mid-1990s. We find that the main problems with these regional agreements lie with their enforceability. Even though the agreements appear to be far reaching, they often contain underlying clauses that allow members to delay or opt out of implementing certain measures. The most obvious are the temporary exclusions and sensitivity lists that are present in almost all ASEAN investment agreements in the past.[2]

This suggests that these agreements, by themselves, are insufficient. While ASEAN regional actions and agreements can be helpful for attracting FDI, they can at best be only supplementary, not substitutes to the individual country actions. Each ASEAN country will need to have well considered policies and carefully thought out incentives. Strong country factors in each ASEAN nation complemented by solid ASEAN agreements could make the ASEAN region an FDI magnet again.

Potential Benefits of the AEC in the Private Sector

Despite the shortcomings, it is important to realize that such top-down initiatives have been beneficial in encouraging bottom-up integration processes which will allow the region to emerge increasingly like a single market over time. Essentially, private businesses have signalled plans for investment and jobs in the region that is become more closely interlinked and they have realized the need to provide support to the AEC's ambitious plans in order to tap into the value of economic integration. For instance, Air Asia is working towards its goal of a single ASEAN aviation authority by setting up an office in Jakarta to engage with the ASEAN Secretariat and CEOs from major private sector companies like CIMB Bank and Bangkok Bank. Air Asia and the Ayala Group have jointly launched the ASEAN Business Club (ABC) in order to engage in ASEAN community building efforts.

Apart from companies furthering their own integration agendas, top-down initiatives have also increasingly spurred cross-border mergers and acquisitions and joint ventures within ASEAN. For example, Singaporean and Malaysian banks and telecommunication firms have invested heavily in the region and Siam Cement is gearing up to invest 75 per cent of its 2012–16 investment fund to acquire assets in ASEAN countries. Even companies outside ASEAN have started to take notice, as shown by Shin

Shin-Etsu Chemical — Japan's largest chemical producer — which has invested US$64 million to build two chemical plants in Vietnam with the hope of serving a large base of customers in the region.

V. Solutions and Recommendations

Assessment of Trends

Put simply, the foregoing discussion suggests that several countries in ASEAN had enjoyed an attractive investment climate up to the 1990s. But since then, the region's attractiveness relative to emerging economic powers has diminished; a diminution which successive efforts at the ASEAN level to promote investment have not fully rectified.

What is Likely to Improve in Time?

In looking forward, it is important to bear in mind that some factors are coming into play which will help raise ASEAN's investment attractiveness over time. First, ASEAN had been ahead of China and India in attracting FDI for the simple reason that most ASEAN countries had been much more open to FDI than China or India and were able to attract a large stock of FDI that was outsized in relation to the size of ASEAN economies in comparison with the accumulated stock of FDI in China and India. As China, especially, and India to some extent opened up to FDI, global companies had to re-evaluate their portfolio of foreign investment. There began a process of re-adjustment within these portfolios to increase the under-represented stock of Chinese and Indian investment, which inevitably meant reduced flow of FDI to ASEAN for so long as this re-adjustment process was unfolding. With the stock of FDI in China now substantial and more reflective of its size, competitiveness and other economic fundamentals, this re-adjustment process can slow, allowing some recovery in FDI into ASEAN.

Second, the one-off political and financial adjustments which created uncertainties for investors or created obstacles for investors such as difficulties in securing bank loans in the post-1997 crisis period are mostly over now. With fewer headwinds, both domestic as well as foreign investors have fewer disincentives to invest. As political, financial and other uncertainties diminish and remain low for an extended period of time, the hurdle rates for an investment project to be approved by a company will tend to fall in line with a declining risk premium. This should help improve investment over time.

Third, under-investment in critical power, transportation and other infrastructure since 1997 has reached a point where congestion and risks of power shortages are spurring a new wave of investment in infrastructure. Major policy-led infrastructure programmes have been announced in Indonesia, Thailand, and Malaysia for instance, while even Singapore with relatively good infrastructure has been stepping up investment in mass transit schemes. In other words, ASEAN could be poised to enjoy a rebound in investment rates in coming years.

What Needs to be Put Right?

However, such a rebound is not a given. Unlike before 1997, ASEAN now faces competition with China and India and not just with each other. The above discussion also raises several issues which need to be addressed if this rebound is to materialize.

The Need for Economies of Scale

One major challenge for ASEAN is in scale economies. ASEAN needs to offer scale economies for businesses that are unique or competitive with those offered by China and India. Individually, each ASEAN economy cannot provide anything close to the market size that the two Asian giants can offer businesses, as Table 5.6 brings out. However, the collective weight of ASEAN is considerable and sufficient to offer attractive scale economies.

Therefore, any recommendations should not only focus on reforms that individual economies should undertake to improve its investment climate but also include ways to encourage progress in the fulfilment of the AEC goal in order to rebrand ASEAN as a region which businesses can thrive and be excited about.

Creating a Sense of Opportunity: The ASEAN Brand

Many recommendations for improving ASEAN's competitiveness in attracting investments focus on improving specific areas like infrastructure or raising the savings rate or leveraging more effectively on ASEAN's investment plans. These are important but not likely to be the critical factor. Instead ASEAN needs to recapture the sense of opportunity and the promise of high returns that the core ASEAN economies were offering from around 1986 to 1996. The way to do this is to change investors' perceptions so that they believe that ASEAN can also offer not just scale economies that are fairly strong compared to China and India, but also

TABLE 5.6

Population and Economic Size —
ASEAN compared to China and India

	Population	2010 GDP, US$ billion	2010 GDP Per Capita, US$
China	1,338,300,000	3,246.0	2,430
India	1,224,615,000	963.4	787
ASEAN	591,814,000	1,496 (2009)	2,532
Brunei	399,000	7 (2009)	17,092 (2009)
Cambodia	14,139,000	7.9	558
Indonesia	239,870,000	274.4	1,140
Laos	6,201,000	3.4	555
Malaysia	28,401,000	147.3	5,180
Myanmar	47,963,000	25 (2009)	419 (2009)
Philippines	93,261,000	129	1,380
Singapore	5,077,000	165.1	32,500
Thailand	69,122,000	187.5	2,710
Vietnam	86,928,000	62.8	723

Source: World Bank (GDP in constant 2000 prices), ASEANstats (Brunei, Myanmar, and ASEAN figures updated as of 2009).

unique opportunities that are equally exciting. For this, it needs to have a new approach to economic integration.

Hence, ASEAN must strive to behave like a single market whenever possible in a bottom-up approach towards the formation of the AEC. In fact, there are some successful examples of joint investment programmes between member countries that can either be expanded so that they are more inclusive of other members or replicated with other member states such that the overall level of investment can be maximized.

We also think that national governments have also not fully appreciated the benefits of economic integration and a campaign to re-emphasize these benefits is necessary to provide the impetus to move forward in terms of realizing the AEC. With regards to investment, it is clear that economic cooperation and integration can create synergies and economies of scale such as market size which are essential to attracting investment. An additional benefit is improved ties between cooperating countries where an increased reliance on legal mechanisms like treaties and memoranda of agreement help to resolve potential disputes.

Recommendations — ASEAN Wide Level

A practical approach to improving ASEAN's investment climate must be realistic in appreciating that the political obstacles towards full blown integration will take time to dissipate. On too many occasions, ASEAN countries compete with each other rather than act in unison. This boils down to the fact that ASEAN governments choose to retain their sovereignty instead of engaging in shared decision-making that transcends national boundaries. Such an outcome is difficult to avoid considering that conflicts in ideologies regarding economic growth models, political systems, and lingering suspicions of each other due to unresolved territorial or other conflicts will not go away soon and will maintain the strong unwillingness to cede power for joint efforts that could produce collective economic benefits. This is why ASEAN members sign bilateral agreements separately, undermining the cohesiveness of the group.

The practical answer is to focus on bite-sized regional integration — where the case for substantial synergies from integration can be realized more easily. Once these synergies are released and the benefits of regional integration demonstrated, the larger efforts at regional integration can proceed with less opposition. The Iskandar project and Greater Mekong Subregion are examples of sub-regional integration that could be extended to include other regions. The successful implementation of these integration efforts can also inspire similar projects that will benefit overall investment in ASEAN.

Focus on New Forms of Economic Integration such as Sub-regional Integration

Iskandar Region

The Iskandar Region was established in 2006 as part of the 9th Malaysia Plan and includes Johor Bahru and its surrounding towns of Pontian, Senai, and Pasir Gudang. The intention is to create a thriving development area with a wide economic base and which by 2030 is projected to have a per capita income of a developed country. The project is in the interest of both Singapore and Malaysia as there are huge benefits and synergies which can be gained through closer integration between Singapore and the Iskandar Region. It is a culmination of a natural, symbiotic and historical relationship between Singapore and Malaysia which is much more complementary than competitive due to the fact that:

- Singapore always had a close relationship with Johor. Even before the British rule in 1819 and up till 1967, despite different political systems and jurisdictions, there was a seamless flow of goods and people between both countries. After 1967, the integration between Singapore and Malaysia began to wither as they followed separate economic and political paths. From 1986 to mid-1990s, there was an outward relocation of manufacturing activities from Singapore and Singapore tourism ventured into Johor. The proximity and historical relationship makes renewed cooperation between the two areas more viable and attractive;
- There exist clear complementarities. For Singapore to attain its desired status as a global city, it needs to grow bigger as the mass within the Singapore territory is insufficient. In comparison with other global cities with multiple airports, Singapore is lagging behind with just one. However, it is highly constrained by its limited land and it is impossible to have another large airport or seaport in its territories. In addition, Singapore is also constrained by population density limits which will cause it to lose its competitive edge. Iskandar's youthful demographic profile and abundant land present Singapore with the ideal hinterland that will provide it with the necessary economies of scale and critical mass to continue its drive towards becoming a global city; and
- From Malaysia's point of view, it can also take advantage of the critical mass and connectivity, such as transportation facilities, that are available in Singapore. Cooperation and investment from Singapore will also help to boost Malaysia's competitiveness which is way below the level of Singapore. Furthermore, Singapore's tourism products can complement with Iskandar's so that the total product is compelling and varied enough to keep bringing tourists back for repeat visits. In addition, economic integration would lower business costs for SMEs. Lower cost of living will significantly ease the burden of lower income groups and heightened economic cooperation would also improve the overall quality of life for people of both countries, as congestion may be

reduced and the increase in diversity would create greater choices for consumers.

Thus, the synergies released from integration will be huge and the net benefits visible. The demonstration effect of visible benefits will help push the case for wider integration efforts over time. The results have been encouraging too. According to official figures, the Iskandar Malaysia development region has brought in RM77.82 billion in new investments by September 2011, much higher than the target of RM47 billion and approximately 60 per cent are domestic investments, while the rest are from foreign sources. Singapore's cumulative committed investments into Iskandar Malaysia have totalled RM4.13 billion as of the end of June 2011.

A Push for More Cross-border, Sub-regional Integration Recommended

ASEAN leaders should study the results and implementation process of the Iskandar Region and the Greater Mekong Subregion and draw lessons from them so that more cross-border, sub-regional integrations could take place that would allow member states to gain competitiveness and enhance their investment climates. Ideally, "One Economy, Many Countries" model should be used wherever possible. This will require massive deregulations across industries and modifications of existing legislations concerning labour, immigration and commercial matters so as to ensure:

- Companies registered in one country could operate freely in the other;
- There was reasonably free flow of labour;
- People movements were made easy — little in the way of immigration checks, for example;
- Goods continued to flow across the borders as in the pre-separation days; and
- The Stock Exchange and currency were unified.

The list above is not exhaustive yet it already demonstrates the difficult challenges that confront governments when pushing for integration between areas of diverse economic statuses, cultures, and ideologies. For example, Singapore has a much more welcoming stance towards foreign companies compared to Malaysia who places various restrictions on how a foreign firm can operate there. In addition, countries have different tolerance towards issues such as the level of environmental responsibility or immigration requirements. All these suggest that much political will is needed for participating governments to engage in thorough discussions to iron out differences and come up with compromises so that sustainable integration can commence.

Cooperation and integration with other Asian economies should also be considered as long as there are mutual economic benefits to be reaped. We briefly discuss two options that have the potential to achieve deep integration for ASEAN. The ADB has approved a regional technical assistance (RETA) to strengthen regional cooperation and promote links between BIMP-EAGA, IMT-GT, GMS, and ASEAN to help implement the Master Plan on ASEAN Connectivity and realize the AEC by 2015.

First, the rise of China as an economic giant and the corresponding liberalization of its economy present challenges for ASEAN economies, such as competition for investment as discussed in Section 1. However, its emergence also produced opportunities including increased trade and complementarities to exploit. ASEAN is a region well-endowed with natural resources and could help China meet its increasing demand for oil, gas, and minerals to drive its rapid industrial expansion. Likewise, China can serve as an export platform for ASEAN manufactured exports and also as a profitable final market due to its vast consumer market. It can also absorb manufacturing operations from Singapore and Malaysia who are looking to move up the value chain while shifting low-level textile operations to lower-wage economies like Cambodia and Myanmar. One initiative that seems to have lost steam in recent years is the Pan-Beibu Gulf Economic Region (PBG). Authorities should immediately revive talks to accelerate the realization of this project. The PBG is a proposed integrated zone that the Pan-Beibu Gulf Economic Cooperation Zone, the two plates of the GMS and the Nanning-Singapore Economic Corridor linking to form the alphabet M. The entire region will cover parts of China, Vietnam, Malaysia, Singapore, Indonesia, Brunei, and the Philippines. The geographical location and environmental conditions of the PBG mean that it has great potential to become a transportation hub for China and ASEAN via air, coastal, and land. Once the transportation infrastructure is in place, the PBG can then be developed into a dedicated centre for trade and logistics between China and ASEAN.

Second, a sizeable effort should be undertaken in Cambodia, Laos, Myanmar, and Vietnam (CLMV) to help them integrate better with the more developed ASEAN economies. Although the CLMV countries have grown rapidly in recent years, they still lag behind the other ASEAN economies considerably in terms of social, infrastructure, economic, and financial sector development. We think that there are a lot of potential for the CLMV to cooperate and jointly develop industries that are useful and competitive. For example, a combined state-enterprise between the countries could be set up to expand, upgrade and modify infrastructure in a way such that more complementarities between the countries can be created, producing more opportunities for future cooperation. This could be within the framework of special economic zones (SEZs) that integrate the CLMV countries underlined by demarcated production sites, efficient administrative rules to expedite processes, and business services to provide financing, legal, logistics, and labour training support for businesses that operate within the SEZs. For this to happen, the annual CLMV Summit must work to create and operationalize action plans instead of remaining a largely symbolic forum.

Make a Big Push for Increased Physical Connectivity

One crucial strategy to achieve cross-border integration is to establish efficient transport links for increased physical connectivity between two regions. This would facilitate the flow of labour, raw materials, and goods so that intra-regional trade and production could be optimized. The experiences of other iconic connectivity projects shows that improving physical connectivity can have tremendously positive benefits as the synergies from connecting complementary sub-regions are released. For example, the Øresund Bridge that connects Copehnagen and Malmö was built in 2000 and carries over 60,000 commuters daily between the two cities. The bridge has facilitated incredible access for the Danes and the Swedish to each other's countries. Rising house prices in Copenhagen has encouraged many Danes to relocate to Malmö yet enable them to maintain jobs back in Denmark due to easy commute between the two towns, mitigating any labour force shortage in Copenhagen. At the same time, Danish employers also found it easier to recruit Swedish employees and vice versa, leading to a peak in employment numbers for both countries in 2007. We note some ongoing projects that strive to achieve increased connectivity.

Another example of connectivity is the high-speed train link between Kuala Lumpur and Singapore. Under Economic Transformation Programme (ETP), PM Najib's administration is planning a high-speed rail (HSR) system linking Penang, KL and Singapore. The project is estimated to cost RM8–14 billion. A feasibility study has found that the HSR journey from KL to Singapore could take 2.4 hours, the train travelling up to 280 kilometres per hour. Through fast and efficient physical connectivity, the realization of the project would facilitate trade flow, alleviate the flow of manpower, build up tourism potential and link the two countries to become a prime economic hub.

Showcase Iconic Projects and Successful Industries to Entice Investors

These projects and industries will serve to highlight to investors the potential of ASEAN economies.

Master Plan for the Acceleration and Expansion of Indonesia's Economic Development (MP3EI), Indonesia

MP3EI, unveiled on 13 May 2011, is coordinated by a committee chaired by President Yudhoyono. The plan provides a framework for achieving Indonesia's aim of becoming one of the ten major economies in the world by 2025. The plan aims at boosting GDP to US$4.5 trillion by 2025. The Master Plan includes eight main programmes, each consisting of twenty-two main economic activities including commodities, agriculture, and defence. Three implementation strategies have been recognized: (i) developing regional economic potential in six Indonesia Economic Corridors, (ii) strengthening national connectivity, and (iii) strengthening human resource capacity, and science and technology to support development of main programmes. The Master Plan was designed to support and complement currently ongoing economic development plans by the government, such as the Long Term National Development Plan and the Medium Term National Development Plan.

Infrastructure projects are to be the focus for the next five years, including the expansion of airports, a rig project, power plants and highways. The government set aside US$464 billion to be invested for the next fourteen years, including infrastructure, but the private sector is expected to take the lead in the longer-term. As of August 2011, thirty-nine projects worth RP400 trillion have officially started. Even in the economic crisis, Indonesia remains attractive to investors — foreign direct investment has shown positive increases. Korea, Japan, and China, the three leading investor countries, will establish secretariats to support Indonesia's Master Plan.

Pharmaceutical Industry, Singapore

Between 2003 and 2008, Singapore's pharmaceutical sector received around 30 to 40 per cent of total FDI in the manufacturing industry, reaching a record 41.1 per cent in 2007. World-class organizations such as GlaxoSmithKline, Roche, Merck Sharp, and Baxter are among the pharmaceutical companies who have significant investments in biological facilities or established regional headquarters in Singapore. These foreign investors have profited from their investments. The return on investment (ROI) for the pharmaceutical sector is one of the most profitable sectors and is consistently above the ROI of the manufacturing industry in general.

Singapore is the fourth largest foreign exchange trading centre in the world and is a leading provider for a wide array of service such as international banking, insurance, wealth management, legal services, and trade financing. Investors also get to enjoy a politically sound environment, protection of ideas and innovations and the many FTAs and Investment Guarantee Agreements that the country has in place.

The Singapore government has also rolled out specific incentives catered to the pharmaceutical and biomedical sector to increase foreign participation. It has ensured that top quality infrastructure is available for R&D purposes by spending S$295 million on a Biopolis hub which is a designated cluster aimed to bring together research and medical communities to encourage collaboration so that synergies can be achieved. The EDB has strived to secure a steady stream of highly qualified workforce for the sector by setting up A*STAR which aims to produce more Ph.D. graduates, both local and foreigners, in related disciplines. Finally, generous government subsidies are provided for research purposes in order to bolster R&D capacities in Singapore.

Minimize the Exclusion and Sensitive List

There should be minimum gap between what is committed and what is implemented if business trust and confidence are to be earned. In other words, it is more beneficial to focus on implementation of agreements rather than promising fantasy reforms that cannot be fulfilled. One way is for ASEAN leaders to urgently compromise to reduce the exclusion and sensitive lists that have greatly reduced the incentives for some members to enact the necessary reforms to become competitive in. For such lists to be minimized, the richer and more competitive countries may need to agree to monetary compensation or other conditions to make it economically viable for the other party to drop certain exclusion conditions.

Better Adherence to Existing Frameworks

It is important to make better use of the existing Agreements than adding more Agreements to the list. Member states must make use of existing frameworks that can help further promote FDI in the region. This means adhering to previously agreed frameworks such as free trade agreements and bilateral treaties. In particular, the ACIA, which has only been entered into force at the end of 2009, must be fully utilized and disciplinary mechanisms must exist to punish parties that veer from it. According to the ERIA, insufficient information on investment impediments and the small sample size of surveyed firms restrict the ability to identify a relationship between the specific FDI impediments which a particular type of firm faces. This is required in order to formulate optimal policies to attract broad-based invest-ments. Hence, ASEAN leaders must ensure two things: a well-functioning entity to deal with treaty enforcement and disputes and better research and disclosure of investment impediments within region countries.

Recommendations — Country-Specific

Have a Strong Investment Promotion Organization

Each ASEAN member should establish a strong investment promotion organization. It should be based on strong commitment from the political leadership, enabling it to get other government agencies in line whether it be immigration, universities and education ministries, labour ministry, and so on. The organization must be well-resourced in terms of funding, talented staff and led by a strong, forward-looking leader. In this respect, ASEAN members should model themselves against Singapore's Economic Development Board (EDB) and Hong Kong's InvestHK — two of the most successful investment promotion organizations in Asia and the world.

- The EDB is a great example. It works in conjunction with the Ministry of Trade and Industry to provide long-term strategic solutions by identifying and attracting investors within sectors that are important to Singapore's economic development at each point in time. The organization does not only focus on multinational corporations, but also places much emphasis on individual investors and domestic start-ups through a myriad of programmes and incentives tailored for each category of investors. For example, the EDB has enacted a wide range of flexible financial schemes that offer affordable loans for equipment and machinery, international expansion and rebates for small-medium enterprises, among many others. It is also responsible for encouraging and arranging networking between local and foreign enterprises to explore joint ventures and business opportunities. Much of EDB's success is attributed to its ability to constantly evolve with the changing global economic conditions and spotting new industries that Singapore could have competitive advantages over its competitors and entice them aggressively. Overall, the restructuring of Singapore's economy from a low-skilled, labour-intensive industrial hub to a research-driven knowledge economy is testament to the EDB's achievements.

Identify Weaknesses in Ease of Doing Business and Address Them Aggressively

A proactive and efficient investment promotion organization is not enough and will have problems attracting investment if the investment climate of a country is poor. Therefore, it is fundamental that ASEAN countries also work aggressively to improve their investment conditions. The hardware and software constraints at the country level need to be addressed. ERIA's study clearly indicates the areas that the ASEAN countries need to improve at individual country level. After all ERIA findings are based on the interviews with the business people who are supposed to bring FDI.

NOTES

1. This chapter is drawn from a longer paper on "The ASEAN Economic Community: The Investment Climate", which is a part of the ISEAS-ADB Project on "Assessment of Impediments & Actions Required for Achieving AEC by 2015". The papers of the project is a forthcoming publication (*The ASEAN Economic Community: A Work in Progress*) by the Institute of Southeast Asian Studies.
2. The complete Temporary Exclusion and Sensitive Lists may be accessed at the following link: <http://www.aseansec.org/22218.htm>.

6

FREE FLOW OF SKILLED LABOUR IN ASEAN

Chia Siow Yue

I. Introduction

The AEC provides for market access for ASEAN skilled labour, that is, professionals and skilled manpower. "Free flow of skilled labour" affects the implementation of the ASEAN Framework Agreement on Services (AFAS) through allowing foreign service suppliers, and the ASEAN Comprehensive Investment Agreement (ACIA) through allowing employment of foreign corporate personnel to accompany FDI.

The AEC Blueprint focuses on action to implement Mutual Recognition Arrangements (MRAs) for major professional services which, as discussed in the chapter, is highly inadequate to achieve the AEC objective of "free flow of skilled labour". The AEC Scorecard Report on skilled labour for the 2008–11 period is extremely brief:

> To support greater mobility of qualified professionals in the region, the MRAs for engineers and architects have been implemented, while work is underway to effectively operationalize the other professional MRAs

(nursing, medical, dental, accountancy and surveying). To facilitate the movement of persons engaged in trade and investment, the ASEAN Agreement on Movement of Natural Persons (MNP) has been drafted and is expected to be finalized in 2012.

An example of the legal hurdles to implement MRAs is given by Tilleke & Gibbins (1 March 2012) in the case of Thailand. Thailand was the second last member (after Laos) to ratify the ASEAN Framework Agreement on MRA in May 2002, which came into effect in December 2002. But Thailand has yet to ratify any of the seven MRAs signed, and in engineering services, it came short of ratification by merely sending a "notification of participation" to the ASEAN Secretary-General. Thailand has to revamp its two major legal stumbling blocs:

- The Foreign Business Act (FBA) restricts the participation of aliens in certain business activities according to three lists. List 1 principally contains agriculture and land-dealing activities. List 2 includes businesses related to national safety or security or involving art and culture, tradition, folk handicraft, or natural resources and environment. List 3 contains most services, including legal and accounting. Foreigners cannot engage in List 1 activities at all, while the activities under List 2 and List 3 may be pursued if the foreigner obtains an alien business license. Tilleke and Gibbins argue that a major overhaul of the FBA would cause delays in the implementation of Thailand's AEC commitments. Alternatively, Thailand could expand the list of projects eligible for investment promotion by the Board of Investment (BOI), which is empowered to grant a wide range of incentives and guarantees to qualified investment projects.
- The Alien Employment Act requires a work permit for all aliens working in Thailand. Only a few exceptions are granted, such as to members of diplomatic or consular delegations, the United Nations and other international agencies, as well as pursuant to certain treaties and authorization by the Council of Ministers. Tilleke and Gibbins argue that more exemptions should be enacted in order for Thailand to be able to commit to the various MRAs.

It is obvious that recognition of qualifications is not enough to ensure market access in ASEAN. We need to also look at policies and regulatory frameworks affecting skilled labour mobility, and highlight the various policy and regulatory constraints and impediments.[1] For comparison with the AEC, this chapter also includes a discussion of movement of natural persons provisions in General Agreement on Trade in Services (GATS) and selected regional and bilateral trade agreements.

II. Skilled Labour Mobility and Issue of Brain Drain and Brain Gain

Movement of Natural Persons in the GATS

Barriers to cross-border skilled labour mobility or Movement of Natural Persons (MNP) in WTO language include:

1. Restrictive immigration visa requirements and employment passes and work permits, other administrative constraints and processing costs;
2. Quality assurance: pre-employment requirements, health and security clearance, personal and professional references;
3. Educational and professional qualifications and regulations and licensing requirements by receiving country professional associations;
4. National treatment limitations: qualifications and restrictions based on nationality; economic needs test; numerical quotas for each profession; ethnic and religious preferences; and language requirements; and
5. Measures to discourage and prevent brain drain.

MNP under GATS Mode 4 refers to cross-border mobility of professionals and skilled individuals on a temporary basis either as self-employed individual service providers or as employees of foreign companies supplying services. MNPs cover:

1. Business visitors: engage in business without seeking employment;
2. Traders and investors: natural persons carrying out specific trading and investment activities;
3. Intra-corporate transferees: employees of MNCs that move their staff across borders; and
4. Professionals: include doctors and nurses, lawyers, accountants, engineers, IT personnel and other professions.

Issue of Brain Gain and Brain Drain

Globally, there has been a net flow of highly skilled professionals and executives or "brains" from the less developed countries to the more developed countries and this phenomenon has gained importance in the past two decades, although their numbers are still small relative to the large cross-border flows of semi-skilled and unskilled workers. Many developed countries as well as advanced developing countries now have deliberate policies of attracting "brains". At the same time, liberalization of the "movement of natural persons" in GATS and growing FDI presence have resulted in significant labour mobility of the professionals and skilled from developed to developing countries as well as flows among developing countries.

Receiving countries of skilled labour are generally regarded as enjoying "brain gain", as inflows augment and supplement domestic supplies, remove domestic shortages, improve economic competitiveness and productivity, and facilitate structural transformation and industrial upgrading. Yet not all countries are unreservedly open to skilled labour inflows. Most countries have measures to manage and even restrict such inflows. Reasons include the political, economic and social pressures to "reserve" jobs for nationals, the "closed shop" licensing practices of professional bodies, and the security aspects of critical and sensitive jobs.

Brain drain occurs when professionals and skilled manpower emigrate because some countries have been unable to efficiently employ them because of sluggish economic growth and high unemployment as well as skill mismatches. Also, many of these skilled emigrants started the migration process when they left for the OECD countries to pursue tertiary education and then stayed on to gain work experience and were attracted by the job opportunities, better remuneration and working conditions and quality of life. The developing countries generally have a scarcity of skills and a sizeable brain drain would adversely affect their development potential. At the least, the brain drain represents losses to past educational investments. In most cases these human resources would have been trained at great public expense and emigration often leads to the loss of a country's "best and brightest". Some of the negative effects of skills depletion are seen in the Philippines, where success in sending nurses abroad has depleted its healthcare services of experienced nurses. Some developing countries have restrictive emigration policies that make it difficult for their nationals to take jobs abroad, such as bonding scholars on government scholarships to ensure their return to serve their country. A proposal to impose a brain drain tax[2] on receiving countries to compensate the sending country for the brain drain has failed to take off, as it present problems of estimating the appropriate amount of such a tax, who should pay the tax (the receiving country, the employer or the migrant professional himself), who should benefit from the tax (sending country government and how should the tax revenue be used). Many developed countries have tried to mitigate the developing countries problem with temporary entry programmes that require workers or students to return to their source country after a period of stay.

It is also increasingly recognized that the brain drain could also have positive effects on the sending countries, as emigrants can make a greater contribution to development of their home countries. For those who stay abroad, they send back remittances; transfer technology and knowledge; and provide crucial networks for trade and investment. Prospects of emigration for work can also lead to a higher level of human capital formation in the sending country. For example, more Filipinos seek education and training as nurses to facilitate their employability abroad. Also, there are significant gains when the "brains" eventually return and bring with them greater experience, knowledge, savings and business and social networks. Thus, an initial brain drain may become a long term brain gain. The Asian diaspora is increasingly viewed by their origin countries as a valuable resource to be tapped for national economic development — for their remittances and investments, entrepreneurial and professional skills, and business and social networks. For example, returnees have contributed much to the technological development and industrial upgrading of South Korea and Taiwan. The "overseas Chinese" communities in Hong Kong and Taiwan and to a lesser extent in Southeast Asia have been major foreign investors in China, particularly in the first decade of China's open-door policy. In its current phase of development India is also trying to tap its diaspora for their investments and expertise.

III. Policies and Regulatory Frameworks on Skilled Labour Mobility in and among ASEAN Countries

ASEAN governments have allowed or facilitated inflows of professionals and skilled manpower for various reasons, including to: facilitate FDI by permitting entry of foreign business people and professionals to accompany FDI; meet short-term skills shortages; facilitate structural/ industrial upgrading; meet commitments under GATS and FTAs; and promote health and education services.

Provisions in AFAS

AFAS provides, inter alia, for regulatory convergence and regulatory harmonization including MRAs. ASEAN countries may recognize the education or experience obtained, requirements met and licensing or certification granted by other ASEAN countries. The 2003 Bali Concord II called for completion of MRAs for qualifications in major professional services by 2008 to facilitate the free movement of professionals and skilled labour. With MRAs, each country may recognize education and experience, requirements, licenses and certificates granted in another country. However, progress in Mode 4 on MNP and progress in MRAs have been slow

AFAS Article 5 — Domestic Regulation (on qualifications):

With the objective of ensuring that measures relating to qualification requirements and procedures, technical standards and licensing requirements do not constitute unnecessary barriers to trade in services, the Parties shall jointly review the results of the negotiations on disciplines in these measures pursuant to Article VI.4 of GATS, with a view to their incorporation into the Agreement. In sectors where specific commitments regarding professional services are undertaken, each Party shall provide for adequate procedures to verify the competence of professionals of any other Party.

AFAS Article 6 — Recognition (on qualifications):

- For the purposes of fulfilment of their respective standards or criteria for the authorization, licensing and certification of service suppliers, each Party may recognize the education or experience obtained, requirements met, or licenses or certification granted in another Party. Such recognition, which may be achieved through harmonization or otherwise, may be based upon an agreement or arrangement between the Parties or the relevant competent bodies or may be accorded autonomously;

- Two or more parties may enter into, or encourage their relevant competent bodies to enter into, negotiations or recognition of qualification requirements, qualification procedures, licensing and/ or registration procedures for the purposes of fulfilment of their respective standards or criteria for the authorization, licensing or certification of service suppliers;
- A Party to an agreement or arrangement of the type referred to in paragraph 1 shall afford adequate opportunity for other interested Parties to negotiate their accession to such an agreement or arrangement or to negotiate comparable ones with it. Where a Party accords recognition autonomously, it shall afford adequate opportunity for any other Party to demonstrate that education, experience, licenses or certifications obtained or requirements met in that other Party's territory should be recognized; and
- A Party shall not accord recognition in a manner which would constitute a means of discrimination between countries or a disguised restriction on trade in services.

AEC Blueprint on "Free Flow of Skilled Labour"

ASEAN countries can be divided into three main groups with respect to the mobility of professionals and skilled manpower. First, where inflows of skills far exceeded outflows of skills there will be net brain gain. Singapore, Brunei and to a lesser extent Thailand are in this category. Thailand has explicit laws that restrict employment of foreigners. Second, where outflows of skills far exceeded inflows of skills there will be net brain drain. Philippines and Malaysia are in this category. Most ASEAN countries do not have an active policy towards outward migration of its professionals and skilled workers except for the Philippines. Malaysia has historically large outflows of skills to Singapore but also increasingly to the English-speaking developed countries, reflecting dissatisfaction with Malaysia's ethnic-based education and employment policies. In recent years Malaysia is also actively promoting inflows of talents, including red-carpet treatment for its diaspora, as part of its economic restructuring strategy. Third, in the other ASEAN countries of Indonesia, Cambodia, Laos, and Vietnam, skilled and professional manpower inflows and outflows do not figure prominently. In these countries, inflows have been limited by restrictive regulations, while outflows have not been significant because of the small pool of professional and skilled manpower and their inadequate English proficiency that restricts their international mobility. Myanmar has the English language proficiency but outflows are restricted by the political regime.

In general, types of natural persons allowed, with certain conditions, for temporary presence in ASEAN countries are: business visitors for sales negotiations; intra-corporate transferees (executives, managers, specialists, others), executives, managers, specialists, technical experts, certain professionals, certain types of skilled workers, and other types of persons such as consultants and chefs. The free flows of skilled labour have important implications for trade in services and FDI flows.

Article 33 of the AEC Blueprint provides that "in allowing for managed mobility or facilitated entry for the movement of natural persons engaged in trade in goods, services and investments, according to the prevailing regulations of the receiving country, ASEAN is working to facilitate the issuance of visas and employment passes for ASEAN professionals and skilled labor who are engaged in cross-border trade and investment activities". Article 34 goes on to provide that in facilitating the free flow of services, ASEAN is also working toward harmonization and standardization with a view to facilitate the movement of skilled labour within the region. As such the ASEAN Framework goes beyond a push to simplify visa and work permit processing, as it also involves the establishment of mechanisms by which member states can recognize the professional qualifications issued within each.

Reference to the free flows of skilled labour in the Blueprint may be found in A2. Free Flow of Services and A5. Free Flow of Skilled Labour:

- On the free flow of services by 2015, ASEAN is working towards recognition of professional qualifications. Actions include: Mode 4 and limitations on horizontal commitments; complete MRAs currently under negotiation, with architectural services, accountancy services, surveying qualifications, medical practitioners by 2008 and dental practitioners by 2009; implement the MRAs expeditiously according to the provisions of each respective MRA; identify and develop MRAs for other professional services by 2012, to be completed by 2015. ASEAN is also working towards harmonization and standardization, with a view to facilitate their movement within the region and actions include: enhance cooperation among ASEAN University Network (AUN) members to increase mobility for both students and staff within the region; develop core competences and qualifications for jobs/occupations and trainers skills required in the priority services sectors (by 2009) and in other services sectors (from 2010 to 2015); and strengthen the research capabilities of each ASEAN country in terms of promoting skills, job placements, and developing labour market information networks among ASEAN countries; and

- On the free movement of skilled labour, according to the prevailing regulations of the host country, ASEAN is working to facilitate the issuance of visas and employment passes for ASEAN professionals and skilled labour who are engaged in cross-border trade and investment related activities; facilitate the free flow of services, particularly, develop core competencies and qualifications for job/occupational and trainers skills required in the priority service sectors by 2009 and in other services sectors by 2015; enhance cooperation among ASEAN University Network (AUN) members to increase mobility for both students and staff within the region; and strengthen the research capabilities of each ASEAN Member Country in terms of promoting skills, job placements, and developing labour market information networks among ASEAN member states. The timelines are:
  - o Complete MRAs for major professional services, including Priority Integration Services (PIS) sectors of e-commerce, healthcare, air travel, tourism and logistics by 2008;
  - o Develop core competencies (concordance of skills and qualifications) for job/occupational skills required in PIS by 2009; and
  - o Develop core competencies (concordance of skills and qualifications) for job/occupational skills in all service sectors by 2015.

ASEAN University Network (AUN)

The AEC Blueprint lists as one of its actions towards free flow of skilled labour as enhancing cooperation among ASEAN University Network (AUN) members to increase mobility for both students and staff within the region. The specific objectives of AUN are to promote cooperation and solidarity among professionals, academicians, scientists, and scholars in the region; develop academic and professional human resources in the region; and promote information dissemination including electronic networking of libraries, exchanges and sharing of appropriate information among members of the academic community, policy-makers, students, and other relevant users.

The AUN structure comprises a Board of Trustees, Participating Universities and Secretariat.[3] Academic institutions of any ASEAN member country may be admitted to the AUN upon submission of application for such membership to the Board of Trustees. The AUN Secretariat is based at Chulalongkorn University in Thailand. At the Second AUN Rectors' meeting in March 2010, progress of the implementation of the ASEAN Credit Transfer System (ACTS) was discussed. Quality of the courses offered by AUN member universities is essential to the success of ACTS. ACTS face severe problems of differences in the languages of instruction, differences in standards of faculty members and student entry requirements among universities (not only across countries, but also within countries), and differences in university resources to fund exchanges of staff and students.

Hence, significant exchanges of staff and students are limited. In the meantime, Singapore's universities have proceeded to establish joint programmes and staff and student exchanges with top universities in the U.S., U.K., Europe, Japan, and China. Singapore is also offering scholarships to ASEAN students (those that meet the university entrance requirements) to study at its universities. There is also a sizeable number of ASEAN nationalities among the faculty of Singapore's universities.

Malaysia has established many private universities, often in collaboration with universities in Australia and U.K. and attracting an increasing number of paying students from ASEAN countries.

ASEAN Mutual Recognition Arrangements (MRAs)

At the 7th ASEAN Summit in November 2001, ASEAN heads mandated the start of negotiations on MRAs to facilitate the flow of professional services under AFAS. Bali Concord II in 2003 called for completion of MRAs for qualifications in major professional services by 2008 to facilitate free movement of professionals/skilled labour/talents in ASEAN.

AFAS Article V (Mutual Recognition) states that a member state may recognize the education or experience obtained, requirements met, or licences or certifications granted in another member, for the purpose of licensing or certification of service providers. Normally there are five primary/basic components of an MRA — definition, recognition provision, recognition mechanism, dispute settlement provision, and capacity building provision.

- Definition normally defines a practitioner of professional in a particular service subsector in terms of a natural person who has not only completed the required professional training and conferred professional qualification in that particular area, but also has been registered and/or licensed by the relevant professional regulatory authority in his home country as being technically, ethnically and legally qualified to undertake professional practice in that particular area of expertise. There are normally six mutual recognition criteria provided in the framework — education, examination, registration and licensing, experience, continuing professional education, code of ethics (professional conduct);
- Professional regulatory authority, as the recognition mechanism, refers to a body vested with the authority by the government in each ASEAN country to regulate and control practitioners and their practice of each professional. Mutual exemption is normally provided. E.g. in Medical and Dental Services, there is a provision stating that "any arrangement which would confer exemption from further assessment by the PMRA/PDRA of the host country may be concluded only with the involvement and consent of that PMRA/ PDRA. (PMRA refers to Professional Medical Regulatory Authority; PDRA refers to Professional Dental Regulatory Authority);
- In terms of dispute settlement, the following provision is normally found in ASEAN MRAs — ASEAN countries shall at all times endeavour to agree on the interpretation and application of this MRA and shall make every attempt through communication, dialogue, consultation and cooperation to arrive at a mutually satisfactory resolution of any matter that might affect implementation of this MRA. The provision is based on the ASEAN Protocol on Enhanced Dispute Settlement Mechanism which applies to disputes concerning the interpretation, implementation, and/or application of any of the provisions under this MRA upon exhaustion of the abovementioned mechanism;
- For capacity building, it is essential in the ASEAN context. This is due to varying levels of development in each sector/subsector of professional services within the region;

- Pre-arrangements to an MRA are a normal practice in ASEAN. They include an agreed pre-determined and published methodology providing guidelines for the ASEAN wide recognition/accreditation process. Certain sector/subsector of professional services are without a common ASEAN-wide understanding (definition) of the services and its scope of responsibilities, nor specific Central Product Classification coding; and
- In general, types of natural persons allowed with certain conditions for temporary presence in ASEAN countries are: business visitors for sales negotiations; intra-corporate transferees (executives, managers, specialists, others), executives, managers, specialists, technical experts, certain professionals, certain types of skilled workers, and other types of persons such as consultants and chefs.

The AEC Blueprint's strategic schedule for MRAs are:

- 2008–09: Complete MRAs currently under negotiation, that is, architectural services, accountancy services, surveying qualifications, medical practitioners and dental practitioners (2008);
- 2010–11: Identify and develop MRAs for other professional services by 2012–13; and
- 2014–15: Full implementation of completed MRAs (2015).

The following MRAs have been concluded:

1. Engineering services, signed in December 2005;
2. Nursing services, signed in December 2006;
3. Architectural services, signed in November 2007;
4. Framework for surveying qualifications, signed in November 2007;
5. Medical practitioners, signed in February 2009;
6. Dental practitioners, signed in February 2009;
7. Framework for accountancy services, signed in February 2009; and
8. Ongoing negotiations on tourism professionals.

Major difference between MRA and MRA Framework is in terms of objectives — while the MRA aims at facilitating the mobility of designated professionals, the MRA framework limits itself to facilitating only the negotiations of MRAs, by providing a structure towards the conclusion of such MRAs. For accountants and surveyors, member countries agreed to a framework by which their qualifications could be recognized, and have encouraged member states to negotiate MRAs among themselves covering these lines of work. Additionally, an MRA also aims at promoting the exchange of information and enhance coopera-ion in respect of the mutual recognition to promote the adoption of best practices on standards and qualifications in a particular profession and to provide opportunities for capacity building and training.

Typical processes in implementation preparation of MRAs involve setting up implementation committee and its rules and procedures; setting up secretariat for implementation; establish recognition/assessment mechanism; compilation of related domestic rules and regulations. Typical processes in implementation involve review of recognized institutions, review of applicants, and the establishment of work programme.

The Economic Community Scorecard (May 2012) reported that MRAs for engineers and architects have been implemented, "while work is underway to effectively operationalise the other professional MRAs (nursing, medical, dental, accountancy, and surveying). To facilitate the movement of persons engaged in trade and investment, the ASEAN Agreement on Movement of Natural Persons (MNP) has been drafted and is expected to be finalised in 2012." The report's Table 1 showed that "ASEAN has implemented 85.9 per cent of measures under Pillar 1 (single market and production base) with significant achievements in free flow of skilled labour and capital, and integration of priority sectors." On free flow of skilled labour, there was full implementation in the 2008–11 period. The implementation rate is defined as the ratio of measures that are fully implemented to total number of measures targeted. This result is somewhat puzzling, as Tilleke & Gibbins reported (see paragraph below) that Thailand has yet to adopt domestic legislation to implement the ASEAN MRAs.

Tilleke & Gibbins (29 February 2012) note that on MRAs, the general approach is that, to be eligible to work in the host country, the skilled worker must meet the requirements applicable in the skilled worker's country of origin. These would include appropriate qualification, pro-fessional registration and/or licence, minimum experience, satisfaction of continuing education requirements, lack of professional misconduct and no pending investigations thereof, and perhaps other requirements such as medical examinations or competency assessments. Tilleke & Gibbins cautioned that these agreements do not function to override local laws. The agreements are applicable only in accordance with prevailing laws and regulations of the host country. Practically, this means that member countries can still impose significant restrictions on skilled labour mobility. For example, in Thailand the Alien Employment Act remains in force. And Thailand has yet to adopt domestic legislation to implement the ASEAN MRAs. Moreover, for some lines of work, it may be impractical to comply with applicable professional obligations of the host country, given host country issues such as language barriers.

A major challenge is certification of professional qualifications skills across ASEAN countries with different educational systems and standards. MRAs are designed to facilitate mobility of professionals in the regulated or partially regulated occupations. Medical doctors and nurses clearly belong to the first category in all ASEAN countries. IT professionals belong to an unregulated category with no legal requirements for registration or licensing, or even a requirement to comply with professional standards set up by a corresponding professional body. Aside from the need to amend domestic law, the development of MRAs presents significant challenges for some lines of work, given the differences in educational standards across member countries. To address this issue, there are also efforts to develop core competencies and qualifications for various lines of work.

Quality assurance refers to pre-employment requirements, health and security clearance, personal and professional references. These are normally required by receiving countries and prospective employers.

Language proficiency (in the national language of receiving country) is usually required in certain professions, such as medical, nursing, teaching and legal to ensure efficient delivery of service and protect consumers. It acts as a serious barrier to skilled labour mobility. In countries where English is one of the state languages and a language of instruction in the tertiary system (Singapore and Philippines) the mobility of healthcare and teaching professionals is greatly facilitated. Likewise, prospects of working abroad for healthcare professionals from Myanmar are greatly facilitated by their English language skills. On the other hand, lack of English language skills is a major impediment to international mobility of Indonesian and Thai professionals. Entry into Japan of healthcare professionals under various bilateral EPAs with ASEAN member states, requires that the foreign nurses undergo appropriate language training before they qualify for a Japanese licence/registration.

Other Factors in ASEAN Skilled Labour Mobility

There are two types of cross-border labour flows in ASEAN. First, the much larger flow of unskilled and semi-skilled workers on short term contracts. Second, the much smaller flow of professionals and skilled manpower. The AEC covers only the second type of flows. Cross-border skilled labour mobility reflects an interplay of various forces that include the following:

- *Large disparities in wages and employment opportunities*: The more advanced countries, with higher wages and better employment opportunities, tend to attract labour migrants from less developed neighbouring countries. Among the ASEAN countries the per capita income rankings (reflective of wage and salary rankings) in descending order are Singapore, Brunei, Malaysia, Thailand, Philippines, Indonesia, Vietnam and CLM. Singapore, Brunei and Malaysia are experiencing general labour shortages as well as skills shortages, while the other countries are experiencing skills shortages to varying degrees;
- *Geographic proximity and social-cultural-linguistic environment*: Historically there was much free movement among the populations of Southeast Asia, both across the seas and across land borders. In particular, people moved freely between Malaysia and Singapore as the two countries shared a long common history (including under British colonial rule) and social-cultural-linguistic ties. So when educational and job opportunities for ethnic Chinese in Malaysia became restrictive, many of them sought such opportunities in nearby Singapore and stayed on as permanent residents and Singapore citizens. Likewise, there have been sizeable labour movements along the sea and land borders of Cambodia, Indonesia, Malaysia, Myanmar, Laos, Philippines, and Thailand. However, in this day of globalization and the internet, geographic proximity and its accompanying ready access to information and socio-cultural affinities are no longer strong pulls for skilled migrants, while language and educational links have become more important. Hence, many English-speaking professionals from ASEAN found employment in English-speaking countries in North America,

United Kingdom, and Australia-New Zealand. On the other hand, professionals conversant in the various European and Japanese languages tend to seek employment in these countries;

- *Disparities in educational development*: Countries in East Asia (Philippines, South Korea, Taiwan) that adopted the American and Japanese educational systems have long had broad-based tertiary education and produced large numbers of university and college graduates. With this foundation, South Korea and Taiwan were able to transit towards knowledge-based economies with little difficulty. On the other hand, Philippines economic development has been less robust, and the large numbers of Filipino university and college graduates had difficulties in securing remunerative employment at home and hence sought overseas employment with their advantage of English language proficiency. In contrast, Singapore, Malaysia, and Hong Kong adopted the more restrictive British educational system. Singapore only rapidly expanded its university and polytechnic intakes from the 1980s and hence there is a shortage of experienced mid-level professionals and managers. ASEAN students studying in developed countries in North America, Europe, Japan, and Australia-New Zealand are often attracted to stay on after graduation because of better-paying jobs, career-development prospects, and quality of life. The capacity of ASEAN professionals to secure overseas employment often depends on the quality of education received and the foreign language (particularly English) proficiency;
- *Policy factors* (discussed below).

Policies and Regulatory Frameworks on Outward Skills Mobility (Chia 2011)

Policies range from "laissez faire" in which out-migration is regarded as a matter of individual choice, to specific policies to promote labour export, such as in Vietnam and Indonesia to ease domestic unemployment and earn foreign exchange. Advances in modern transportation and ICT have greatly weakened the barrier of distance in choice of destination, while social and cultural links continue to bias migration in favour of certain locations. Measures to prevent brain drain by some countries include bonding of scholars on government scholarships — practised in Cambodia, Indonesia, Laos, Malaysia, Myanmar, Singapore, and Vietnam.

Philippines Outflows:

Philippines stand out as the main supplier of skilled (also unskilled) labour to ASEAN countries and to developed countries. This reflects a surplus supply of Filipino professionals from its educational and training institutions as employment opportunities within the country are inadequate, and facilitated by Filipinos' English language proficiency. The Philippines government does not officially encourage overseas employment. But through the POEA (Philippines Overseas Employment Administration), it promotes, facilitates and regulates the movement abroad of Filipino professionals, while TESDA (Technical Education and Skills Development Agency) provides the accreditation. In particular, Filipino nursing and teaching professionals are in great demand in various advanced countries. This has attracted more Filipinos to take up nursing qualifications to improve their "exportability". Tullao (March 2008) argued that when the more productive human talents are employed abroad, the less qualified and inexperienced are left domestically. Inefficiencies of these young and inexperienced service providers contribute to increase labour costs in the Philippines. Also, the Philippines has to spend more to produce the same calibre of professionals that will in time leave the country. The large remittances received by the Philippines are usually cited as a benefit from its out-migration. However, such remittances have also created the "Dutch disease" effect on the exchange rate.

Malaysia Outflows:

Kanapathy (March 2008) noted that Malaysian migration outflows are predominantly professional and technical manpower while migration inflows are almost entirely temporary low-skilled contract labour. Out-migration began in the early 1960s with migration for both work and long-term settlement, but recent trends suggest migrants are mostly temporary and in search of better opportunities. Malaysians working abroad were estimated at 784,000, with nearly half in Singapore, followed by Australia, Britain, and the US (Star Online, 1 November 2010). In 2010, the government created the Talent Corporation to attract, motivate, and retain talents and help agencies to ease the entry of skilled workers into the country. Actions include facilitating the diaspora to return as well as engaging them to contribute to Malaysia from wherever they are; focuses on government scholars in local universities and abroad and chart out their professional development when they return and join the workforce; and looks into retaining highly skilled and talented foreign expatriates as well as enticing foreign experts who used to work in Malaysia to return.

Singapore Outflows:

Singapore does not have a policy of restricting outward migration, but has two regulations that impede it. One is the obligation for compulsory military service for Singapore males. The other is the bonding of all tertiary students funded by government scholarships. Severe penalties are meted out to defaulters. A growing number of Singaporean professionals are also working abroad, reflecting the internationalization of the Singapore economy and Singapore enterprises and the growing number of Singaporeans working for foreign MNCs, as well as Singaporean tertiary students studying abroad. Some have chosen to settle permanently abroad, particularly in the advanced countries. However, the inflow of brains exceeds the outflow. Nonetheless, given the small population size of Singapore, the government is concerned over the loss of the domestic talent pool and has supported networks to connect them with Singapore in the hope that they may one day return.

Policies and Regulatory Frameworks on Inward Skills Mobility (Chia 2011)

Labour receiving countries are usually apprehensive of the impact of large inflows of foreigners on their labour markets, and the demand pressures on social infrastructure and services. As a result, they attempt to control the volume and source of labour inflows. Policies are usually two-tracked and asymmetric, with liberal policies towards inflows of professionals and skilled manpower and highly restrictive policies towards inflows of unskilled and semi-skilled workers. Political-social-cultural considerations may also lead some receiving countries to prefer sourcing from particular regions and countries.

Policies and regulations that facilitate and encourage inflow of professionals and skilled manpower:

Foreign professionals and skilled manpower are attracted by:

- Better salaries and expatriate packages that include housing, medical benefits, education for children, and duty-free importation of household goods and vehicles;

- Better working conditions, job experience, career development prospects, and research opportunities;
- Lower tax liabilities compared to home country;
- Better quality of life compared to home country; and
- Prospects of permanent residence and citizenship.

The main receiving countries are Singapore, Malaysia and to a lesser extent Thailand. They have adopted different policy mixes that seek to balance various goals and differ significantly in the breadth and focus of policy. Singapore stands at one extreme, Thailand at the other and Malaysia is in between:

Singapore Inflows:

Singapore has a large net inflow of professionals and skilled manpower (and an even larger inflow of unskilled and semi-skilled workers). It has a national strategy to attract inflows of professionals and executives to augment its limited domestic "talent pool" so as to facilitate economic upgrading and ensure sustainable economic growth. Potential migrants consider salaries, career opportunities, the quality of life, amenities and the environment as well as personal income tax regimes. A perennial question for Singapore is whether its quality of life and tax regime are as attractive as that of Hong Kong.

Professionals and skilled foreigners seeking employment in Singapore require an Employment Pass, valid for up to five years and renewable. Singapore's foreign skilled manpower is associated with the large presence of FDI in manufacturing and in services. Traditionally most of them are from the advanced industrial countries of U.S., Western Europe, Australia, and Japan, reflecting the important role of intra-corporate transferees from the thousands of foreign MNCs operating in Singapore. The Singapore public sector and Singaporean domestic enterprises also employ large numbers of foreign professionals and skilled workers. Foreign talent is being recruited through liberalized immigration policies, easing requirements for permanent residence and citizenship, offer of scholarships and research fellowships, recruitment missions to the main centres of learning by government agencies, and improving the living and cultural attractions, and tax regime of Singapore for foreign expatriates. Active recruitment of these professionals for the public service is undertaken by the Professionals' Information and Placement Service (PIPS) formed under the Public Service Commission, while for the private sector, the

Committee for Attracting Talent to Singapore (CATS) helps with the recruitment.

The very rapid growth of foreign professionals (including permanent residents and new citizens) in 2008–09, coupled with the impact of the global recession on the job market for Singaporean professionals, led to rising public concerns over the influx of foreign professionals (as well as low-skilled workers) crowding out jobs, public civic space, public transport, education and healthcare facilities, and contributing to a real estate bubble. This has led the government to slowdown the intakes of permanent residents, new citizens, and employment pass holders since 2011 and a promise to cap foreign workers (professionals as well as lowly skilled) at around one third of the Singapore workforce.

Malaysia inflows:

Less than 2 per cent of in-migration comprises high-skilled labour. The government argues that the lack of skilled and qualified workers was impeding its economic programmes. By end of 10th Malaysia Plan, the percentage of skilled workers in the country must rise to 37 per cent, highlighting ICT as a priority sector; the target is to increase GDP per capita to RM 38,000 by 2015. To encourage FDI and upgrade towards skill and knowledge intensive industries, policies on intake of foreign professionals and skilled manpower have been liberalized. Expatriates are allowed to work in almost all sectors, except those that impinge on national security and some restrictions are imposed on their numbers in banking and finance. However, manufacturing firms located in the various Economic Growth Regions can hire as many expatriates as required. Expatriates can bring along their dependents.

Thailand inflows:

Under the Investment Promotion Law, aliens are allowed to enter Thailand to investigate investment opportunities, or for other matters which might benefit investment. BOI will grant permission to stay in Thailand for not more than six months at a time. A promoted company will be allowed by BOI to bring in foreign personnel as skilled technicians/experts together with their families. Duration of one-year at a time for the work permit will be allowed except for positions that have been approved to work in the promoted company for more than two years. However, BOI encourages the employment of Thai nationals as managers/technicians.

The largest share of occupations given work permits are managers and executives, followed by elementary occupations and professionals. BOI has a One-stop Centre to handle all aspects of visa extensions and issuance of work permits, including work permit extensions, issuance of re-entry permits and changes in type of visas to non-immigrants.

Barriers to and regulations on employment of foreign professionals/skilled manpower:

These cover constitutional provisions reserving such jobs for nationals; requirements and procedures for employment visas, employment passes and permits; sectors and occupations closed or with numerical caps on foreign professionals and skilled manpower; economic test to justify the need for employment of foreigners; requirement to have foreign professionals and skilled labour replaced by locals within a stipulated time period; lack of recognition of foreign professional education, training and experience; and licensing regulations of professional associations.

(a) Legal and Administrative Framework on Inflows of Skilled Labour

Singapore: The government introduced several legislations since the 1980s for regulating the entry, employment, management, and departure of foreign labour. These include the Employment of Foreign Workers Act, Immigration Act, Employment Agencies Act, Employment of Foreign Workers (levy order), Employment of Foreign Workers (fees) regulation, and Work Permit (exemption) (consolidation) notification. The main government agencies involved are the Ministry of Home Affairs (MOHA) which exercises border controls under the Immigration and Checkpoint Authority, and the Ministry of Manpower (MOM) which issues work passes, enforces the regulations, and sees to the well being of foreign workers. Information regarding the different kinds of work permits and employment passes are available on the MOM website. There is extensive use of online information and applications resulting in transparency, efficiency, and convenience. In January 2010, MOM launched the new Employment Pass Services Centre (EPSC) to register and issue new Long Term Pass (LTP) cards to pass holders and their dependents entering Singapore on the various types of employment passes, providing a seamless and convenient service upon arrival in Singapore. Apart from MOHA and MOM, other agencies involved with managing and servicing foreign labour include the housing, physical planning and environmental authorities, the labour movement, and NGOs.

(b) Constitutional Provision Reserving Jobs for Nationals

Philippines: As a general rule, the Republic of the Philippines (RP) Constitution reserves the practice of licensed professions to RP citizens save in cases prescribed by law. These include engineering; medicine and allied professions; accountancy and architecture. Philippine law (RA 8182) also requires that preference be given RP citizens in the hiring of consultants and other professionals necessary for the implementation of projects funded by foreign assistance. Legislation in February 1998 (RA 8555) gives the RP President the authority to waive this and other preferences applicable to the procurement of goods and services funded with foreign assistance. Although the constitutional language states that "the practice of all professions in the Philippines shall be limited to Filipino citizens", this statement is immediately followed by "save in cases prescribed by law". However, the Philippines constitution is not a strict legal barrier to the participation of foreign professionals. Most of the laws regulating professions contain reciprocity provisions. There are 45 laws governing the practice of specific professions, and 40 contain "reciprocity" provisions allowing foreigners to practise their profession in the Philippines, provided their countries of origin also allow Filipinos to practise these. However, the provisions are administratively difficult to satisfy and very few foreign professionals apply to the Professional Regulatory Commission (PRC) other than for temporary permits. In addition, a Supreme Court rule limits the practice of law to Philippine nationals. Five laws regulating criminologists, environmental planners, foresters, pharmacists, and radio and x-ray technologists state the profession is restricted to Philippine nationals and contain no reciprocity provisions.

(c) Visa Requirements, Employment Passes and Permits

Market access faces difficulties in getting visas. While ASEAN countries have implemented visa-free rule for social visits among themselves, business and employment visas are required for foreign businesses and professionals seeking employment. Visa costs include fees for single and multiple visas, complexity of the application procedure and processing time. In addition, countries require foreigners to be issued with employment passes or employment permits. The inward movement of professionals seem to be most restrictive in Indonesia, Cambodia, Laos, and Myanmar, which require an employer hiring a foreigner to ensure that some capacity-building and skills-transfer activities are conducted so as to eventually replace the foreigner with a local staff member.

Indonesia: Foreign managerial and expert personnel are allowed in positions that cannot yet be filled by Indonesian nationals. There are incentives on employment and stay of foreign workers for companies with export ratio of at least 85 per cent. Three requirements must be met by all foreigners seeking employment — a minimum five-year educational or job experience relevant to the position sought, a willingness to state that the foreign professional will relinquish his position to nationals, and a capacity to communicate in the Indonesian language. Bureaucratic procedures which underlie processing of work permits and visa applications include cumbersome documentation requirements seeking to protect domestic professionals from foreign competition, and to ensure rapid replacement of foreign workers with nationals through regulation.

To employ foreign workers, a company must submit a Plan of Using Foreign Manpower (RPTKA) to Ministry of Manpower and Transmigration. The company must ask for visa recommendation from Director of Provision and Use of Manpower and bring the recommendation to the Ministry of Law and Human Rights. After obtaining the approval letter of granting a visa, the company must submit request for Employing Foreign Workers Permit (IMTA) to Ministry of Manpower and Transmigration and have it signed. Criterion for issuing passes and permits are education and professional qualifications; skills accreditation requirements; relevant work experience requirements; salary offered by prospective employer as indicator of level of skills and relevant work experience. Duration of the foreign expatriate's term to work in Indonesia is subject to government regulation, based on expertise and the availability of an Indonesian to replace the expatriate position. There is no quota or numerical cap by sector or profession.

Malaysia: Immigration processing time of several months often proves to be too long for prospective job seekers. Visa processing delays is often the reason for their acceptance of an alternative destination. Employment pass is issued to any foreigner who enters the country to take up a contract of employment with a minimum period of two years. There are different types of employment passes and permits for professionals, academics and managers.

A company with foreign paid-up-capital of less than US$2 million will be considered for expatriate posts on the basis of the following: first, key posts can be considered where the foreign-paid-up capital is at least RM 500,000 and the number of key posts allowed depends on the merits of each case. Second, for executive posts which require professional qualification and practical experience, expatriates may be employed up to a maximum period of nineteen years, while for non-executive posts which require technical skills and experience, expatriates may be employed up to a maximum period of five years, subject to condition that Malaysians are trained to eventually take over the posts. Third, employment of other foreign workers is allowed in construction, plantation, services (domestic maids, restaurants, hotel industry, trainers and instructors), and manufacturing sectors. Fourth, the Foreign Workers Division of Immigration Department is the approving authority for the employment of foreign workers belonging to the skilled, semi-skilled and unskilled categories (i.e. excludes expatriates under the management, professional, and technical/supervisory categories). Fifth, approval is based on the merits of each case and subject to conditions that will be determined from time to time. An employer's application to employ foreign workers will only be considered after efforts to find qualified local citizens and permanent residents have failed. Sixth, to ensure that foreign labour is employed only when necessary, an annual levy on foreign workers is imposed, but those who pay income tax are exempt from paying the worker levy.

There are quota or numerical caps for each profession/sector — not more than 30 per cent in any particular sector. There are also restrictions on employment of nationals from certain countries with no diplomatic relations (such as Israel). Criteria used for issuing passes and permits — contract of employment with a minimum period of two years' education and professional qualifications; skills accreditation requirements; relevant work experience requirements; salary offered by prospective employer as indicator of level of skills and relevant work experience. Preference is given to education and qualifications from first world countries in the British Commonwealth, North American and EU.

Singapore provides largely visa-free entry for business and social visitors, but has three types of visas for employment. First, semi-permanent residents with semi-permanent work passes who are allowed to take any job anywhere in Singapore (valid for five years); they can apply for citizenship and face no restrictions in the labour market and can bring their families. Second, there are foreign professionals with employment passes, which are issued only for specific jobs and for a specific duration (valid for one to five years); although tied to a specific company, such employment pass holders enjoy limitless opportunities to get their permits extended. Third, there are short-term contract workers with permits usually valid for two years (subject to renewal).

Singapore has an elaborate structure of employment passes (EP) for foreign professionals and skilled manpower which are defined by educational/skills qualifications and salaries. Employment passes are valid for up to five years and are renewable. There is no foreign worker levy or dependency ceiling quota as with lower-skilled work permit holders. They are also eligible to apply for dependent pass (DP) for spouse and unmarried children and may apply to become Singapore permanent residents or citizens. Except for the Q and S pass holders, they may also apply for Long term social visit pass (LTSVP) for parents, step-children, spouse, handicapped children and unmarried daughters. Employment pass is also tied up with the specific employer, except for the Personalised Employment Pass.

Thailand: The Investment Promotion Law allows aliens to enter Thailand to investigate investment opportunities or for other matters which might benefit investment. BOI will grant permission to stay in Thailand for not more than six months at a time. The Alien Occupation Law requires all aliens working in Thailand to obtain a Work Permit. The Work Permit is subject to renewal or extended visa. A Work Permit is valid for one year but extendable. The number of foreign workers allowed in a company is determined by its registered capital — 2 million baht per foreign worker with a maximum of ten workers or 3 per cent of the firm's full-time workforce.

If the company is registered with BOI, it can obtain multiple work permits without needing to increase registered capital, depending on the agreement reached with BOI. However, BOI companies need to be set up with minimum of 1 million baht of registered capital. If the company does not have BOI approval and the foreign employee is not married to a Thai national, then 2 million baht of registered capital per work permit holder will be required. If applicant is married to a Thai national, then the required amount of registered capital is 1 million baht.

Vietnam: Enterprises with foreign owned capital and parties to a business cooperation contract have the right to recruit and employ labour in accordance with business requirements and must give priority to Vietnamese citizens, only recruit and employ foreigners for jobs which require a level of technical and management expertise which a Vietnamese citizen cannot satisfy but must train Vietnamese citizens as replacements. Criteria used for issuing passes and permits are education, professional qualifications and relevant work experience.

IV. Conclusion

Skilled labour mobility is essential for effective implementation of services liberalization and FDI liberalization as well as a goal in itself for deeper ASEAN economic integration. Further, as more ASEAN countries strive to move up the technological ladder, liberalizing trade in goods and services and in FDI is not enough, and a larger pool of professional and skilled manpower becomes necessary. Until such time when domestic educational and training institutions are able to supply the necessary high level manpower, countries will have to depend on "foreign talents". Even with adequate domestic supply there is still a need for foreign talents, as they will provide the competition, stimulation and synergy to improve the quantity, quality and productivity of domestic talents. Some countries, particularly Singapore and to a lesser extent Malaysia, are regarding foreign talent as an upgrading and competitive tool and to enhance their roles as education and medical hubs, and have active policies to promote inflows of foreign professionals and skilled manpower. Most ASEAN countries, however, have yet to move away from policies, regulations and practices that aimed at protecting domestic professionals and skilled workers from foreign competition.

Effective cooperation among the ASEAN University Network in terms of mobility of students and staff remain limited, reflecting the sharp differences in curricula and standards among the institutions, lack of an ASEAN "role model" and the limited financial resources for student and staff exchange. Cooperation and exchange tend to be with universities and institutions from the advanced countries of North America, Western Europe, Australia and Japan rather than intra-ASEAN.

It does not help that the medium of instruction in the ASEAN countries is usually the national language, except for the use of English in the Philippines and Singapore. A greater use of the English language as a medium of instruction would facilitate student and staff exchanges among ASEAN countries, and in the process gain wider recognition of ASEAN academic and professional qualifications. After all, in recognition of the different national languages that exist among ASEAN countries, the working language at all ASEAN meetings and for all ASEAN documents and publications is, pragmatically, English. Institutions should redouble their efforts to achieve cooperation and integration in education and adopt policies across countries that will facilitate the exchange of students and staff, and eventually the mobility of skilled workers. It would be useful if ASEAN adopted concerted approaches to improve the efficacy of their education and training institutions in providing the necessary skills for the labour market.

MRAs appear to be the main tool for skilled labour mobility in ASEAN. However, negotiating for recognition is a complex and time-consuming process given the wide differences in development levels among ASEAN countries. Effective implementation of these MRAs poses even further problems. Moreover, negotiations of MRAs cannot be equated with market access and effective intra-ASEAN skills mobility. There are many domestic regulations and practices that impede such mobility. These include constitutional and other legal provisions reserving such jobs for nationals; requirements and procedures for employment visas and employment passes and permits; sectors and occupations closed to or with numerical caps on foreign professionals and skilled manpower; economic and labour market tests to justify the need for employment of foreigners and requirement by employers to have them replaced by locals within a stipulated period; lack of recognition of foreign professional education, training and experience; licensing regulations of professional associations; and language proficiency requirements.

ASEAN member states should try, as far as possible, to remove the various regulatory impediments to freer flow of skilled labour. For a start, more information exchange and transparency and simplifying visa and employment pass applications would help. Amending constitutional provisions would be extremely difficult.

However, it would be hard to envision an ASEAN single market and production base by 2015 or later without the free flow of skilled labour to deliver on services and FDI liberalization. The ASEAN Agreement on the Movement of Natural Persons was signed in November 2012, providing for the rights and obligations additional to those set out in AFAS; facilitating the movement of natural persons engaged in the conduct of trade in services and investment; establishing streamlined and transparent procedures for applications for immigration formalities for the temporary entry or stay of natural persons; and protecting the integrity of ASEAN member states' borders and protecting the domestic labour force and permanent employment in the ASEAN member states.

NOTES

1. See Chia (2011) for detailed analysis of these impediments to ASEAN skilled labour mobility.
2. Jagdish Bhagwati, *Taxing the Brain Drain Challenge*, vol. 19, no. 3 (July/August 1976): 34–38.
3. The initial participating leading universities of ASEAN are Universiti Brunei Darussalam; Gadjah Mada; Universiti Sains Malaysia and Universiti Malaya; University of the Philippines; National University of Singapore and Nanyang Technological University; Burapha University of Thailand.

REFERENCES

Asia Now blog. *Cross Border Mobility: Its Shortcomings in ASEAN* (accessed 21 April 2012).
ASEAN Secretariat. *The ASEAN Economic Community Blueprint* (accessed 2009).
————. *ASEAN Integration in Trade in Services: Developments, Challenges and Way Forward* (accessed June 2011).
————. *ASEAN Economic Community Scorecard* (accessed March 2012).
Chia Siow Yue. "Demographic Change and International Labour Mobility in Southeast Asia: Issues, Policies and Implications for Cooperation". In *Labour Mobility in the Asia-Pacific Region: Dynamics, Issues and a New APEC Agenda*, edited by Graeme Hugo and Soogil Young. Singapore: Institute of Southeast Asian Studies, 2008.
————. "Free Flow of Skilled Labor in the AEC". ERIA Final Report, 2011.

Kanapathy, Vijayakumari. "Managing Cross-border Mobility in Malaysia: Two Decades of Policy Experiments". Paper presented at the PECC-ABAC Conference on Demographic Change and International Labor Mobility in the Asia Pacific Region: Implications for Business and Cooperation, Seoul, 25–28 March 2008.

Plummer, Michael G. and Chia Siow Yue, eds. *Realizing the ASEAN Economic Community: A Comprehensive Assessment.* Singapore: Institute of Southeast Asian Studies, 2008.

Tilleke and Gibbins. *Thailand: Movement of Natural Persons under AEC: Labor Market Issues* (accessed 29 February 2012).

———. *Thailand: ASEAN Economic Community 2015 and Thailand* (accessed 1 March 2012).

Tullao, Tereso S. "Demographic Changes and International Labor Mobility in the Philippines: Implications for Business and Cooperation". Paper presented at the PECC-ABAC Conference on Demographic Change and International Labor Mobility in the Asia Pacific Region: Implications for Business and Cooperation, Seoul, 25–28 March 2008.

Wong Li Za. "Talent Corp out to stem brain drain". Star Online, 1 November 2010.

7

INFRASTRUCTURE DEVELOPMENT IN ASEAN

Mahani Zainal Abidin and Firdaos Rosli

I. Introduction

Since the formation of ASEAN Free Trade Area (AFTA) in 1992, ASEAN has made significant strides in transforming the region into an area for free movement of capital, goods, services, and its people. In 2003, ASEAN moved a step closer towards a greater regional integration by adopting the Bali Concord II that comprises three pillars — ASEAN Economic Community (AEC), the ASEAN Political-Security Community (APSC), and the ASEAN Socio-Cultural Community (ASCC). ASEAN leaders later agreed to accelerate the establishment of the AEC from 2020 to 2015, with the belief that integration can close the development gap amongst its member states.

The AEC vision is to ensure that the ASEAN region be a single market and a production hub by 2015. One of the measures for achieving this vision is the level of regional intra-trade. The intra-ASEAN trade is stagnant at around 25 per cent, with trade between

Malaysia and Singapore accounting for more than half of the total. Economists believe that to ensure self-reliance, ASEAN has to achieve at least 40 per cent of intra-regional trade. The availability of a good physical infrastructure system that connects ASEAN member states is an important and necessary factor that can increase intra-regional trade and contribute to regional integration.

According to the Asian Development Bank Institute,[1] there are four reasons why infrastructure can generate a higher cycle of higher demand, productivity and growth, consistent with ASEAN's long-term development goals. These are:

1. Infrastructure plays a significant role in promoting and sustaining economic growth in the region;
2. Infrastructure development is necessary to accelerate economic integration within the region, particularly in the area of trade and investment;
3. Addressing inequalities in infrastructure development is critical to the wider objective of reducing development gaps among ASEAN countries and income inequality and poverty within each country; and
4. Infrastructure development is necessary to improve resource sharing and efficiency in the region to provide basic needs, such as water and electricity.

Realizing the importance of infrastructure, ASEAN countries initiated cooperation in the areas of transport, ICT and energy facilities even before the AEC. However, more progress needs to be made. In addition, ASEAN countries have built national infrastructure but the level of achievement varies between countries, depending on the stage of development and the availability of resources. Acknowledging the importance of having a good national as well as cross-border infrastructure, ASEAN launched the Master Plan on ASEAN Connectivity (MPAC) in 2009. The Plan, which focuses on improving regional connectivity through national and cross-border infrastructure development, will hopefully bring ASEAN countries closer together towards the realization of the AEC.

This chapter will examine the ASEAN infrastructure cooperation in transportation (roads, bridges, and railway) as well as in energy (electrical power network, gas, and petroleum pipelines), water (pipes and storage reservoirs systems) and communication (telephone cables, satellite, and undersea cables) facilities. The issues discussed will include the evaluation of the current status and the framework of cooperation and assessment of progress towards the milestones as set out in the AEC Blueprint. There are gaps between the progress made and the targets set and hence there is a need for policy reforms to ensure that the goals are met.

Section II of this chapter will examine the infrastructure policy framework in ASEAN, while Section III assesses the infrastructure achievements in the AEC Blueprint. Section IV will analyse the progress towards a well-connected region including the Master Plan on ASEAN Connectivity and Infrastructure Financing. Issues, challenges and policy recommendations will be discussed in Section V and Section VI concludes with some thoughts on future initiatives.

II. Infrastructure Policy Framework in ASEAN

Seven out of the ten of ASEAN members are geographically connected by land and as such, cooperation in the transport sector represents the biggest subset of the region's infrastructure development. Besides building national and regional infrastructure, a key challenge is to ensure the smooth movement of goods and services across borders, which have to undergo various processes that complicate the flow and increase the cost of trade. Evidently, ASEAN is continuously building a more effective mechanism to reduce the physical barriers for better movement of trade and people that can further strengthen connectivity, where member states operate according to the same standards.

ASEAN began its infrastructure policy framework that will eventually assist regional connectivity through developing common commitments and priorities in transportation, energy, and information and communication technology (ICT).

Cooperation in the Transport Sector

Prior to the formation of AFTA in 1992, ASEAN adopted sectoral approach in dealing with its transport cooperation whereby shipping, ports, rail, road, and air networks were developed independently. There was little push to develop a comprehensive transport model within the region. As a result, little effort was made towards the realization of a single regional transport market. However, as tariff rates were being reduced in AFTA, it was realized that if trade facilitation was not improved, intra-regional trade would not increase. Hence, trade facilitation became the main policy drive, which results in the formation of a comprehensive transport policy. Since then, ASEAN had recognized that transport cooperation in logistics and service support sector was critical in achieving regional economic integration and international competitiveness (see Table 7.1).

ASEAN Plan of Action in Transport and Communication (1994–96) was the region's starting point in achieving the objectives of transport cooperation. The Action Plan, endorsed by the Senior Economic Officials Meeting (SEOM) in March 1995, identified six key objectives for ASEAN cooperation in transport and telecommunications, namely:

1. Development of multimodal transport and trade facilitation;
2. Development of ASEAN interconnectivity in telecommunications; including fixed and mobile voice and data and EDI services, for trade and business communications and to enhance land, sea, and air transport;
3. Harmonization of road transport laws, rules, and regulations in ASEAN;
4. Improvement of air space management in ASEAN;
5. Development of ASEAN rules and regulations for carriage of dangerous goods and industrial wastes by land and sea; and
6. Human resources development in transport and communications.

ASEAN Transport Ministers met for the first time in March 1996 in Bali to further institutionalize its transport cooperation programmes and to endorse the Ministerial Understanding on ASEAN Cooperation in

TABLE 7.1
Policy Commitments in Transport Cooperation in ASEAN

Programmes	Timeline
ASEAN Plan of Action in Transport and Communications	1994–96
ASEAN Plan of Action in Transport (Ministerial Understanding)	1996–98
Successor Plan of Action in Transport	1999–2004
ASEAN Transport Action Plan	2005–10
ASEAN Strategic Transport Plan	2011–15

Source: ASEAN Secretariat.

Transportation. The Ministerial Understanding has four main objectives, namely to:

1. Establish and develop a harmonized and integrated regional transport system in order to provide safe, efficient and innovative transportation infrastructure network;
2. Enhance cooperation in the transport sector amongst member states in order to contribute towards the achievement of the objectives of the AFTA;
3. Establish a mechanism to coordinate and supervise cooperation projects and activities in the transport sector; and
4. Promote interconnectivity and interoperability of national networks and access thereto taking particular account of the need to link islands, land locked, and peripheral regions with the national and global economies.

The 1997/1998 Asian Financial Crisis did not decelerate much ASEAN's push for greater integration in transport cooperation. In fact, ASEAN continued to strengthen its transport commitments by adopting the Successor Plan of Action in Transport 1999–2004 to translate the Hanoi Plan of Action's Transport Priorities into action. The Plan had 55 projects and activities during the six-year period with four sectoral working groups in Transport Facilitation, Air Transport, Land Transport, and Maritime Transport. During that period, ASEAN transport cooperation was focused on the development of the trans-ASEAN transportation network, transport facilitation agreements, cooperation with private sectors (most noticeably in amongst airlines, forwarders, ports, shippers' councils, and ship owners) and strategic partnerships with ASEAN Dialogue Partners such as China, India and Japan. ASEAN needed to realize the leaders' goal of AEC by 2020 (which was subsequently accelerated to 2015) and the ASEAN Transport Action Plan 2005–10 was endorsed as the foundation to achieve this aim.

The Policy Agenda under the ASEAN Transport Action Plan (ATAP) 2005–10 were carried out through 48 proposed actions, goals and strategic thrust as shown in Table 7.2. Out of these 48 actions, 13 actions are for land transport, 10 actions for air transport, 14 actions for maritime transport, and 11 actions for transport facilitation. The Action Plan was complemented by three sectoral roadmaps, i.e. Roadmap for Integration of Air Travel Sector (RIATS), Roadmap towards an Integrated

TABLE 7.2

Goals and Strategic Thrust Area in ATAP 1999–2004

	Goals	Strategic Thrust
Land transport	• Establishing efficient, integrated, safe and environmentally sustainable regional land transport (road and railway) corridors linking all members and neighbouring trading partners.	• Improving land transport infrastructure integration and intermodal interconnectivity, with principal airports, ports, and inland waterways, and ferry links. • Promoting concerted and coordinated efforts at policy and operation level to develop ASEAN land transport trade corridors.
Air transport	• Establishment of a regional open sky arrangement to support regional economic integration. • Achieving globally-acceptable standards in aviation security and safe.	• Implementing the regional plan on the ASEAN Open Sky Policy, on a staged and progressive basis. • Promoting satellite-based air navigational and automatic sensing systems to effectively control air traffic and improve safety in airspace.
Maritime transport	• Creating a more efficient and competitive regional maritime transport sector. • Achieving globally-acceptable standards in maritime safety and security and protection of marine environment.	• Formulating and implementing a common regional shipping policy. • Improving maritime safety and security and protection of the marine environment by enhancing cooperation amongst AMSs to facilitate the acceptance and implementation of IMO conventions.
Transport facilitation	• Creating an integrated and efficient logistics and multi-modal transportation system, for cargo movement between logistics bases and trade centres within and beyond ASEAN.	• Operationalizing the ASEAN Framework Agreements on the Facilitation of Goods in Transit, Interstate Transport and Multimodal Transport. • Enhancing capacity and skills development to further progress regional transport facilitation cooperation. • Conceptual planning for an integrated inter-modal transport network.

Source: ERIA.

and Competitive Maritime Transport in ASEAN and Roadmap for the Integration of Logistics Services (RILS).

Under ATAP, the transport cooperation went beyond comprehensive roadmaps, collaboration with Dialogue Partners and other sub-regional initiatives. However, sub-regional transport cooperation made little progress due to, mainly, financial constraints.

In 2010, ASEAN Transport Ministers endorsed the Brunei Action Plan, or ASEAN Strategic Transport Plan (ASTP) 2011–15, to provide the main reference that would guide the ASEAN transport cooperation and integration over the next five years. The ASTP's goals are shown in Table 7.3. The ASTP identified strategic actions to be implemented in the

TABLE 7.3
Goals under the ASEAN Strategic Transport Plan 2011–15

Transport	Goals
Land transport	• Accomplish the implementation of SKRL project; • Complete the ASEAN Highway network (AHN); • Reduce road fatalities by 50% in AMSs by 2020; • Establish efficient and integrated inland waterways network; • Develop "Intelligent Transport System" (ITS); • Enhance human, technical and institutional capacity in AMSs; and • Establish a sustainable, energy efficient and environmentally-friendly transport system.
Air transport	• Establish an ASEAN Single Aviation Market (ASAM); • Promote environmentally-friendly aviation; and • Enhance engagement with Dialogue Partners to promote greater connectivity.
Maritime transport	• Accomplish an integrated, efficient, and competitive maritime transport system; • Develop safety navigation system and establish advanced maritime security system in line with international standards; and • Accomplish the Eco-Port and environmentally-friendly shipping.
Transportation facilitation	• Establish integrated and seamless multimodal transport system; • Enhance the competitiveness of ASEAN Logistics Industry; • Establish safe and secure inter-state transport system; and • Develop environmentally-friendly logistics.

Source: ERIA.

period 2011–15 to support the realization of the AEC as well as the new priority of enhancing regional connectivity identified in the MPAC.

The specific objectives of ASTP are to:

1. Maintain continuity of actions for the implementation of AEC Blueprint to develop an integrated and harmonized trans-ASEAN transportation network;
2. Enhance connectivity of intra-ASEAN transport networks to support the MPAC;
3. Leverage on the strong Asian economic growth and increased external ASEAN cooperation by strengthening transport connectivity with Dialogue Partners and other regional partners;
4. Capitalize on the strategic geographical location of ASEAN and accelerated pace of globalization to upgrade selected transport infrastructure components and services, which serve as vital links to international supply routes;
5. Incorporate environmental and climate change considerations in planning, development, operations and management of ASEAN transport networks in line with relevant global initiatives; and
6. Enhance regional capability to further improve the level of safety and security in the provision of transport services.

The transport sector infrastructure cooperation cannot be realized in one master plan. Therefore, ASTP is not very much different from earlier plans but rather a continuation of major infrastructure cooperation and projects such as the ASEAN Highway Network and Singapore-Kunming Rail Link (SKRL). These infrastructure projects require large financial investments and involve other critical considerations such as construction, network upgrading and close project monitoring. ASEAN countries are committed in realizing these projects but progress is slow. As most of the basic rail and road networks are already in place, the bigger task now is to finance the interconnection links between participating countries.

Cooperation in the Energy Sector

Since 1999, ASEAN aspires to reach optimum levels of energy security and sustainability in an affordable way and plans to achieve this through two long-term energy cooperation projects, namely the ASEAN Power Grid (APG) and Trans-ASEAN Gas Pipeline (TAGP). As the demand for energy is increasing, and at the same time, supply of energy is decreasing, securing a stable supply of energy at a reasonable cost in an environmentally friendly manner remains ASEAN's biggest challenge in the energy sector.

ASEAN's cohesive cooperation in the energy sector is guided by its five-year ASEAN Plan of Action for Energy Cooperation (APAEC). The first APAEC (1999–2004) blueprint aimed to:

(a) Ensure security and sustainability of energy supply, efficient utilization of natural energy resource in the region and the rational management of energy demand, with due consideration of the environment; and

(b) Institute the policy framework and implementation modalities by 2004 for the early realization of the Trans-ASEAN energy networks covering the APG and the TAGP as a more focused continuation of the medium-term programme of action (1995–99).

During the period 1999–2004, ASEAN's energy security framework was enhanced by the conclusion of Trans-ASEAN Gas Pipeline Master Plan and the ASEAN Interconnection Master Plan Study. The subsequent APAEC (2004–09), saw the advent of APG as well as the establishment of ASEAN Council on Petroleum Gas Centre and APG Consultative Council.

The late 2000s oil crisis and the projection of the region's energy supply sparked greater collaboration in energy security by accelerating the implementation of action plans to bring energy security, accessibility, and sustainability closer together. The third APAEC (2010–15) strategies are shown in Table 7.4 and it contains 26 strategies and 91 actions and expected to reduce regional energy intensity by at least 8 per cent based on 2005 levels and to achieve a 15 per cent collective target for regional renewable energy in the total power installed capacity by 2015.[2]

Energy cooperation in the region appears to have gained some traction over the years due to the price and supply volatility in the global energy market. Achieving the desired level of energy security would be worthwhile if it reduces the costs of electricity generation, regional investment on power development projects and promoting adequate power reserves. ASEAN countries have shown interest in pooling their resources to exploit the collective benefits of energy interdependence. However, domestic political and social dimensions have to be taken into

TABLE 7.4
APAEC 2010–15 Strategies

Programme Area	Strategies
ASEAN Power Grid	• Accelerate the development of the ASEAN Power Grid Interconnection projects • Optimize the generation sector *vis-à-vis* the available indigenous energy resources in the region • Encourage and optimize the utilization of ASEAN resources, such as, funding, expertise and products to develop the generation, transmission, and distribution sector
Trans-ASEAN Gas Pipeline	• Collectively implement the ASEAN MOU on TAGP by ASCOPE Members • PERTAMINA and PSC Partners to undertake detailed feasibility study for East Natuna Gas Field Development • Implement the approved Roadmap for TAGP by respective ASCOPE Members • Implement the approved 5-year ASCOPE Gas Centre Work Program
Coal and Clean Coal Technology	• Strengthen Institutional and Policy Framework and build an ASEAN Coal Image • Promote Coal and Clean Coal Technologies • Promote Intra-ASEAN Coal Trade and Investment • Enhance environmental planning and assessment of coal projects
Energy Efficiency and Conservation	• Develop Energy Efficiency Policy and Build Capacity • Enhance awareness raising and dissemination of information • Promote good energy management practices, especially for industrial and commercial sectors • Facilitate Energy Efficiency Financing
Renewable Energy	• Increase the development and utilization of renewable energy sources to achieve the 15% target share of renewable energy in ASEAN power generation mix • Enhance awareness and information sharing and strengthen networks • Promote intra-ASEAN cooperation on ASEAN-made products and services • Promote renewable energy financing scheme • Promote the commercial development and utilization of biofuels • Develop ASEAN as a hub for renewable energy

Programme Area	Strategies
Regional Energy Policy and Planning	• Enhance energy policy and supply security information sharing network • Conduct capacity building in energy and environmental policy planning and energy supply security assessment • Prepare regional energy outlooks and conducting ASEAN energy policy reviews and analysis series • Strengthen collaboration and dialogues with ASEAN partners and with national, regional and global institutions • Monitor and evaluate the progress of APAEC programmes
Civilian Nuclear Energy	• Conduct capacity building among ASEAN Member States • Strengthen public information and public education on nuclear power generation • Strengthen institutional, legal and regulatory capacities on nuclear energy for power generation

Source: ASEAN Secretariat.

context as energy security is also a part of national security. As APG and TAGP are very intricate cross-border investments, it would take more than just regional energy framework to translate these projects into national priorities.

Cooperation in the Information and Communication Technology (ICT) Sector

The development of ASEAN ICT infrastructure framework started in 2000 when ASEAN leaders endorsed the e-ASEAN Framework Agreement[3] to:

1. Develop the ASEAN Information Infrastructure;
2. Facilitate the growth of electronic commerce in ASEAN;
3. Promote and facilitate the liberalization of trade in ICT products, ICT services and of investments in support of the e-ASEAN initiative;
4. Promote and facilitate investments in the production of ICT products and the provision of ICT services;
5. Develop an e-Society in ASEAN and capacity building to reduce the digital divide within individual ASEAN Member States and amongst ASEAN Member States; and

6. Promote the use of ICT applications in the delivery of government
   services (e-government).

Since then ASEAN has achieved two major milestones in the ICT
sector namely the Ministerial Understanding on ASEAN Cooperation
in Telecommunications and IT (2001) and ASEAN ICT Master Plan
2015 (2011).

Bridging the large gap in digital divide amongst ASEAN members
remains the region's biggest challenge in developing a common region-
wide IT infrastructure. However, as countries continue to embrace the
advancement of IT applications, ASEAN has formed the ASEAN ICT
Master Plan (AIM) 2015. The AIM, whose strategic thrusts and key
outcomes are shown in Figure 7.1, was endorsed in the 10th ASEAN
Telecommunications and Information Technology Ministers Meeting
in 2011 and consists of a set of comprehensive actions and projects to
be implemented from the period 2011 to 2015. The six strategic thrusts
are economic transformation, people empowerment and engagement,
innovation, infrastructure development, human capital development,
and bridging the digital divide.

In addition to the growing number of ICT usage, ASEAN's ICT
framework has provided a platform to benchmark best practices to narrow

FIGURE 7.1

Key Outcomes and Strategic Thrusts of ASEAN ICT Master Plan 2015

| Key Outcomes | ←→ | • Economic transformation
• People empowerment and engagement
• Innovation
• Infrastructure development
• Human capital development
• Bridging the digital divide |

| Strategic Thrusts | ←→ | • ICT as an engine of growth for ASEAN countries
• ASEAN as a global ICT hub
• Enhance quality of life for peoples of ASEAN
• Contribution towards ASEAN integration |

Source: ASEAN Secretariat.

the region's digital divide. As a result, the level of ICT advancement by the least developed ASEAN countries are catching up fast. This is largely contributed by internet service providers that are investing in higher bandwidth technologies to keep prices low.

ASEAN's infrastructure framework in the ICT cooperation sector cannot be static and has to move along with the rapid advances in the global technology to remain relevant. However, infrastructure investment in this sector is very dependent on the economic condition and income level of its people. There are also ICT operators who are not keen to invest due to economic viability of investing in costly hardware ICT infrastructures. As these ventures require large capital outlay, operators will find it hard to assess returns on investment.

Additionally, ASEAN's progress in ICT infrastructure development will also depend on political and legal institutions, which must be ready to embrace the exponential growth rate of information flow as a result of rapid changes in ICT advancement and applications. There needs to be a balance ICT privacy and security requirements and suitable legal frameworks that do not impede the basic freedom to information.

III. Assessment of Infrastructure Development in the AEC

In 2007, ASEAN leaders adopted the AEC Blueprint that sets out specific priorities and targets towards achieving the AEC by 2015. The AEC Scorecard, developed to monitor the progress of AEC measures serves as a checklist of actions that are specified in the AEC Blueprint is under the responsibility of the ASEAN Secretariat. The progress of the scorecard is presented to the ASEAN Economic Ministers (AEM) in four biennial phases from 2008 to 2015.

As of December 2011, the overall implementation rate under Phases 1 and 2 of the AEC Scorecard were 67.5 per cent.[4] ASEAN did better in Phase 1 where it completed 86.7 per cent of measures.[5] It fared much lower in Phase 2 with 55.8 per cent implementation rate with 76 outstanding measures.

The Infrastructure Development checklist falls under the second pillar of the AEC Scorecard — "Competitive Economic Region" — as illustrated in Table 7.5. In Phase 1, all outstanding measures are under the transport sector. At the time of writing, none of ASEAN countries have ratified Protocol 2 (Designation of Frontier Posts) and Protocol 7

TABLE 7.5

Competitive Economic Region Scorecard (2008–11)

Key Areas	Phase I (2008–09)		Phase II (2010–11)		TOTAL MEASURES	
	Fully Implemented	Not Fully Implemented	Fully Implemented	Not Fully Implemented	Fully Implemented	Not Fully Implemented
Competition Policy	2	0	2	0	4	0
Consumer Protection	2	0	5	4	7	4
Intellectual Property Rights	0	0	4	1	4	1
Transport	15	10	6	8	21	18
Energy	0	0	2	1	2	1
Mineral	1	0	7	0	8	0
ICT	2	0	4	0	6	0
Taxation	0	0	0	1	0	1
E-Commerce	0	0	1	0	1	0
Total Number of Measures	22	10	31	15	53	25
Implementation Rate*	68.7%		67.4%		67.9%	

Note: * Implementation rate is calculated as the ratio of measures that are fully implemented to total number of measures targeted.
Source: ASEAN Economic Community Scorecard, Charting Progress Toward Regional Economic Integration Phase I (2008–09) and Phase II (2010–11).

(Customs Transit System) of the ASEAN Framework Agreement on the
Facilitation of Goods in Transit (AFAFGIT). In addition, there are three
ASEAN countries that have yet to ratify Protocol 1 (Designation of Transit
Transport Routes and Facilities) of AFAFGIT.

In Phase 2, transport sector continues to be the biggest laggard
in the competitive economic region scorecard as per Table 7.6. Under
the Infrastructure Development sub-heading, problem areas for full
implementation are in the enactment of necessary domestic legislations for
the ASEAN Framework Agreement on Multimodal Transport, ratification
of ASEAN Framework Agreement on Inter-State Transport, ratification of

TABLE 7.6

**Implementation of AEC Scorecard under the Transport Sector
by Country under Phases I and II**

ASEAN Countries	Transport Cooperation	
	Phase I (2008–09)	Phase II (2010–11)
Brunei Darussalam	○	○
Cambodia	○	○
Indonesia	○	●
Lao PDR	○	○
Malaysia	○	○
Myanmar	○	○
Philippines	○	○
Singapore	○	○
Thailand	○	○
Vietnam	○	○
ASEAN	○	●

◍ Indicates that all measures targeted in this area were implemented
○ Indicates that more than half of the measures targeted in this area were
   implemented
● Indicates that less than half of the measures targeted in this area were implemented

Source: ASEAN Economic Community Scorecard, Charting Progress Toward Regional
Economic Integration Phase I (2008–09) and Phase II (2010–11).

ASEAN Multilateral Agreement on the Full Liberalization of Passenger Air Services (MAFLPAS), conclude Protocol 6 under the AFAFGIT, complete activities scheduled under ASEAN Single Shipping Market and implement the ASEAN Interconnection Projects. In addition, ASEAN countries find it hard to reach a common position on implementing other infrastructure-related initiatives such as in trade facilitation and customs integration.

Overall, the shortfall in the implementation rate is due to the delay in ratification of ASEAN's existing soft infrastructures (regional agreements) and translating them into respective national laws. Most of these regional agreements are signed after years of consultation with respective capitals. It is imperative for ASEAN countries to intensify efforts and aligning regional goals into national priorities.

Having said that, ASEAN cannot risk putting all its eggs in one basket, as all outstanding measures will "snowball" to the subsequent phase of the AEC Scorecard. It is very optimistic for ASEAN to believe that it will implement all outstanding measures on top of the current year of AEC Scorecard prior 2015. Without immediate attention in addressing this shortfall, ASEAN would find itself in a position to rush implementing them in the final phase of the Scorecard. This would weaken ASEAN's relevance as a regional organization as it will be criticized for having limited drive to pull its resources in achieving its goals.

IV. Progress Towards a Well-connected Region

Complementary Policy Framework for Infrastructure Development in ASEAN

In addition to the infrastructure policy frameworks as discussed earlier, there are also other similar initiatives outside the scope of the AEC. Since the inception of ASEAN in 1967, various sub-regional initiatives have been introduced to physically link ASEAN countries. These include the Greater Mekong Sub-Region initiative (GMS), Brunei-Indonesia-Malaysia-Philippines East Asia Growth Area (BIMP-EAGA), Indonesia-Malaysia-Thailand Growth Triangle (IMT-GT), and the Indonesia-Malaysia-Singapore Growth Triangle (IMS-GT). There are also other projects under the transport sector such as the ASEAN Highway Network and the Singapore-Kunming Rail Link, as well as in the energy sector such as ASEAN Power Grid and Trans-ASEAN Gas Pipeline. These initiatives have somewhat facilitated the movement of economic resources and supported the increase in intra-ASEAN trade by 70 per cent over the period of 2004–09.

On 20 December 2011, the ministers of GMS countries endorsed the Third GMS Economic Cooperation Program Strategic Framework 2012–22 that includes strengthening transport linkages and telecommunications and ICT development. Together with assistance from the ADB, the resource-rich region is expected to grow at a faster rate after Japan pledged its support by providing financial aid of US$7.5 billion over the next three years.[6] In addition to the financial aid, Japan also presented a list of fifty-seven infrastructure projects planned in the region, estimated to cost around US$28 billion.

In April 2012, leaders of BIMP-EAGA adopted the Implementation Blueprint 2012–16 with a greater emphasis on project implementation and to follow through the progress made under the BIMP-EAGA Roadmap to Development (2006–10). The new blueprint will be aligned with the projects under the MPAC.[7]

For the IMT-GT, the ADB, as a development partner and regional advisor of the sub-region, is formulating the Implementation Blueprint 2012–16 for the sub-region. It was reported that the new blueprint will consist of forty-three projects in which half of them will be on infrastructure and transportation cooperation.[8]

Notwithstanding these planned initiatives, economic activities in these sub-regions remain slow. The issue of connectivity (availability of infrastructure) remains the biggest challenge that hinders these sub-regional initiatives as it adds to the high cost of doing business as indicated by the private sector. Participating countries requires a very large sum of funds to realize the infrastructure investments. Presently, it is difficult to justify with the returns on investment based on the level of economic activity in these underdeveloped regions. It is estimated that the BIMP-EAGA sub-region alone requires at least US$1 billion to fund its priority projects.[9]

In addition to financing problems, another difficulty is the close coordination required in implementing these connectivity projects because many of the projects involve cross-border infrastructure investments. This demands agreement in prioritizing these investment projects as there are more infrastructure development projects than financial resources available.

Master Plan on ASEAN Connectivity (MPAC)

In July 2009, Thailand proposed the idea of enhancing ASEAN connectivity as a strategic goal of ASEAN in building a more competitive ASEAN Community by 2015. It aims to bring people, goods, services and capital closer together in accordance with the ASEAN Charter. The idea behind the MPAC is to allow freer travel passage for goods, services, investment and people, with minimal impediments within the ASEAN region. The MPAC will cover physical, institutional, and people-to-people connectivity in fifteen prioritized projects.

The MPAC is a result of two overarching needs. First, it aims to consolidate the existing three pillars of ASEAN (political-security, economic, and socio-cultural) and prioritize actions toward achieving the ASEAN Community by 2015. Second, to put in place a well-coordinated infrastructure system that will produce an integrated physical, institutional, and people-to-people link within as well as outside the region. A well-functioning ASEAN connectivity will ultimately yield higher intra-regional trade and economic growth.

According to ADB and ADBI's study, ASEAN needs about US$60 billion a year for infrastructure investment for the 2010–20 period.[10] With a well-developed physical infrastructure, ASEAN is envisaged to increase its intra-regional trade to 40 per cent, at the very least (currently at 24.5 per cent).

Under the MPAC, there are fifteen priority projects to enhance ASEAN connectivity:

A. Physical connectivity projects:

1. Completion of the ASEAN Highway Network (AHN) Missing Links and Upgrade of Transit Transport Routes;
2. Completion of the Singapore Kunming Rail Link (SKRL) Missing Links;
3. Establish an ASEAN Broadband Corridor (ABC);
4. Melaka-Pekan Baru Interconnection (IMT-GT: Indonesia);
5. West Kalimantan-Sarawak Interconnection (BIMP-EAGA: Indonesia); and
6. Study on the Roll-on/Roll-off (RoRo) Network and Short-Sea Shipping.

B. Institutional connectivity projects:

1. Developing and Operationalizing Mutual Recognition Arrangements (MRAs) for Prioritized and Selected Industries;
2. Establishing Common Rules for Standards and Conformity Assessment Procedures;
3. Operationalize all National Single Windows (NSWs) by 2012;
4. Options for a Framework Modality towards the Phased Reduction and Elimination of Scheduled Investment Restrictions/Impediments; and
5. Operationalization of the ASEAN Agreements on Transport Facilitation.

C. People-to-people connectivity projects:

1. Easing Visa Requirements for ASEAN Nationals;
2. Development of ASEAN Virtual Learning Resource Centres (AVLRC);
3. Develop ICT Skill Standards; and
4. ASEAN Community Building Programme.

In order to successfully implement these priority projects, a technical assistance must be available to facilitate project identification, preparation, monitoring, and evaluation. ASEAN also needs to determine an indicative funding size and sources for technical assistance from ASEAN-led institutions, Dialogue Partners and other multilateral bodies such as the World Bank and the ADB. This will also involve the development of a clear funding mechanism for these infrastructure needs. Moreover, ASEAN has to address other externalities that arise from a region with a well-connected infrastructure, namely national priorities and social impact.

Infrastructure Financing

There is clearly a need for a large amount and continuous flow of capital to finance ASEAN infrastructure projects. In the past, national governments provided most of the capital outlay for infrastructure development. But today, a hybrid model of public-private partnership for infrastructure financing is becoming more practical as constraints and priorities of national governments change over time.

In May 2012, the long-awaited ASEAN Infrastructure Fund (AIF) commenced operations following the first meeting of its Board of Directors on the side line of the ADB 45th Annual Meeting. The AIF is the largest ASEAN-led initiative in the association's history with a planned start-up capital of US$485.2 million. The idea was first mooted in May 2005 by then Malaysian Prime Minister Tun Abdullah Ahmad Badawi in the hope that each ASEAN country would utilize more than US$700 billion of their foreign exchange reserves to promote infrastructure development and support the realization of the AEC by 2015.[11]

The AIF, domiciled in Malaysia, is a limited liability company owned by ASEAN governments and the ADB. It will subsequently issue bonds for additional funding. AIF's basic equity structure comprises of Member States' contribution, a hybrid capital of US$162 million and debt. All AIF shareholders have agreed that the disbursement will not commence unless and until at least 80 per cent of the first tranche equity contributions, i.e. US$129.4 million, have been contributed.

Malaysia, followed by Indonesia, is the largest contributor to the AIF from ASEAN. The ADB plans to contribute US$150 million to the AIF but it seems that it will be contributing even more to the fund than the stipulated amount because each project under the AIF will also be co-financed by the Bank (see Table 7.7).

Although the proposal of AIF was mooted some time ago, its implementation took quite a while to be realized. Reaching a consensus

TABLE 7.7

Structure of ASEAN Infrastructure Fund

Assets (US$ millions)	Equity (US$ millions)
Various assets 647.2	ASEAN contribution 335.2
	ADB's contribution 150
	Hybrid capital 162
647.2	**647.2**

Source: ADB.

on the establishment of AIF took more than six years and without a clear institutional set-up, ASEAN member countries may not be able to utilize the fund fully.

However, ASEAN cannot just depend on AIF to fund its infrastructure financing as its fund size of US$485.2 million is too small and will not be sufficient to finance major infrastructure projects. Thus, there is a need for a larger funding through the participation of Plus Six partners, which may give a sizable financing to effectively implement these planned infrastructure projects.[12]

Apart from the conventional multilateral development banks such as the ADB and World Bank, the role of ASEAN dialogue partners is also important in providing sufficient financing infrastructure projects. The idea to establish an East Asian Infrastructure Development Fund and the newly set-up US$10 billion China-ASEAN Fund on Investment Cooperation will provide a much needed boost for a bigger financing mechanism than the AIF. In addition, China is also considering setting up a US$4.7 billion "ASEAN Bank" with the aim to promote SMEs development, as well as financing infrastructure projects within ASEAN and south-western China.[13] Member states of ASEAN, Japan and South Korea are invited to take a stake in the ASEAN Bank.

V. Issues, Challenges and Policy Recommendations

(a) The Need for an Effective Regional Institutional Mechanism to Implement Infrastructure Cooperation and Projects

Over the years, ASEAN has introduced various infrastructure development frameworks and projects to make the region a truly integrated single market and production base. This vision is supported by ASEAN Dialogue Partners and multilateral development institutions. But the latest AEC scorecard shows that there is still a lot more improvements that can be made in infrastructure development in ASEAN. The fundamental ASEAN concept of non-interference and national sovereignty remains the key reason why infrastructure development remains low and progress is slow.

It is noted that despite various initiatives made by ASEAN, the level of cooperation among member countries remain low, most notably amongst GMS countries. The GMS project, although initiated by the ADB in 1992, was started much earlier in 1957 under the auspices of

United Nations Economic and Social Commission for Asia and the Pacific (ESCAP). The Xayaburi Dam Project, for example, although is not part of any of regional initiatives, highlights the differences amongst GMS countries in finding an agreement for a collective and shared benefit.[14] Another example, the operationalization of the AFAFGIT under the AEC Scorecard 2008–09, which was initially signed in 1998, remains as a stumbling block in increasing intra-trade within ASEAN. If ASEAN delays the implementation of key measures in the AEC Scorecard, they will be added to the next phase of the scorecard with a shorter implementation period.

Thus, ASEAN needs a stronger institutional implementation mechanism to ensure that the AEC datelines are met. This implementation mechanism should supersede national government in matters of implementation of infrastructure policies and projects already agreed by the Leaders at the regional level. As long as the regional implementation body is unable to converge or mediate national concerns and interest, there may be a possibility of delaying the implementation rate of AEC Scorecard even further. To establish such a mechanism, ASEAN needs to decide on the issue of giving up some degree of non-interference and national sovereignty to regional body.

(b) Limitations to the Regional Infrastructure Planning and Monitoring

Although ASEAN has vast experience in infrastructure planning at the national level, it has limited capability in such planning at the regional level. Most of the planning of cross-border infrastructure projects in ASEAN is done by multilateral development institutions. Infrastructure planning is complex because the projects are large and they require long-term payback periods, project operators are exposed to revenue risks, due to pricing and currency fluctuations and related socio-economic externalities such as environmental and societal impact.

In this context, national planning and regulatory coherence amongst ASEAN member states is important to ensure convergence and streamlining of national projects with regional infrastructure plans. This is important to:

- Avoid duplication, conflicting or burdensome enforcement systems to facilitate smoother movement of goods, services, capital and people;

- Promote economic growth in a transparent, effective, enforceable and mutually coherent regulatory system based on international best practices; and
- Greater transparency and consultation process in national and regional infrastructure plans.

Regional infrastructure projects usually involve additional project management that complicates the implementation process. In some cases, the lengthy process of vetting, appraisals, tendering practices can significantly delay implementation with some being aborted due to a variety of reasons, including unrealistic cost assumptions, poor technical design, and inability to realize adequate financial returns.

Thus, it is crucial for ASEAN to establish a planning mechanism that can coordinate and streamline national and regional infrastructure planning and needs. Likewise, ASEAN has very little capacity at the regional level to monitor effectively the implementation of the infrastructure projects. In this case, it may have to seek assistance from multilateral development institutions such as the ADB to assist in this work.

(c) Financing Requirements

As the financing needs are large, ASEAN may face stiff competition in securing the sufficient funds for implementing its infrastructure projects. One source is the Plus Three partners, namely China, Korea, and Japan. However, these funds will likely be invested in the GMS region because of the rising trade and investment links with China and Japan. Another source of funds is the recycling of the significant reserves held by East Asian countries including some ASEAN members. This idea has been raised since the Asian financial crisis in 1997/98 but little progress has been made.

Another source of funding is of course the private sector. However, the cost may be higher because the funds are raised commercially and the risks are set at a higher level. Often, to mitigate the risks associated with infrastructure projects, private investors would seek support or guarantees from governments. In addition, the higher costs are also due to the reasonably high returns demanded by these private sector investors.

Despite being backed by ASEAN governments, the AIF has similar limitations as other sources of financing. There are risks associated to the AIF's capital structure and operations that may affect its ability to raise fund. Firstly, the AIF has to attain a high investment-grade rating in order to ensure that the lending rate, lending volume and return on equity can keep borrowing cost low. Secondly, as the AIF will finance risky and complex non-sovereign projects, the issue of disbursement and prioritizing infrastructure projects will further complicate the allocation of the fund. Thirdly, currency mismatch may increase the project cost and ability of a country to pay back the loans. The long gestation of infrastructure project will expose borrowing countries to currency fluctuations that some time can go beyond the estimated range of currency movement. This is further aggravated when borrowing countries may face difficulties when project revenues are in local currencies while the loans are in foreign currencies.

Besides challenges in raising and costs of funds, AIF is also exposed to additional risks that may delay the implementation of projects. Prioritizing cross-border infrastructure projects requires coordination between two or more sovereign countries, particularly when there is a mismatch between countries and regional interests for infrastructure projects. For example, preliminary projects for 2012 and 2013 are still subject to further approval by recipient countries even after being agreed by the AIF Board.

The issue of duration of mismatch and size of investment plays an important role in the complexities of cross-border infrastructure financing. Infrastructure investments can take a long time to yield financial returns. Furthermore, forecasting accurately potential traffic outcome of usage of infrastructure developed that could give the financial returns especially in less developed or populated areas is always difficult. This will make the estimation of future costs and revenue streams hard to ascertain and potential investors may demand financial support, which often pose a heavy burden on the government.

Since financing is a key factor in the successful implementation of ASEAN infrastructure projects, its leaders should take a bold approach in getting member states with strong financial capacity to invest in AIF. For this to work, ASEAN leaders should then come to an agreement in terms of balancing countries' financial contribution with having a role in the prioritizing and effective implementation of projects.

(d) National Priority Versus Regional Benefit

A major challenge in regional infrastructure development is coordinating the various national needs with the regional vision and plans. Often, member countries' priorities do not coincide with the regional plans. Overlapping projects will result in non-optimal use of resources and in some cases can even produce negative outcomes. Although member states are committed to join regional initiatives, national needs often take precedence because governments have to fulfil the aspirations and demands of its own constituencies. The task for governments is how to rationalize national infrastructure needs so that it corresponds and fits in with the regional vision. In other words, if regional benefits are a total sum of national priorities, then there will be a greater commitment by ASEAN members to achieve regional infrastructure vision.

Each member state has its own infrastructure plans and programmes. The challenge is how to coordinate these national plans into a regional framework with minimum investments. A good example is the road projects: a good standard ASEAN road network can be built by linking the various national road systems. Additional investments may be needed to link the missing parts of the national road systems, which can be undertaken by a regional body.

Another important element for developing a regional infrastructure network is the harmonization of the various national infrastructure standards into a regional one. Without harmonized regional standards, a free flow of movement of vehicles, people, goods and services cannot take place. As such an urgent initiative is to accelerate the work on harmonizing infrastructure standards among the ASEAN member states.

VI. Conclusion

A more globalized world will present greater challenges for ASEAN in sustaining economic prosperity and well-being. The achievement of AEC vision of being a truly integrated market and a production base is very important for ASEAN to enhance its economic prosperity and competitiveness. Infrastructure development and cooperation are essential to attaining the AEC vision for without it there will not be the seamless flow of goods, services, investment, and people.

ASEAN's effort in this area started with cooperation in transport, energy, and ICT. Under the AEC, these initiatives have been expanded to include cross-border infrastructure projects and the creation of region-wide infrastructure networks. The progress of infrastructure measures under the AEC made so far could be further improved.

It is imperative that ASEAN overcome the challenges and accelerate the implementation of the committed cooperative work plans and infrastructure projects. Among the key issues for consideration is the establishment of regional institutional mechanism for project implementations, enhancing regional planning and monitoring capacity, meeting financing needs, streamlining national infrastructure priorities with regional visions and accelerating the work to harmonize infrastructure standards. ASEAN also needs a more effective mechanism in further strengthening information sharing and close the legal, regulatory and capacity gaps.

Without doubt, closer regional cooperation and integration will benefit everybody in the region. For this, the infrastructure development and cooperation requires the involvement of all parties — the ASEAN governments, Dialogue Partners, public sector, private sector and multilateral development institutions.

NOTES

1. Biswa Nath Bhattacharyay, Infrastructure Development for ASEAN Economic Integration, ADBI Working Paper Series No. 138, May 2009.
2. ASEAN Plan of Action for Energy Cooperation (APAEC) 2010–15 — "Bringing Policies to Actions: Towards a Cleaner, more Efficient and Sustainable ASEAN Energy Community".
3. e-ASEAN Framework Agreement, Article 3, The Fourth ASEAN Informal Summit, Singapore, 22–25 November 2000.
4. Source: *ASEAN Economic Community Scorecard — Charting Progress Toward Regional Economic Integration Phase I (2008–09) and Phase II (2010–11).*
5. Ibid.
6. "Japan Pledges US$7.4b for Mekong Development", 21 April 2012, <http://www.channelnewsasia.com/stories/afp_asiapacific/view/1196663/1/.html>.
7. "BIMP-EAGA Underscores Strong Connectivity within the Region", *Borneo Post*, 4 December 2011, <http://www.theborneopost.com/2011/12/04/bimp-eaga-underscores-strong-connectivity-within-the-region/>.
8. "Indonesia, Malaysia, Thailand Sepakat Tak Ada Proyek Baru", Okezone.com, 13 April 2012, <http://economy.okezone.com/read/2012/04/13/320/610865/indonesia-malaysia-thailand-sepakat-tak-ada-proyek-baru>.
9. "EAGA Airlines Complement Efforts for Sub-regional Connectivity", Philippine Information Agency, 25 April 2012, <http://www.pia.gov.ph/news/index.php?article=1701335315743>.

10. "Infrastructure for a Seamless Asia", Asian Development Bank and Asian Development Bank Institute, 2009.
11. Dato' Dr Mahani Zainal Abidin, "Fiscal Policy Coordination in Asia: East Asian Infrastructure Investment Fund", ADBI Working Paper Series No. 232, July 2010.
12. H.E. Abhisit Vejjajiva, "One ASEAN: What Must We Do? And How Close Are We?", *Bangkok Post*, 13 October 2011.
13. Reuters, "EXCLUSIVE — China Eyes Creation of ASEAN Bank", 27 October 2011.
14. "Opening the floodgates, A giant dam is about to be built. Protests are about to erupt", *The Economist*, 5 May 2012, <http://www.economist.com/node/21554253>.

REFERENCES

Abidin, Mahani Zainal, Dato' Dr. "Fiscal Policy Coordination in Asia: East Asian Infrastructure Investment Fund". ADBI Working Paper Series No. 232 (July 2010).
Bhattacharyay, Biswa Nath. "Infrastructure Development for ASEAN Economic Integration". ADBI Working Paper Series No. 138 (May 2009).
"BIMP-EAGA Underscores Strong Connectivity within the Region". *Borneo Post*, 4 December 2011. <http://www.theborneopost.com/2011/12/04/bimp-eaga-underscores-strong-connectivity-within-the-region/>.
"EAGA Airlines Complement Efforts for Sub-regional Connectivity". Philippine Information Agency, 25 April 2012. <http://www.pia.gov.ph/news/index.php?article=1701335315743>.
"EXCLUSIVE — China Eyes Creation of ASEAN Bank". Reuters, 27 October 2011.
"Indonesia, Malaysia, Thailand Sepakat Tak Ada Proyek Baru". Okezone.com, 13 April 2012. <http://economy.okezone.com/read/2012/04/13/320/610865/indonesia-malaysia-thailand-sepakat-tak-ada-proyek-baru>.
"Infrastructure for a Seamless Asia". Asian Development Bank and Asian Development Bank Institute, 2009.
"Japan Pledges US$7.4b for Mekong Development", 21 April 2012. <http://www.channelnewsasia.com/stories/afp_asiapacific/view/1196663/1/.html>.
"Opening the floodgates, A giant dam is about to be built. Protests are about to erupt". *The Economist*, 5 May 2012. <http://www.economist.com/node/21554253>.
Vejjajiva, Abhisit, H.E. "One ASEAN: What Must We Do? And How Close Are We?". *Bangkok Post*, 13 October 2011.

8

SME DEVELOPMENT IN ASEAN: A Cambodian Case Study

Chap Sotharith

I. Introduction

Small and medium enterprises (SMEs) are an important part of ASEAN economic integration. Hence, their development is prioritized in the Pillar 3 "Equitable Economic Integration" of the ASEAN Economic Community (AEC) Blueprint. As ASEAN is committed to accelerate the establishment of the AEC by 2015, the 18th ASEAN Summit, under the chairmanship of Indonesia, has reaffirmed the important role of SME development as a critical element towards narrowing the development gaps amongst and within the ASEAN member states.

SMEs are integral to the economic development and growth of the ASEAN member states, as they largely outnumber large enterprises in both quantity of establishments and share of the labour force that they employ. Within ASEAN, SMEs account for more than 96 per cent of all enterprises and 50 to 85 per cent of domestic employment. The contribution of SMEs to total GDP is between 30 and 53 per cent and the contribution of SMEs to exports is between 19 and 31 per cent. They are important in terms of income and employment generation, gender and youth empowerment through business participation, and their widespread presence in non-urban and poorer domestic regions. SMEs are the backbone of ASEAN and SME development is integral in achieving sustainable economic growth.[1]

The Strategic Action Plan for ASEAN SME Development 2010–15 envisions that "by 2015, ASEAN SMEs shall be world-class enterprises, capable of integration into the regional and global supply chains, able to take advantage of the benefits of ASEAN economic community building, and operating in a policy environment that is conducive to SME development, exports and innovation".

Concrete and detailed policy measures, implementation time-frame, and indicative outputs have been identified in ASEAN Policy Blueprint on SMEs Development (APBSD). Even though the APBSD is no longer the working framework for ASEAN, its reference to AEC and the review of its implementation up to 2009 would provide some useful insights and lessons for regional efforts in SME policy development and coordination in ASEAN. The review would not entirely refer to what is in the AEC, since there are only a few priority actions with respect to SME development in the AEC. What is required now is that ASEAN member states must have common curricula for entrepreneurial training, service centres at national and subregional level, and financial facilities. What is to be done from now till 2015 is to have in place an internship scheme and exchange for skilled training, and the establishment of an ASEAN SME development fund.

According to a study by Tambunan (2008), it shows that both real gross domestic product per capita and government development expenditure (especially that used to finance SME development promotion programmes) have positive impacts on SME growth. With this finding, the research argues that SMEs in least developed countries (LDCs) can survive, and even grow in the long-run, for three main reasons: (a) they create a niche market for themselves, (b) they act as a "last resort" for the poor, and (c) they will grow along with Large Enterprises (LEs) because of their increasingly important production linkages with LEs in the form of subcontracting.[2]

With the strong forces of globalization, it is therefore essential to build the capacities of SMEs in the region in order to ensure that they are highly competitive, innovative, and are able to utilize the regional economic initiatives and incentives provided by the government. This chapter examines the status of SMEs development in ASEAN and highlights a case study from Cambodia.

II. ASEAN Strategic Action Plan for SME Development (2010–15)

ASEAN established its SME Working Group in 1995. The Working Group is the main driver to formulate policy and strategy for SME development in ASEAN. The Strategic Action Plan for ASEAN SME Development 2010–15 outlines the framework for SME development in the ASEAN Region. The Plan covers mandates stipulated in the AEC Blueprint, and the current and future work of the ASEAN SME Working Group (ASEAN SMEWG), which is composed of the SME Agencies of all ASEAN member states. In partnership with donor agencies and the private sector, the ASEAN SMEWG seeks to ensure the advancement of SMEs in the region.

The ASEAN SMEWG has established joint consultations with the SME Agencies of the ASEAN Plus Three (China, Japan and the Republic of Korea), which enables valuable exchanges of best practices and fruitful cooperation on several SME projects and workshops.

There are five major deliverables targeted for SMEs under the AEC Blueprint, namely the establishments of: (a) a common curriculum for entrepreneurship in ASEAN (2008–09), (b) a comprehensive SME service centre with regional and subregional linkages in member states (2010–11), (c) an SME financial facility in each member state (2010–11), (d) a regional programme of internship scheme for staff exchanges and visits for skills training (2012–13), and (e) a regional SME development fund for use as a funding source for SMEs that are doing business in ASEAN (2014–15).

III. ASEAN Policy Blueprint for SME Development (APBSD) 2004–14

After two years of preparation by ASEAN SME Working Group, the APBSD 2004–14 was submitted to, and endorsed by, the Senior Economic Officials Meeting (SEOM) meeting on 12–14 February 2004 in Siem

Reap, Cambodia. It was then submitted to, and approved by, ASEAN Economic Ministers at the Thirty-Sixth Meeting on 3 September 2004 in Jakarta, Indonesia.

The APBSD outlines the framework for SME development in the ASEAN region. It comprises strategic work programmes, policy measures, and indicative outputs.

The APBSD has its mission:

- To develop and sustain a culture of entrepreneurship and innovation within the SME sector in the region;
- To assist and ensure that ASEAN SMEs become and remain learning, dynamic and outward-looking enterprises;
- To encourage collaboration and networking among SMEs within ASEAN as well as with business enterprises outside the region;
- To accelerate the pace of SME development, optimizing on the diversities of member states;
- To enhance the competitiveness and dynamism of ASEAN SMEs by facilitating their access to information, market, human resource development and skills, and finance as well as technology;
- To strengthen the resilience of ASEAN SMEs to better withstand adverse macroeconomic and financial difficulties, as well as the challenges of a more liberalized trading environment; and
- To increase the contribution of ASEAN SMEs to the overall economic growth and development of ASEAN as a region.

The APBSD has its **Focus Programmes and Activities** as follows:

Human Resources Development and Capacity Building

1. Entrepreneurship Development Programme
- Regional training programme in SME entrepreneurship development during the period of APBSD;
- Regional pilot project in entrepreneurship development in ASEAN. The timeframe is 15 months; and
- Subregional pilot project in entrepreneurship development for ASEAN-6 (or ASEAN-4). The timeframe is 9–12 months.

2. Enhancing SME-sector Skills in Management and Organization on a Self-reliant Basis

- Regional programme in developing system packages on 31 areas of enterprise management and organizational skill requirements during the period of APBSD;
- Regional pilot project in system development in: (i) quality control and certification, and (ii) quality, cost, and delivery improvements. The timeframe is 24 months;
- Regional project in the simplification and standardization of basic terminologies for SME training courses, business plans, and business project preparations, system developments, etc. The timeframe is 3–6 months; and
- Regional programme for the promotion of internship schemes, workers' and entrepreneurs exchanges, and study visits for skill training and enhancement, and inter-firm linkages during the period of APBSD.

3. Fostering SME Capabilities for Inter-firm Networking and Linkages

- Regional tracking of SME readiness and compliance as subcontractors in domestic, regional, and global production networks and supply chains during the period of APBSD;
- Regional pilot project in compiling compliance requirements for SME subcontracting. The timeframe is 12–15 months; and
- Regional research study on the key drivers and processes of enterprise clustering, and on related policy issues, implications, and options. The timeframe is 6 months.

4. Tracking and Benchmarking SME Capabilities, Dynamism and Competitiveness

- Regional programme in surveying, monitoring, and benchmarking the evolution of SME capacities, dynamism, and competitiveness in various priority sectors and industries within ASEAN during the period of APBSD; and
- Regional pilot project in surveying and benchmarking SME capabilities, dynamism, and competitiveness in selected priority industries and sectors within ASEAN. The timeframe is 18 months.

Enhancing SME Marketing Capabilities

5. Setting up Regional and Subregional Networks of Interlinked, Online Clearing Points or Trading Houses for SME Businesses

- Regional programme in establishing interlinked, online networks for SME products and services during the period of APBSD.

6. Enhancing SME Capabilities in and Reliance on ICT and E-commerce

- Regional programme to promote SME e-commerce during the period of APBSD;
- Regional and subregional programmes to build basic skills and capabilities for internet-based e-commerce during the period of APBSD; and
- Research on an enabling regional or subregional framework of policies and regulations for ICT and e-commerce. The timeframe is 6–9 months.

7. Tracking and Benchmarking SME Readiness as Subcontractors and Compliance to Non-negotiable Subcontracting Preconditions or Compliance Requirements on the Demand-side

- Regional tracking of SME readiness and compliance as subcontractors in domestic, regional, and global production networks and supply chains during the period of APBSD; and
- Regional pilot project in compiling compliance requirements for SME subcontracting. The timeframe is 18 months.

Access to Financing

8. Capacity Building for Improved SME Access to Financing

- Regional and subregional capacity building in the proper maintenance and reporting of accounting and financial information by SMEs during the period of APBSD; and
- Regional and subregional capacity building in the preparation of business plans to the bankable stage by SMEs during the period of APBSD.

9. Financial Institutional Capacity Building for Improved SME Financing

- Regional and subregional capacity building in credit rating system for SMEs within the financial sector. The timeframe is in the medium term (3 to 5 years); and
- Regional and subregional capacity building in the establishment and maintenance of credit information reference and referral systems with a focus on the special needs of SMEs. The timeframe is in the medium term (3–5 years).

10. Widening and Deepening SME Access to Credit

- Regionalization and subregionalization of financial schemes and alternative financial sources (credit guarantee scheme, seed and venture capital, inventory financing, equipment leasing, etc.), and external investor base during the period of APBSD.

Access to Technology

11. SME Technology Upgrading and Transfers of Innovative Technologies

- Collection and dissemination of best practices at the enterprise and policy levels in technology upgrading and transfers, and intellectual property matters involving SMEs within and outside the region during the period of APBSD;
- Regional pilot project in system development for technological upgrading to enhance quality control and certification. The timeframe is 12 months; and
- Regional pilot project in system development for technological upgrading to enhance quality, cost, and delivery. The timeframe is 12 months.

Creating Conducive Policy Environment

12. Simplification, Streamlining, and Rationalization of the Procedures for SME Registration, and the Process for SME Support Services

- Collection and dissemination of best practices in SME registration and support services within and outside the region during the period of APBSD;

- Regional or subregional research study on ways and means to simplify procedures, and reduce costs and delays in the formal registration of SMEs. The timeframe is 6–9 months; and
- Establishment of a one-stop SME office in the respective countries emphasizing on seven functional areas: facilitation, monitoring and evaluation, outreach, advocacy, research, information systems, and liaisons. The timeframe is in the medium term (3–5 years).

13. Fine-tune Policy and Regulatory Framework for SME Development

- Collection and dissemination of best practices in policy and regulatory framework for SME development within ASEAN and outside the region during the period of APBSD; and
- Regional or subregional research study to review and fine-tune existing policies and regulatory framework for ASEAN SMEs. The timeframe is 9–12 months.

14. Promotion of Public-private Synergies and Partnership for SME Development and Integration

- Collection and dissemination of best practices in the promotion of: (i) public-private synergies and partnership, and (ii) closer interaction and more frequent dialogues between the public and private sectors for SME development and integration within and outside the region during the period of APBSD; and
- Regional or subregional research study in the promotion of public-private synergies in providing business development services and extension activities. The timeframe is 9–12 months.

IV. SMEs in the ASEAN Economic Community

To further enhance the competitiveness and resilience of SMEs toward a single market and production base, ASEAN implemented the Strategic Action Plan for the ASEAN SME Development (2010–15). Endorsed in August 2010, the Plan gives guidance on the current flagship projects and other SMEs initiatives in the region. The ASEAN SME Advisory Board was established to provide strategic policy inputs on SME development to the Ministers and guidance on high priority matters to the ASEAN SME Working Group (SMEWG). Recognizing the importance of financing facilities for SMEs, ASEAN started to work on the development of the Conceptual Framework for Regional SME Development Fund.

Two projects under the Strategic Action Plan have recently been completed, namely the ASEAN Multi-media Self-reliant System Toolkit Package, and the Feasibility Study of the SME Service Centre. The Multi-media Toolkit project seeks to develop a quality culture in SMEs and create awareness on the necessity of providing high quality products or services to customers. The Toolkit follows the quality system (control, quality, and cost) based on the ISO 9000: 2008. The Feasibility Study of the ASEAN SME Service Centre examines best practices in integrating SME Service Centres, disseminating services to SMEs, and providing services to SMEs at the local, national, and regional levels.

The Study has proposed two sustainable frameworks to integrate the ASEAN SME Service Centres. In line with the promotion initiatives under the Strategic Action Plan, the "Directory of Outstanding ASEAN SMEs 2011" which lists more than 800 top SMEs from all ASEAN member states, was launched on the sidelines of the ASEAN Business and Investment Summit (ASEAN BIS). The Directory seeks to promote linkages of SMEs to the regional and global supply chains and production networks. The Directory has also been uploaded onto the ASEAN website, and can be accessed via the following links: <http://www.asean.org/20440. htm> and <http://www.asean.org/23238.htm>. The ASEAN SMEWG is working toward the establishment of the "Directory of ASEAN Innovative SMEs" by 2012, to encourage innovation and creativity among ASEAN SMEs.[3]

Whilst the application of the focused programmes under the APBSD is currently up to each ASEAN member state, depending on their domestic needs and level of economic development, five outputs, which are aimed at addressing SMEs' lack of access to markets, technology and finance, are expected to be achieved by 2015 under the AEC.

The first is to establish a common curriculum for entrepreneurship in ASEAN. This will primarily ensure that ASEAN's curriculum for entrepreneurship is in line with international standards and, thus, provide ASEAN SMEs with the latest information on standards and market trends.

The second and third will, in particular, address the needs of the newer ASEAN member states, as well as less developed regions of ASEAN, which are unable to ably assist aspiring entrepreneurs. They are to establish a comprehensive SME service centre with regional and subregional linkages in ASEAN member states and establish an SME financial facility in each member state. For the realization of these outputs, the more developed member states, ASEAN Dialogue Partners, as well as donors could help by sharing their experiences and resources.

The fourth is to establish a regional programme for the promotion of an internship scheme for staff exchanges and visits for skills training. Through these exchanges, ASEAN nationals will not only learn from the experiences (including new ways of doing things and technology) of their counterparts, but also greatly contribute to community building as they are able to obtain an understanding of each other's cultures.

The last but not least is to establish a regional SME development fund that would be used as a financial resource for SMEs that are undertaking business in the ASEAN region. This aims to stimulate entrepreneurship at the regional level. Under this output, ASEAN would like to learn from the experience of the European Union, which has successfully set up regional development funds aimed at start-ups and fledgling companies.

V. Challenges

The SME sector in ASEAN is confronted with a wide-range of fiscal and non-fiscal issues and challenges, particularly limited access to finance, technology, and markets.

Access to finance is one of the daunting challenges in SMEs development in ASEAN. Findings from the Economic Research Institute for ASEAN and East Asia's (ERIA) SME research project in 2009 confirmed that access to finance is amongst the most critical factors determining the competitive readiness of regional SMEs and their ability to fully exploit and participate in the global economy and business opportunities from regional economic integration and, in particular, participation in regional production networks (Vo, Narjoko, and Oum 2009).

With greater competition, rapid technological advances, more demanding market requirements, and constant changes in consumer demands require SMEs to be innovative and creative in order to face the challenges of the global market.

There is also insufficient entrepreneurial spirit and management skill among ASEAN SMEs. These problems are compounded with the lack of information, compliance to standards and certification, and a conducive business environment. In addition, a new trend of conducting business utilizing information and communication technology (ICT), as well as outsourcing and networking strategies adopted by large enterprises and multinational companies (MNCs) require SMEs to undertake proactive measures to ensure their business sustainability.

SMEs in ASEAN also have a weak competitive position compared to other countries such as China, Japan, and Korea. Despite the fast-approaching regional single market under the AEC, SMEs in ASEAN are not well prepared for economic integration which will be realized in 2015. As an example, according to a survey, more than half of Thai small and medium-sized enterprises have still not prepared themselves for the challenges of trade liberalization.[4] This puts many of them at risk of being forced out of business in the not-too-distant future, according to the University of the Thai Chamber of Commerce (UTCC). A report by the UTCC's Centre for International Trade Studies, released on 14 February, showed that 57.2 per cent of SMEs across eleven sectors in Thailand did not understand the benefits of regional integration.

Consumer preferences and market standards have become more sophisticated and exacting. Competitive advantage is now determined by several non-price parameters such as quality, health and safety, social equity in employment and production, and ecological compatibility of products and processes.[5] Furthermore, market demand is constantly changing, a trend facilitated not least by the rapid advances in ICT, bioengineering, and new materials sciences. In consequence, there are more frequent introductions of new products and processes, faster and more innovative design changes, shorter product cycles and smaller output batches, higher quality and greater mass customization, more just-in-time sourcing, and greater punctuality in delivery.

VI. A Case Study: Cambodia's SME Development

(a) Background

The number of enterprises in Cambodia has been increasing gradually, tracking the expansion of the economy, especially during the period of high positive growth from 1999 to 2008. In 1999, the number of SMEs was estimated at about 25,000, and reached 36,000 in 2009. The growth in the number of establishments was, therefore, about 44 per cent in ten years. During this period, employment in the industrial sector was observed to expand, and labour productivity in the sector increased significantly.[6]

Cambodia's production base remains weak. The manufacturing sector is dominated by food processing, garments, and furniture. According to the establishment listing, wholesale and retail trade account for more than 50 per cent of all establishments, while only slightly more than 20 per cent are in the manufacturing sector. Hotels and restaurants comprise around 8 per cent of total establishments. However, in terms of employment, manufacturing provides around 35 per cent of total employment, while wholesale and retail trade activities account for 30 per cent. Hotels and restaurants and educational institutions each generate 8 per cent of employment. More than half of Cambodia's micro enterprises are involved in wholesale and retail trade, and only 20 per cent are engaged in manufacturing. More than half the large enterprises are in manufacturing.[7]

An analysis of the SME sector shows that the major obstacles for its development relate, first, to an inadequate legal and regulatory framework. Thus, many of the necessary institutions, laws, and regulations needed for an efficient private sector are missing or are currently being developed. Furthermore, some of the existing institutions and regulations need reforming to improve the enabling environment for business. Second, there is limited access to finance. The primary causes of poor access to finance are the lack of suitable collateral, uncertain land titles, the lack of a comprehensive legal framework, poor contract enforcement, and the lack of diversity in financial institutions. Third, there is a lack of support services in the form of private sector business development services and the provision of public goods and services.

Given these constraints, the framework sets out a vision for the Inter-Ministerial SME Sub-Committee that promotes an environment conducive to business. This will lead to a competitive SME sector, contribute to the creation of quality employment, and improve the range of goods and services available for drawing on the experience of other countries, particularly those in the region facing similar problems.

(b) Small and Medium Enterprises Development Framework

The Royal Government of the Kingdom of Cambodia has embarked on an ambitious programme of development and reform to meet the needs of country development. A primary goal is to reduce poverty. In the fight against poverty, the government recognizes that SMEs play a significant role in promoting economic development and creating sustainable employment and income.

In order to give force to the vision, and the strategy, the Inter-Ministerial SME Sub-Committee was established, with private sector representation. The committee has a secretariat located in the Ministry of Industry, Mines and Energy to support its function and coordinate its activities. Implementation of the road map will also require the government to coordinate with donors, as well as support the development of and coordination with business associations.

In order to implement the government's Rectangular Strategy and to achieve an environment conducive to business, the SME Development Framework focuses on three key areas: (i) the regulatory and legal framework, (ii) access to finance, and (iii) SME support activities. Several issues are identified and discussed within each of these three key areas. The discussion includes background information and the constraints and objectives faced by SMEs. For each sub-topic, the discussion then shifts to actions to be taken in two phases (Phase I in 2005–07 and Phase II in 2008–10).

In regard to the regulatory and legal framework, a significant issue is the need for streamlining and reducing the cost of company registration. Currently, this represents one of the highest costs and time expenditures in the region. A second priority is establishing a regulatory review process and a recourse mechanism. This would focus on the numerous and overlapping licenses issued by most ministries, a situation that imposes a severe burden on SMEs. Third, the need for establishing a commercial legal framework is highlighted as an important part of the strategy. As of mid-2005, the commercial legal framework remained incomplete.

The second key area in the strategy is improving access to finance. Access to finance is a critical issue for all businesses and remains a problem particularly for SMEs. Among the issues that the strategy addresses are: (i) collateral and land titling, (ii) leasing, (iii) credit information sharing, (iv) simplified accounting for SMEs, and (v) non-bank financial institutions. Addressing these issues is seen as critical for improving SME access to credit.

Finally, the third key area is to improve support activities for SMEs. In the delivery of support services, there is a role for the government to play in addition to that played by the private sector. Where public goods and services are involved or there is market failure, the government should take the initiative, either by itself or in partnership with the private sector. Where private sector Business Development Services (BDS) markets do not exist, there is a role for the Inter-Ministerial

SME Sub-Committee to work with donors and business associations to stimulate demand and develop private sector supply. In particular, support activities should focus on improving access to markets, upgrading technology and human resources, and developing linkages necessary for SME growth.

The SME Development Framework will require significant effort by the committee and its secretariat. It will also require the cooperation and coordination of donors, business associations, and other stakeholders. Moreover, the framework should be periodically reviewed and revised to reflect changing conditions and priorities for Cambodian SMEs.

Therefore, the SME Development Framework has been designed to improve and coordinate the government's efforts in promoting SME activity in a market economy. In doing so, it incorporates and elaborates the government's key SME policies, including those set out in July 2004 in the so-called "Rectangular Strategy".[8]

The SME Development Framework is intended to serve the government as a road map for the development of the SME sector. In doing so, it should be seen as a "living document" which will be amended as conditions faced by SMEs and the government's capacity to deliver services change. The framework also provides a focal point around which government and donor discussions and activities can be coordinated. The Framework is divided into five interrelated chapters and one appendix. Chapters 1 and 2 provide background information and identify the major issues faced by SMEs. Chapter 3 provides the policy context and institutional structure for the SME Development Framework. Chapters 4 and 5 set out a strategy for dealing with each of the major issues identified. It divides the strategy into two phases and by issues. The appendix provides a summary road map of action needed to be taken.

(c) Small and Medium Enterprises Development in Cambodia

In order to promote the private sector, the Royal Government of Cambodia established the Government-Private Sector Forum (GPSF), which is composed of eight Technical Working Groups (TWG). The SME TWG is co-chaired by H.E. Suy Sem (Minister of Industry, Mines & Energy) and Okhna Te Taing Por (First Secretary General of the Cambodia Chamber of Commerce).

As in most countries, SMEs play a significant role in the local economy and in Cambodia, they employ over 1.5 million people. Okhna Te Taing

Por and Oknha Hun Lak, two prominent businessmen decided to take up the challenge in setting up Federation of Associations of SME of Cambodia (FASMEC) with the support from MIME (Ministry of Industry, Mines & Energy).

FASMEC is a recent initiative to gather round various business associations and commercial enterprises throughout the country sharing the same vision and was officially registered with the Ministry of Interior on 22 December 2010 under No. 1817 Sor Chor Nor.[9]

FASMEC is committed to fulfilling the following mission:

- Promote SMEs in Cambodia;
- Be the main conduit for dialogue on SME issues with the government through the GPSF;
- Seek technical and financial support from government, multilateral, and bilateral aid agencies for SMEs improvement;
- Facilitate SMEs problem solving with the government;
- Provide relevant vocational training and capacity building for SMEs;
- Partner with government institutions to improve productivity, standards, export procedures, etc.; and
- Assist SMEs in business registration, licensing, and permit acquisition in the most cost effective way.

FASMEC held its first Annual General Meeting (AGM) on 19 November 2010 and elected thirty-four Council Member Representatives. It is possible to recognize that Cambodia is dominated by SMEs and that the largest numbers of these are found in the rural sector. According to the SME framework, an SME can be identified or defined by the number of employees and/or by capital as shown in Table 8.1.

According to a study which was conducted to emphasize the significant role of SMEs in Cambodian economic development, especially in the context of the global economic crisis, it was found that regional integration in Southeast and East Asia has created both opportunities and challenges for Cambodia's SMEs.[10] Their limited capacity for business expansion and integration in production networks restrains Cambodia's SMEs from making use of regional integration. There are certain different characteristics for those SMEs that participate in production networks from those which do not, such as their higher productivity, business capability, and ability to innovate. Most surveyed SMEs are operating

TABLE 8.1

Criteria for Defining SMEs in Cambodia

Statistical (Determined by Labour)

Micro	Less than	10 employees
Small	Between	11–50 employees
Medium	Between	51–100 employees
Large	More than	100 employees

Financial (Determined by Assets), excluding land

Micro	Less than	US$50,000
Small	Between	US$50–250,000
Medium	Between	US$250–500,000
Large	Over	US$500,000

Source: Royal Government of Cambodia Sub-Committee on SME (2005).

under severe internal constraints. For those that are not in production networks, the majority of the constraints are in their functional barriers (management and financial capability), ability to compete (product and price barriers), and "information". For SMEs that are in production networks, both the detailed and main category ranking of constraints is consistently high on "functional barriers" and "product and price barriers". Though SMEs receive some assistance, they still need support in the fields of "business linkages and networking" and "financing". Since access to financing is consistently viewed as one of the biggest constraints faced by SMEs, specialized SME banks, which are very common in the region, should be established, or a loan or mortgage guarantee scheme provided by the government as practised in Indonesia, should be considered. An SME Development Fund and SME Business Development Services (BDS) could be further options for tackling these constraints.

The development of SMEs in Cambodia is facing many challenges:

- Electricity cost is a big part of SMEs' cost structure. The electricity tariff remains high compared to neighbouring countries, and is a big obstacle in strengthening Cambodia's competitiveness as well as attracting investment and improving livelihoods. Access to electricity in rural areas is still limited;

- The shortages of technicians and skilled workers are a major obstacle to accelerating SMEs in both urban and rural areas;
- SMEs find it difficult to access supporting finance. Though it is accessible, SMEs have to pay with very high interest loan, especially from informal loan providers; and
- Support from the government to SMEs is still limited, especially in human resources development, market information, market access, and technological innovation.

VII. Conclusion

ASEAN's share in the global economy, especially in trade and investment, is becoming larger and more important. ASEAN is becoming a single market and production base. With 2015, there is expected to be free flow of goods and services and freer flow of investment with the realization of the ASEAN Economic Community (AEC). Therefore, ASEAN SMEs have many opportunities to reap benefit from economic integration. There are many forms of mechanisms and strategies in SME development in ASEAN such as ASEAN Policy Blueprint for SME Development 2004–14 with well-structured actions. However, the implementation of the Blueprint is still limited due to a lack of funding and awareness.

There are many daunting challenges in realizing SME development in the context of AEC. The SME sector in ASEAN is faced with daunting challenges both fiscal and non-fiscal, particularly limited access to finance, technology, and markets. With greater competition in the region and the world, rapid technological advances, and constant changes in consumer demands require SMEs in ASEAN to be innovative and creative in order to face the challenges of the global market. Both ASEAN as a whole and each of member states should work together in SME development, especially in strengthening competitiveness of SME in quality products, access to technology and finance, and to be an important part of global supply chains.

VIII. Recommendation

Access to Finance with Low Interest Rates

Cambodia SMEs have difficulty in expanding businesses or starting new ones. Government support in providing low interest rate loans or monetary policy to support SMEs is really crucial for their development. Since access to finance is consistently viewed as one of the biggest constraints faced by SMEs, specialized SME banks, which are very common in the region, should be established, or a loan or mortgage guarantee from the government, as practised in Indonesia, should be considered. An SME Development Fund could be established, and set aside to be managed by private banks, and could be another option to iron out these constraints. The best practices in SME Business Development Services (BDS), for example, provided by the Penang Skills Development Center of Malaysia, should be explored. The BDS could provide partial or full support services such as training; counselling and advice; technology development and transfer; information; business linkages; and financing.

Technology Transfer

SMEs should be provided with help to get technology transfer, especially through Multinational Corporation if SMEs are sub-contractors.

Strengthening SMEs Support Mechanism

More funding and technical support should be provided by the government and development partners to support SME related agencies such as departments dedicated to SMEs in the Ministry of Industry, Mines and Energy, SMEs Association, and others.

NOTES

1. <http://www.aseansec.org/12877.htm>.
2. Tulus Tambunan (2008).
3. ASEAN (2012) AEC Scorecard.
4. <http://www.nationmultimedia.com/business/More-than-half-of-SMEs-unprepared-for-AEC-UTCC-30175872.html>.
5. Thitapha (2002).
6. Luyna Ung and Sovuthea Hay (2010).
7. Ibid.
8. Ministry of Industry, Mines and Energy at <http://www.gdi.mime.gov.kh/index.php?option=com_content&view=article&id=15%3Asmall-and-medium-enterprise-development-framework&catid=31%3Apolicystrategy&Itemid=181&lang=en> (accessed 14 May 2012).

9. FASMEC website: <http://www.fasmec.com/> (accessed 1 June 2012).
10. Chheang V., et al. in Vo, C.T. et al. (2009).

REFERENCES

Association of Southeast Asian Nations (ASEAN). *ASEAN Economic Community Scorecards: Charting Progress toward Regional Economic Integration*, 2012.

Chheang, V., S. Oum, and T. Leng. "Constraints on SMEs in Cambodia and their Participation in Production Networks". In *Integrating Small and Medium Enterprises (SMEs) into the more integrated East Asia*, edited by T.T. Vo, D. Narjoko, and S. Oum. ERIA Research Project No. 8. Thanh, Jakarta, <http://www.eria.org/research/y2009-no8.html> (accessed 2009).

International Finance Corporation. *SME Finance Policy Guide* (accessed October 2011).

Luyna Ung and Sovuthea Hay. "SMEs Access to Finance in Cambodia". In *Small and Medium Enterprises (SMEs) Access To Finance In Selected East Asian Economies*, edited by Charles Harvie, Sothea Oum, Dionisius Narjoko. ERIA Research Project Report 2010, No. 14.

Tambunan, Tulus. "SME Development, Economic Growth, and Government Intervention in a Developing Country: The Indonesian Story". *Journal of International Enterpreneurship*, vol. 6, no. 4 (2008): 147–67.

Uchikawa, Shuji and Souknilanh Keola. "Small and Medium Enterprises in Cambodia, Laos, and Vietnam". Economic Research Institute for ASEAN and East Asia (ERIA) at <http://www.eria.org/pdf/research/.../chapter_10Uchikawa_and_Keola.pdf> (accessed 2008).

Vo, T.T., D. Narjoko, and S. Oum, eds. *Integrating Small and Medium Enterprises (SMEs) into the more integrated East Asia*. ERIA Research Project No. 8. Thanh, Jakarta. Available at <http://www.eria.org/research/y2009-no8.html> (accessed 2009).

Wattanapruttipaisan, Thitapha. "Promoting SME development: Some Issues and Suggestions for Policy Consideration". *Bulletin on Asia-Pacific Perspectives 2002/03* (accessed 2002).

———. "Four Proposals For Improved Financing of SME Development in ASEAN". *Asian Development Review*, vol. 20, no. 2 (December 2003).

9

EFFECTIVENESS OF INITIATIVE FOR ASEAN INTEGRATION

Vo Tri Thanh

I. Introduction

In December 1997, after years of expansion and cooperation, the ASEAN adopted its Vision 2020, emphasizing the objective of "... transforming ASEAN into a stable, prosperous, and highly competitive region with equitable economic development, and reduced poverty and socio-economic disparities". In October 2003, the ASEAN member states agreed on the establishment of the ASEAN Community by 2020, with the three pillars of the political-security community, economic community, and socio-cultural community. To accelerate the realization of the Vision, in 2007 the ASEAN leaders expressed their commitment to establish an ASEAN Economic Community (AEC) by 2015 as a single market and production base, and later on signed the AEC Blueprint as an action plan for advancing the AEC. Within such a context, the Initiative for ASEAN Integration (IAI) was launched in 2000, seeking to narrow intra-regional development gap by providing assistance to the CLMV in accelerating their integration and development.

With such a big move, ASEAN member countries certainly have a sizeable workload. There remain challenges and impediments to each country and the region as a whole, the most pressing of which lies in whether the less developed members can catch up with more advanced ones. Yet the progress of ASEAN so far, particularly in amalgamating themselves as a single block in negotiating and implementing free trade agreements (FTAs) with other major trading partners, brought about hopes for in-time realization of the AEC goal.

There are several notes regarding the implementation of IAI. First, the scope of priority areas to be addressed by the IAI has been expanded. In the IAI Work Plan for the first phase (2002–08), priority is given initially to only four areas, namely infrastructure, human resources development, information and communication technology (ICT), and capacity building for regional economic integration. In 2005, this Work Plan was extended to cover seven areas, with the three additional areas being tourism, poverty and quality of life, and general coverage projects. The Work Plan for the second phase (i.e. 2009–15) retains all the seven priority areas. Both phases have emphasized the focus on public sector capacity building. However, the first Work Plan also contributed significantly in the area of ICT, while the second one currently supports projects in infrastructure development, regional economic integration, and tourism.

According to a recent report by the ASEAN Secretariat,[1] the IAI, as a key area in the AEC pillar III of Equitable Development Scorecard, has made some progress, especially in the first phase. Under this pillar, 66.7 per cent of targeted measures have been achieved (see Table 9.1).

Second, the IAI serves not only as the platform for identifying and implementing technical assistance and capacity building programmes, but also for recognizing the need to have other regional initiatives to support the CLMV countries. ASEAN-6 is to play their leading role in realizing the IAI programmes. However, neither the efforts of ASEAN-6 nor those of the CLMV are sufficient by any means. Instead, ASEAN needs to mobilize necessary support from dialogue partners and international organizations (such as the Asian Development Bank, World Bank, etc.).

Third, ASEAN needs to conduct periodic socio-economic studies to monitor and/or evaluate the impact of economic integration. On one hand, such studies permit the assessment of IAI programme's effectiveness

TABLE 9.1

Equitable Economic Development Scorecard

Key Areas	Phase I (2008–09)		Phase II (2010–11)		Total Measures	
	Fully Implemented	Not Fully Implemented	Fully Implemented	Not Fully Implemented	Fully Implemented	Not Fully Implemented
SME development	1	0	4	3	5	3
IAI	2	0	1	1	3	1
Total number of measures	3	0	5	4	8	4
Implementation rate	100%		55.5%		66.7%	

Source: ASEAN Secretariat (2012; Table 9.3).

thus far in realizing IAI objectives. On the other hand, the studies will facilitate the identification of contemporary challenges, as well as the way forward to address such challenges.

This chapter serves two purposes. First, the chapter attempts to provide a survey-based perspective of the progress and challenges for ASEAN in implementing the IAI. Second, on the basis of analysed progress and challenges, the chapter develops some proposals as to how the IAI can be carried forward. Apart from the introduction, the remainder of the chapter consists of three sections. Section II assesses the overall effectiveness and relevance of the IAI programme. Section III then discusses the key issues for the IAI. Finally, Section IV makes some recommendations on further deepening IAI efforts.

II. Assessment of IAI's Effectiveness and Relevance

The overall effectiveness of the IAI can be seen in an analytical framework, which looks first at the role of IAI in enhancing CLMV development and regional integration, and second at the factors affecting IAI's effectiveness. The development and integration levels of CLMV are dependent upon not only the IAI programmes and assistance of other donors, but also the CLMV's own domestic reforms and policies, and cooperation among the CLMV themselves. The effectiveness of IAI can be analysed in relations to choice of areas/projects, modality of assistance, monitoring and impact assessment, which are subject to the constraint of available resources (specifically finance and expertise) in ASEAN-6.

Rather than using this framework for a quantitative analysis, this chapter adopts a survey of agencies in Cambodia, Lao PDR, Myanmar and Vietnam about the overall effectiveness of the IAI.[2] Almost all of the survey questions are designated in a way facilitating the concrete answers of either "Yes" or "No" by those surveyed. Using the compiled survey results, the chapter then analyses the effectiveness of IAI programmes in different countries.

Regarding the question of whether the IAI programme areas/projects contribute to narrowing development gap with ASEAN-6, the majority of responses claim that such contribution has been either moderate or substantial, in all surveyed countries. Altogether, the total shares of such answers amounted to almost 85.2 per cent in Cambodia, 70.0 per cent in Laos, 90.8 per cent in Myanmar, and 79.1 per cent in Vietnam. The benefits induced by IAI programmes have thus been arguably inclusive among the CLMV, thereby permitting them to catch up with more advanced ASEAN members.

The IAI programmes, however, produced different patterns of "catch-up" impacts on the CLMV. The proportion of judgement of substantial contribution by IAI programmes/projects is higher than that of answers with moderate contribution in the cases of Cambodia, Laos, and Myanmar, but not in Vietnam. About one fifth of those surveyed in Myanmar and one fourth in Laos failed to make a concrete judgment of the overall IAI effectiveness, while the corresponding figures for Cambodia and Vietnam are 3.7 per cent and 4.2 per cent, respectively. At the other end, none of those surveyed in Myanmar saw the impacts of IAI programmes being of either negligible or modest extent, while no negligible impacts were observed by agencies in Cambodia and Laos.

Table 9.2 depicts how surveyed agencies in the CLMV assess the performance of the IAI programme area(s)/project(s). In all the surveyed countries, the agencies being satisfied with the IAI programme/ project performance make up the largest shares. These findings somehow exhibit consistency with the above perceived contribution of IAI programmes/projects to narrowing the development gap of CLMV with ASEAN-6.

TABLE 9.2

Assessment of Performance of the IAI Programme Area(s)/Project(s)

Question	Percentage (%)			
	Cambodia	Laos	Myanmar	Vietnam
Unsatisfied	–	5.0	3.8	–
Somewhat satisfied	14.8	–	19.2	37.5
Satisfied	48.2	25.0	38.5	54.2
Very satisfied	37.0	15.0	3.9	8.3
Do not know or not applicable	–	55.0	34.6	–
Total	100.0	100.0	100.0	100.0

Source: Author's calculation from IAI survey data.

However, degree of satisfaction with IAI programmes varies significantly across the surveyed countries. Eighty-five point two per cent of the respondents in Cambodia and 62.5 per cent of those in Vietnam were either satisfied or very satisfied with the performance of such programmes. These figures are considerably higher than that in Laos (40.0 per cent) and in Myanmar (42.3 per cent). Fifty-five per cent of those surveyed in Laos and 34.6 per cent in Myanmar were unaware of or could not assess the performance of the IAI programmes/projects. Meanwhile, none of those surveyed in Cambodia and Vietnam found the IAI programmes/projects unsatisfactory, which somehow reflects better performance of such programmes/projects in these countries than in Laos and in Myanmar.

In another aspect, analysis on relevance of IAI Work Plans embodies the needs and development priorities of the CLMV countries. This stems from the fact that the CLMV themselves are different in terms of their economic institutions and the pace of reforms and international integration.

Table 9.3 tabulates the surveyed countries' assessment of IAI Work Plans' relevance to their own needs. The majority of those surveyed appreciate such relevance, albeit to various extents. Altogether, the total share of responses which see partial relevance, relevance, or high relevance of IAI work plans to their needs reaches 100 per cent in both Vietnam and Laos, 92.6 per cent in Cambodia, and 88.5 per cent in Myanmar. Notably, none of the responses claim that IAI Work Plans are irrelevant to their needs. In this respect, the IAI has catered well to the development needs of CLMV countries. The extent of relevance, nevertheless, differs from one host country to another. More than one half of the respondents in Laos, Myanmar, and Vietnam pick 'High' relevance in their judgement of the IAI Work Plan, while the corresponding figure in Cambodia is just one third. Besides, none of the responses in Vietnam and Laos fails to assess such relevance, which is contrary to the situations in Cambodia and Myanmar.

Table 9.4 shows the surveyed countries' assessment of IAI Work Plans' relevance to their own development priorities. Similar to the pattern in Table 9.3, those surveyed largely commend the relevance embodied in the IAI Work Plans. Again, none of the responses considers the IAI Work Plans to completely mismatch their development priorities. That is, while catering very well to the needs of the CLMV countries,

TABLE 9.3

Assessment of Relevance of IAI WPs to the Needs of CLMV

Question	Percentage (%)			
	Cambodia	Laos	Myanmar	Vietnam
Irrelevant to the needs	–	–	–	–
Partly relevant to the needs	11.1	10.0	3.8	4.1
Relevant to the needs	48.2	30.0	30.8	41.7
Highly relevant to the needs	33.3	60.0	53.9	54.2
Do not know or not applicable	7.4	–	11.5	–
Total	100.0	100.0	100.0	100.0

Source: Author's calculation from IAI survey data.

TABLE 9.4

Assessment of Relevance of IAI WPs to the Development Priorities of CLMV

Question	Percentage (%)			
	Cambodia	Laos	Myanmar	Vietnam
Irrelevant to the priorities	–	–	–	–
Partly relevant to the priorities	14.8	5.0	11.5	16.7
Relevant to the priorities	40.8	40.0	26.9	50.0
Highly relevant to the priorities	40.7	40.0	50.0	25.0
Do not know or not applicable	3.7	15.0	11.6	8.3
Total	100.0	100.0	100.0	100.0

Source: Author's calculation from IAI survey data.

the IAI Work Plans are also designed to facilitate the realization of their development priorities, but the degree of relevance varies across the four surveyed countries.

It is worth noting that only some linkages can be observed in Tables 9.3 and 9.4. For Cambodia and Myanmar, the distributions of concrete answers (i.e. Partial Relevance, Relevance, and Highly Relevance) in Table 9.3 do not differ markedly from those in Table 9.4. For Laos and Vietnam, the distributions show some differences. Specifically, more than one half of responses consider the IAI Work Plans to be highly relevant to their needs, but the other half sees the Work Plans to be only relevant to the priorities. As an implication, the Work Plans are perceived to cater well for Lao's and Vietnam's needs, though they may not completely match the key areas which the country has emphasized. For example, those surveyed in Laos noted that the existing assistance is not sufficient for many areas such as services, transport, and customs.

Further exploitation of the survey shows that in general the IAI programmes/projects have targeted appropriate agencies. But the proportion of respondents which deem their IAI programmes/projects to be highly relevant to their needs is significantly higher in Laos and Vietnam than in Cambodia and Myanmar. Besides, none of the respondents in Vietnam fails to assess such relevance, which is contrary to the situation in Cambodia, Laos, and Myanmar. This may imply the ineffective communication of IAI project designs and objectives to the beneficiaries in Cambodia, Laos, and Myanmar. In another aspect, no respondent in Myanmar argues for the irrelevance of their IAI programmes/projects to their needs, but this is not in Cambodia, Laos, and Vietnam. In many cases, it can be seen the different degrees of IAI programme/project relevance at national and implementing agency levels. This implies that there are rooms for improving the contribution of IAI within each host country.

Whilst attaining somewhat consensus about the relevance of IAI programmes and projects, the surveyed agencies have rather judgments of the financial resources dedicated for implementing such programmes and projects (see Table 9.5). More importantly, at the national level, the sufficiency of financial resources relative to IAI activities varied considerably across countries. In Cambodia, none of the surveyed agencies deemed the allocated financial resources as insufficient, while more than two-fifths of them considered such resources to be only partly sufficient.

Meanwhile, the respective shares of agencies regarding financial resources as insufficient are 20.0 per cent, 7.7 per cent, and 20.8 per cent in Laos, Myanmar, and Vietnam, respectively, while partially better sufficiency is only observed by 0.0 per cent, 26.9 per cent and 16.7 per cent of those surveyed in these countries. Conversely, sufficiency or high sufficiency of financial resources has been the case in 55.6 per cent of respondents in Cambodia, whilst being more modest in Laos, Vietnam and Myanmar (accounting for 45 per cent, 29.2 per cent and 23.1 per cent, respectively). In another aspect, only 3.8 per cent of responses in Cambodia were doubtful about the financial sufficiency of IAI programmes/projects, as compared with the corresponding figures of 35.0 per cent, 42.3 per cent and 33.4 per cent in Myanmar and Vietnam, respectively.

Thus, the financial resources committed to the IAI programmes may fail to embody sufficiency. As an implication, the IAI programmes and projects may perform less impressive relative to expectations due to the failure of allocated financial resources to accommodate the activities. Consequently, the IAI programmes may not produce the best impacts on their own. Better coordination of IAI programmes with support by other pro-development donors — such as the World Bank and the ADB — may contribute better to the realization of the IAI activities.

To look further into the coordination between IAI programmes, assistance from other donors and the host country, the survey collected

TABLE 9.5

Sufficiency of Allocated Funds for IAI Programme Areas/Projects Relative to their Expected Results

Question	Percentage (%)			
	Cambodia	Laos	Myanmar	Vietnam
Insufficient	–	20.0	7.7	20.8
Partly Sufficient	40.7	–	26.9	167
Sufficient	33.3	35.0	23.1	20.8
Highly sufficient	22.2	10.0	–	8.3
Do not know or not applicable	3.8	35.0	42.3	33.4
Total	100.0	100.0	100.0	100.0

Source: Author's calculation from IAI survey data.

responses on its role in the process of designing and implementing IAI programme areas and projects. The proportions of agencies which regard donor-host country coordination as partly efficient, efficient, or most efficient add up to nearly 96.7 per cent in Cambodia, 60.0 per cent in Laos, 76.9 per cent in Myanmar, and 87.5 per cent in Vietnam. However, some cross-country differences can be observed. Inefficient coordination is only witnessed by 5.0 per cent and 8.3 per cent of surveyed agencies in Laos and Vietnam, whilst being unobserved in Cambodia and Myanmar. At the other end, only 3.7 per cent of responses in Cambodia have no concrete answer of coordination efficiency with donors, yet the figure increases considerably to 35.0 per cent in Laos, 23.1 per cent in Myanmar, and 12.5 per cent in Vietnam. It appears that coordination efficiency with donors is perceived to be better in Cambodia than in Myanmar and Vietnam. Specifically, the responses tend to concentrate on the choices of "Efficiency" or "Most Efficiency" in Cambodia, whilst being largely "Efficiency" or "Partial Efficiency" in Laos, Myanmar and Vietnam. This observation appears to be consistent with relative financial sufficiency as evidenced in Table 9.5. In other words, compared with Laos, Myanmar and Vietnam, Cambodia could enjoy relatively higher financial sufficiency due to better coordination with donors in designing and implementing IAI programmes and projects.

Overall, the CLMV countries possess rather positive perception of the IAI. Importantly, the IAI programmes and projects are considered to embody significant relevance to development needs and priorities of the CLMV countries. Most of the surveyed agencies in the CLMV countries were somehow satisfied with the performance of the IAI programmes/ projects. Nonetheless, there are also some problems as reflected in the heterogeneity of degree of satisfaction. It appears that better outcomes would have been realized if the design and implementation of IAI Work Plans embark to a larger extent on financial sufficiency and coordination with other donors.

III. Key Issues for IAI

The survey-based analysis shows relatively positive perception of the CLMV countries about the IAI, particularly with respect to its possible contribution to narrowing their development gap with the ASEAN-6. Nevertheless, the IAI programme is not free of problem by itself. First, despite its high relevance, the IAI programme areas may not fully fit with the CLMV countries' key priorities as already noted in Section II. Further evidence may be drawn from the comparison of the IAI-covered areas and the key issues identified by the different country studies. For instance, in the case of Cambodia, economic diversification and agriculture, natural resources, and inadequate institutions and governance may emerge as the key areas to tackle for longer-term growth. Similarly, Lao PDR has to urgently improve macroeconomic management, investment and business climate, natural resources management, while Myanmar and Vietnam must address the respective issues agricultural development and climate change. Yet these areas were not incorporated in the IAI Work Plans, though the multi-period approach to designing such Work Plans allows for flexible adjustment of support activities.

The main underlying reason for this mismatch could be the attempt to adopt a common framework for all CLMV countries, while their heterogeneity has for long been acknowledged. More importantly, whilst trying to bring the CLMV together so as to close the gap with ASEAN-6, the IAI programmes and projects tend to ignore more urgent demand specific to each CLMV country. Consequently, the CLMV countries tend to pay less than sufficient attention to the IAI programmes and projects, which are unfavourable to the realization of objectives set out upon designation of such programmes and projects.

There also exists some gap between the IAI strategic framework and its actual operations. In the status of the IAI Work Plan II by Programme Areas, the actual activities have been concentrated heavily in capacity building. Meanwhile, the use of technical assistance for realizing the Work Plan remains quite rare. The gap is even more significant in such components as labour and employment, higher education, customs and standards — as none of the activity has been even in process. Similar issue is observed with the area of poverty and quality of life. These gaps actually reflect the incompleteness of programme and component designs, which may restrain the effectiveness of the IAI's implementation.

Second, even if the areas and components covered under the IAI are right, they may be too ambitious given the resource and time constraints. As can be seen in Tables 9.6 and 9.7, most of the components under IAI programme areas are perceived as appropriate for the host country's needs and development priorities, aiming at narrowing her development gap with the more advanced ASEAN members. Only in rare cases in Myanmar and Lao PDR was the appropriateness of such IAI components disregarded. Nonetheless, the numbers of both programme areas and

TABLE 9.6

Matching IAI Programme Areas with CLMV's Key Issues and Sample Intended Training by Donors

IAI-covered Areas	ADB Intended Training Programme For CLMV	Country Reports (ADB Project ASEAN Vision 2030)
1. Infrastructure (transport; energy)	1. Macroeconomic stability	*Cambodia*: Human Capital; Economic Diversification and Agriculture; Poverty; Natural Resources; Regional Integration and Connectivity; Institutions and Governance
2. Human resource development (public sector capacity building; labour and employment; higher education)	2. Financial sector development	*Lao PDR*: Human Capital; Macroeconomic Management; Economic Diversification and Agriculture; Investment and Business Climate; Infrastructure; Natural Resources
3. ICT	3. Infrastructure & connectivity	
4. Regional economic integration (trade in goods & services; customs; standards; investment)	4. Regional economic integration	*Myanmar*: Human Capital; Agriculture; Economic Diversification and Industrial Base; Macroeconomic Management; Trade and Foreign Investment; Infrastructure
5. Tourism	5. Poverty and quality of life	*Vietnam*: Institutions and Governance; Infrastructure; Human Capital; Rural Development and Urbanization; Climate Changes and Environment; Social Safety Nets
6. Poverty and quality of life	6. Natural resource management and environmental protection	
7. General coverage projects	7. Governance and institutions	

Source: Author's compilations.

components appear to be overwhelming, whilst still failing to approach reasonable scope for addressing specific and common needs of the CLMV countries. Therefore, one may question the practical feasibility of IAI programmes. The widely acknowledged issue of relative financial insufficiency, as showcased in Section II, provides further support to the question. Furthermore, that the available time for AEC (by 2015) becomes shorter should not be ignored. While the possibility of realizing an economic community by true meaning diminishes to very low probability (Vo 2012), addressing the development gap with a more focused approach under IAI may bring about more meaningful outcomes. As an example, dedicating sufficient efforts to building human and institutional capacity may work out better than merely spreading available resources across a large number of programme areas.

Third, in connection with the above issue, the IAI efforts may not pay enough attention on the issues of institutional building. In fact, institutions do matter for growth and sustainable development, particularly in the perception of CLMV countries (see Table 9.6). Trade liberalization and integration, especially trade and investment facilitation, can be viewed as institutional changes and reform. Meanwhile, the broader economic integration process in East Asia has been rapidly institutionalized, centring on the proactive role of ASEAN. Even in that context, nonetheless, attempts to promote regional economic integration only constitute some substances in the programme areas of IAI. Meanwhile, better developed framework for institutional improvement remains absent. Among the consequences is thus the weak enforcement of institutions at the regional level. Specifically, more advanced economies in ASEAN may wish to accelerate the negotiation and implementation of FTAs to quickly grasp the opportunities from better market access, while less advanced ones want the process to slow down to allow for necessary adjustment.

Another issue lies in the institutions for implementation and realization of the IAI. The issue has several dimensions. On one hand, whether the IAI programme takes fully into account the advantages the member of ASEAN-6 could have in supporting CLMV remains questionable. As an instance, with her profound experiences and foundation, Singapore can take the lead in supporting (and cooperating with) the CLMV in the areas of finance, ICT, health care, education, urban development, institutional building, and logistics. Similarly, Thailand may dedicate some efforts to guide the CLMV countries in promoting tourism, agricultural development, as well as macroeconomic management. The incorporation

TABLE 9.7

Regional and Sub-Regional Development Cooperation Programmes

	Agr.	Energy	Enviro	HR	ICT	Transport	Tourism	Trade	Invest	Involved Countries
EACWP	X	X	X	X	X	X	X	X	X	ASEAN, China, Japan, Korea
IAI		X		X	X	X				ASEAN
GMS	X	X	X	X	X	X	X	X	X	CLMV, Thailand, China
AKBDC	X	X		X	X	X	X	X	X	ASEAN, China
ACPMECS	X			X		X	X	X	X	CLMV, Thailand
BIMP-EAGA	X						X			Brunei, Indonesia, Malaysia, Philippines
IMT-GT		X		X	X	X	X	X	X	Indonesia, Thailand Malaysia

Note: EACW: East Asian Cooperation Work Plan; IAI: Initiative for ASEAN Integration (1st Phase 2002–08); GMS: Greater Mekong Sub-region; AKBDC: ASEAN-Mekong Basin Development Cooperation; ACPMECS: Ayeyarwaddy-Chao Phraya-Mekong Economic Cooperation Strategy; BIMP-EAGA: Brunei, Indonesia, Malaysia, Philippines-East ASEAN Growth Area; IMT-GT: Indonesia, Malaysia, and Thailand-Growth Triangle

Source: Joint Expert Group on EAFTA Phase II Study (2009).

of these areas in the IAI Work Plans has been less than enough by itself. Given the essential objective of helping the CLMV members to catch up with the rest of ASEAN, inducing further leading roles by the latter in designated programme areas may enhance the practical effectiveness of IAI.

On the other hand, the IAI may not follow closely some new issues and challenges. The already complex web of regional/bilateral cooperation and stakeholders' engagements (see Table 9.7) may be added (and complicated) further by new initiatives for regional integration, at both ASEAN and ASEAN+ levels. Besides, ASEAN has to achieve the AEC by 2015, while strengthening their connectivity and centrality. There is some progress towards the AEC but several "AEC Target — Reality Gaps" are still quite significant and vary substantially among the members.[3] Therefore, ASEAN needs to identify the key priorities which need political support for implementation by 2015. These priorities may include trade facilitation measures (customs, ROO, expediting COO), investment facilitation measures (streamlined procedures for permits, etc., best practices, investment promotion), complete tariff phase-out except for very few sensitive ones, and standards and conformance measures (harmonization; mutual recognition agreements, etc).

At this stage, the world and the East Asian region are undergoing a "transition period" of reallocation/redistribution of geopolitical and geo-economic powers. The newly emerging economies, particularly the BRICS,[4] are having a greater voice in the aftermath of the global financial crisis and economic restructuring. The major trade and investment partners of ASEAN member states are also experiencing drastic changes. The new transnational and non-traditional securities issues, such as energy security, food security, and climate change, are also confronting the region. Without sufficient well-coordinated efforts at both regional and country levels, ASEAN can hardly realize its goal of establishing on time the ASEAN Community.

Finally, the design and implementation of the IAI programme appear to embody some limitations. Still, the IAI activities somehow under-estimate the importance of coordinating the support by ASEAN-6 with advantages of the cooperation among CLMV. Meanwhile, promoting South-South cooperation in line with support of more developed/advanced countries/multilateral donor(s) may pave the way for inclusive and non-overlapping development efforts in the CLMV countries themselves. In another aspect, the IAI projects fail to be coordinated with those of other international donors. This casts doubt on actual progress of IAI programmes and projects given the insufficient capacity of the CLMV to absorb wide-scope assistance. That is, simply matching a large scope of assistance efforts with their wide-ranging development needs may not produce the best outcome for the CLMV countries. Moreover, the IAI programme lacks adequate consultation with all relevant stakeholders in the CLMV (i.e. government, business community, think tanks, etc.) which may help identify their needs and the relevant modalities of project delivery.[5] Associated with this comes the smaller possibility to attain cost-effectiveness, not to mention the efficiency as anticipated upon designation of IAI Work Plans.

To add further to the limitations, inadequate efforts have been dedicated for regular and rigorous assessment of the IAI project effectiveness and monitoring the changes in the gap between CLMV and ASEAN-6. This limitation is not new to the IAI implementation itself. In fact, even the monitoring and evaluation of integration progress of ASEAN remain a critical task. The AEC Scorecard may have demonstrated its importance as an instrument to support the implementation of the ASEAN Blueprint; it is, however, less than fully satisfactory by its own. At the sub-regional level, however, even a workable approach to assessing the contribution of IAI projects — particularly with respect to the intra-regional development gap — has not been identified. This represents a room for further, if not urgent, improvement since mere implementation of supporting projects without proper monitoring mechanism may only lead to realization of intermediate targets at its best, rather than the desired final ones.

IV. Policy Recommendations

The discussion in Sections II and III sheds light on the progress so far and challenges perceived at this stage of the IAI implementation. The short time available until 2015 necessitates more effective and targeted attempts for closing the gap between CLMV and ASEAN-6, along with other sets of activities for viable regional economic integration.

Several considerations should be taken in furthering the IAI work plans. It should be recognized that the IAI only constitutes a part of the whole story about how to effectively narrow the development gap among ASEAN members. There are other frameworks for supporting the CLMV countries, i.e. lesser developed members of ASEAN. Even assistance from ASEAN-6 has two major components, namely the special and differential treatment (SDT) notified in ASEAN agreements and the technical assistance for the CLMV. For example, the CLMV may be allowed to enjoy longer period for phasing out tariff, even for the inclusive items. As another note, the practical effectiveness of the IAI is very much dependent upon ASEAN's willingness (i.e. political will), the coordination between all ASEAN members and between ASEAN and other donors, and the understanding of individual CLMV development and institutional reality. Furthermore, the IAI needs to concentrate its efforts to support CLMV in accelerating the realization of AEC commitments by 2015. In doing so, the supporting process should take into account the substantial engagement of many stakeholders and the new challenges for development in the region. The multi-period approach to designing the IAI Work Plans facilitates such accounts, yet the associated benefits may not come in an automatic manner.

Bearing the above notes in mind, the design and implementation of IAI in the forthcoming years should pay more focused attention to certain areas. First, human resources development in both the public and private sectors may play a pivotal role in inducing rapid growth and, accordingly, a catch-up process in the CLMV countries. Along with this comes the narrower gap in labour capability between the CLMV countries and ASEAN, thereby contributing to mutual recognition agreements and ASEAN integration. Second, macroeconomic management and reforms in the CLMV countries, particularly the acceleration of the integration highly correlated with a degree of macroeconomic stability, should receive more assistance. The lesson of macroeconomic instability in Vietnam shortly after her accession to the WTO necessitates the dissemination of experience to the CLM in tackling integration-induced macroeconomic turbulence. Third, the IAI should hinge to a larger extent on investment and trade facilitation. However, the programme areas should be extended to include customs reforms, investment promotion, procedure for permits, and best practices in facilitation. Finally, the IAI needs to improve capacity for financial resource mobilization, particularly public-private partnership (PPP) schemes for infrastructure development. Whilst permitting the private sector to grow up, this direction of efforts also contributes to the attainment of sufficient financial scale required for overall IAI effectiveness. Notably, since these areas of work attain different levels of importance in the CLM, the IAI should perhaps be tailored to specifically meet the needs of each country in this group. In other word, the IAI should incorporate substances of relevance to each

CLM country, considering their aspirational development priorities till 2030 (see Table 9.6).

As for the case of Vietnam-Singapore cooperation, the two governments have been engaged in improving bilateral connectivity for a long time. The Framework Agreement on Connectivity between the two countries has been signed since 2005, with the areas of cooperation being finance, education and training, transport, information-technology and communications, investment, trade and services. Recently, cooperation in some areas — such as finance, information-technology, and trade in goods — has been selected for further deepening efforts. Importantly, these efforts can be streamlined with the commitments of assistance by Singapore for IAI implementation.[6] This example can be replicated between the CLMV countries and ASEAN-6.

Besides, attempts are also required to strengthen the institutions for effective implementation of the IAI. From the experience of ASEAN, setting out good objectives and verbal commitments to make all members inclusive in regional integration and development proves insufficient. As a prerequisite for effective implementation, the IAI Work Plans should have regular consultation with all stakeholders, especially with CLMV. In principle, consultation should yield common understanding which can be readily transformed into concrete and dedicated actions. In this context, specifically, regular consultation permits the configuration of major issues into more specific projects, thereby meeting individual CLMV needs. Simply applying a common Work Plan may not work out at its best given the vast heterogeneity within the CLMV, whilst running the risk of diverting their allocated resources away from relatively more urgent demand.

Moreover, consultation may help clarify the modality of project delivery. In particular, the leading role assigned to members of ASEAN-6 or other donors may bear significant relevance to what extent and how smooth the project outcomes can be realized. In particular, fitting the programme components with advantages of the leading country, as discussed in Section III, may lead to streamlined efforts aiming at closing the intra-regional development gap.

Regarding the delivery of project, technical assistance in combination with training can make good contribution for the CLMV countries. As noted in Section III, the current activities under the IAI Work Plan II are concentrated heavily on capacity-building and training activities, whilst underrating the role of technical assistance. In this respect, technical assistance should be made popular under the IAI Work Plan so as to ensure that the skills and knowledge acquired under the capacity building activities are further internalized by the CLMV countries. Besides, this proposal for project delivery mode includes the attempts to share best practices from ASEAN-6 to CLMV. For instance, Singapore is the champion economy in terms of national single window for trade facilitation, and the country can readily share the related experience with the CLMV, not just in terms of facility development but also in establishing necessary institutional foundations. Other areas for sharing best practices also include budget management system, anti-corruption and smuggling, custom modernization, national single window, effective public services deliveries, etc.

Close consultation plays another important role in that it helps avoid "unnecessary duplications" of supporting efforts to the host country. Allocating too many resources may increase inefficiency in the presence of both resource limitations and diminishing return. Evidences from the surveyed perception of agencies in the CLMV countries, as summarized in Section II, add further ground for enhancing the substances of consultation in IAI process.

In the broader context, East Asia as a whole needs to take into account interests of and cost-benefit assessments of CLMV in any regional initiative and/or arrangement. Failure to do this may slow down regional integration and development cooperation, whilst also magnifies the risks of undermining socio-economic stability in the region (Vo and Nguyen 2010). In line with this, cooperation among the CLMV countries should be enhanced. Several dimensions of this cooperation should be noted. The CLMV countries should make their own efforts for better cooperation among themselves. With a relatively higher development level, Vietnam may take the lead, starting with issues of commonality among the CLMV (e.g. macroeconomic management, see Table 9.6) and with the simplest modality (maybe technical assistance). Through proper and close consultation, the CLMV countries may also coordinate cooperation among themselves with significant support by others — including ASEAN-6 and other multilateral donors.[7]

A number of proposals come up with the idea of expanding the IAI into the Initiative for East Asian Integration (IEAI) to facilitate regional development cooperation.[8] However, in addition to the heterogeneity within the ASEAN itself, the major countries in East Asia (such as Japan,

Korea and China) may also differ in terms of regional development interest. As such, it seems that such an idea of expanding the IAI cannot be materialized at this stage, not to mention the ability to implement the IEAI itself. Alternatively, ASEAN may deepen the engagement in ASEAN+1 dialogues with the regional powerhouses, so that supports from the latter can be harmonized with those within the former for the common sake of narrowing regional development gap. In another direction, the ASEAN (not just the CLMV) should utilize the multilateral mechanism, such as the ASEAN+3 Summit or the ADB, for better coordination of support to the CLMV countries. Accordingly, assistance to the CLMV countries can be better directed to the most prioritized areas in these countries, whilst avoiding the risk of duplication.

Furthermore, ASEAN needs to enforce regular assessment of the IAI project effectiveness and monitoring the changes in the gap between CLMV and ASEAN-6. Even the monitoring over the ASEAN Blueprint implementation should be strengthened with support induced by a more effective scorecard system. Instead, the instrument needs to be complemented by some others which can trace the state, performance, and impact of trade and investment liberalization in the ASEAN region. In line with this comes the secondary analysis of the development gap between CLMV and ASEAN-6 countries.

More broadly, ASEAN may adopt a more rigorous approach to monitoring the regional development gap. In fact, there can be a variety of aspects where development gaps exist, though not all the gaps hinder the ASEAN integration process. Given the limited resources, monitoring all aspects and undertaking related actions in all aspects can never be feasible. Therefore, the ASEAN should identify the most essential and critical dimensions of the development gaps in ASEAN for monitoring and subsequently for policy actions. That is, for some areas, indirect tackle measures are already good enough. As elaborated in Bui and Vo (2007), the four "I" approach — covering income gap, infrastructure gap, integration gap, and institutional gap — may provide a good example of critical development gaps in ASEAN. This may constitute a good foundation on which bridging attempts can proceed and be assessed.

Last but not least, the CLMV countries in cooperation with ASEAN-6 should develop relevant exchange programmes which resemble consistency with the chosen areas. Such exchange programmes may start by taking stock of issues, thereby laying foundations for subsequent experience-sharing activities. More importantly, the exchange programmes should incorporate substances of relevant institutional considerations that may affect actual outcomes of IAI programmes and projects. Such considerations may include, but are not limited to, "rule of games", organizations, and enforcement. Along with exchanging views and sharing information, the CLMV may simultaneously forge closer business linkages among themselves, which incorporates significant feasibility of South-South cooperation.

In a related aspect, ASEAN as a whole needs special consideration of the appropriateness of ODA strategies for the CLMV. A couple of criteria can be employed for assessing such appropriateness. On the one hand, ODA should focus on sectors that can generate significant positive spill-over effects and should create sufficient incentives, rather than burden, to those recipient countries. Thus, the current concentration of IAI Work Plan activities in capacity building should be revised slightly, and at ease, to incorporate better training in terms of project management training for public officials. In turn, this can be transformed into better proposals for IAI-coordinated projects that better serve the needs of the recipient countries. On the other hand, ODA should address the resource gap in these countries, aiming at shortening their development process and avoiding too much reliance on ODA. Eventually, narrowing the development gap in East Asia can only be effective so long as it adheres to regional development targets and embodies substance of credibility over such targets.

NOTES

1. See ASEAN Secretariat (2012). Since 2008, ASEAN has used the so-called AEC Scorecard for monitoring the process of implementation of various AEC measures under four pillars: (1) Single Market and Production Base; (2) Competitive Economic Region; (3) Equitable Economic Development; and (4) Integration into the Global Economy. By the end of 2011, 65.9 per cent, 67.9 per cent and 85.7 per cent of identified measures under Pillars I, II, and IV were implemented, respectively. It is worth noting that the AEC Scorecard is based on reports by member states and not for impact assessment.
2. The survey was conducted in early 2012 in CLMV. We can have only small samples of survey due to time constraint.
3. For more details, see Intal (2011).
4. Brazil, Russia, India, China, and South Africa.

5. Technical assistance, cooperation, training, workshop/seminar, field trips, etc.
6. Including the recent commitment worth S$50 million made during the Bali Summit in 2011.
7. For instance, the cooperation may follow "2 + 1" formula, meaning the cooperation between two developing countries with the support of a more advanced country or an international institution.
8. See Vo and Nguyen (2010).

REFERENCES

ADBI. "ASEAN 2030: Toward a Borderless Economic Community". Draft Highlights. ADBI, Tokyo, 2012.

ASEAN Secretariat. *ASEAN Economic Community Scorecard: Charting Progress Toward Regional Economic Integration*. Jakarta, 2012.

Bui, T.G. and T.T. Vo. "Approach to Development Gaps in ASEAN: A Vietnamese Perspective". *ASEAN Economic Bulletin*, vol. 24, no. 1 (April 2007).

Intal, Ponciano. "ERIA Study to Further Improve AEC Scorecard — Phase II: Draft Report". Paper presented at Hanoi Workshop, 20 September 2011.

Joint Expert Group on EAFTA. *Desirable and Feasible Option for an East Asia FTA*. Final Report on EAFTA Phase II Study, June 2009.

Vo, T.T. "Achieving an Efficient AEC by 2015: A Perspective from Vietnam". In *Achieving ASEAN Economic Community 2015: Challenges for Member Countries and Businesses*, edited by Sanchita Basu Das. Singapore: Institue of Southeast Asian Studies, 2012.

Vo, T.T. and A.D. Nguyen. "Development Cooperation in East Asia". Paper for presentation at pared for the KIEP conference, Seoul, July 2010.

10

MYANMAR IN THE ASEAN ECONOMIC COMMUNITY: Preparing for the Future

Moe Thuzar

I. Myanmar before the AEC: A Brief Background

Myanmar's admission to the Association of Southeast Asian Nations (ASEAN) in July 1997 was accompanied by the country's blanket accession to the treaties and commitments of ASEAN, including measures to be implemented for participation in the ASEAN Free Trade Area (AFTA) through the Common Effective Preferential Tariff (CEPT) Scheme. Myanmar's status as a member of the World Trade Organization (WTO) had facilitated ASEAN's consideration of Myanmar's ability to meet her obligations for multilateral trade relations with other WTO and ASEAN members.[1] In 1997, the other "new" members of ASEAN, i.e. Vietnam (which had joined ASEAN in 1995) and Lao PDR (which was admitted to ASEAN in 1997 together with Myanmar), were not yet WTO members. Myanmar's "potential" to participate in regional economic integration processes was thus seen by the other ASEAN members as the means by which economic development could underpin political change in the country.

However, this potential remained largely unrealized as the military junta in Myanmar hesitated to move forward on its self-styled "roadmap to democracy" and in achieving a functional market economy. ASEAN itself is facing considerable challenges in achieving its goal of regional economic integration. The Asian financial crisis of 1997–98 had set back targets for trade and investment liberalization, and since then ASEAN member states are facing difficulties in gaining the investors' confidence back into the region. The integration challenges of the four "newer" members of ASEAN — Cambodia, Laos, Myanmar and Vietnam (CLMV) — required ASEAN to devise programmes of partnership to help build capacities in the CLMV countries that would facilitate implementation of regional integration goals. In order to move forward, ASEAN adopted an "ASEAN minus x" formula in 2002 for negotiating liberalization of services. This formula can also seen as broadly applied to the respective schedules for ASEAN member states to achieve their commitments for trade and investment liberalization. The newer members were given more time and extended "deadlines" for tariff reduction and service sector liberalization.

With the 9th ASEAN Summit's confirmation in 2003 of the ASEAN Economic Community (AEC) as one of the three key pillars of the ASEAN Community (the other two being the ASEAN Political and Security Community and the ASEAN Socio-Cultural Community), and the announcement by the 11th ASEAN Summit in 2005 to "accelerate" the establishment of an integrated ASEAN Community by 2015, a Strategic Schedule was worked out for realizing the AEC. The schedule, which appears in the AEC Blueprint, lists timelines for ASEAN member states to implement their AEC commitments under each of the key components of AEC. Under this schedule, Myanmar is expected to achieve most of her AEC commitments by 2018, and to implement all undertakings by 2020[2] (the original envisaged date for achieving an integrated ASEAN).

Myanmar was one of the first ASEAN members to publicly state its unilateral endorsement of the Master Plan on ASEAN Connectivity (MPAC).[3] In his congratulatory message on ASEAN's 43rd anniversary in 2010, the then head of military government in Myanmar, Senior General Than Shwe stated his hope that the MPAC would reach "a win-win solution to reflect the interest of all member states and strive for balance between regional and national interest". Clearly, Myanmar policy-makers recognized the country's potential role and capacity in taking advantage of the privileges offered under the ASEAN agreements on trade in goods and the benefits that connectivity with other ASEAN and East Asian economies via the MPAC components.

This chapter assesses how Myanmar — and particularly the business community in the country — could participate in and contribute more effectively to the AEC. It is a broad macro-level assessment, which also takes into account the implications of the political and economic reforms started in 2011. It provides some recommendations for policy-makers to consider in preparing for Myanmar's more active participation in ASEAN, and ultimate integration into the regional and global economic communities.

II. 2011: A Year of Changes

When the Union Solidarity and Development Party (USDP) won the November 2010 elections, the military junta's past record influenced people's perception of the military-backed USDP-led government's accession to executive powers. The release of Daw Aung San Suu Kyi from house arrest on 13 November 2010, though welcomed, was still viewed with scepticism. Although President Thein Sein's inaugural speech on 30 March 2011 highlighted his administration's commitment to economic renewal and poverty alleviation, correcting the human rights record, ensuring good governance, and resolving the decades-long ethnic conflict,[4] many were initially dismissive of these pronouncements and the new government's commitment to initiate change.

2011 saw a slew of reforms — political and economic — in Myanmar under the Thein Sein administration. The broad strokes of reform include the freedom of movement (and speech) of Nobel laureate Aung San Suu Kyi; loosened restrictions on the media; the passing of a law allowing workers to organize and strike; releases of prisoners, including political prisoners; several measures towards opening up the economy; and the National League for Democracy (NLD)'s re-entry into the political process after a watershed by-election in April 2012.

The pace of reforms took the world by surprise, inducing countries such as the United States (U.S.), Britain, Australia and those in the European Union to seek closer engagement with the Thein Sein administration, resulting in the easing of sanctions and, most recently, a landmark visit by the U.S. President on 19 November 2012, the first for a sitting President to do so.

In support of — and to encourage — the reforms in Myanmar, ASEAN has placed its faith in Myanmar's bid to take up its turn for the ASEAN chairmanship in 2014.

The question now to ask is where the reforms would be most effective for Myanmar to catch up with the rest of ASEAN in regional integration efforts and make up for the lost decades. With the reforms now in their second phase, focusing on "people-centred" policies and a comprehensive national development strategy, there is also concern on the continued momentum of the reforms and the commitment of all stakeholders and interest groups.

Myanmar's reforms are taking place in the midst of regional change. ASEAN's economic integration processes can thus reinforce and provide impetus to Myanmar's economic reforms, especially in taking advantage of the assistance available from ASEAN's Dialogue Partners working with the ASEAN member states on implementation of the MPAC priority projects.[5]

Even so, as ASEAN moves closer to the "launching" date of the ASEAN Community (including the AEC) by 31 December 2015, members are grappling with the implications of tensions in the South China Sea, and the Association's own challenges in meeting AEC commitments in the four pillars.[6] Myanmar's ASEAN chairmanship in 2014 is seen as a crucial year, as it falls just before the establishment of the ASEAN Community (including the AEC) by end-2015.

III. How Myanmar Can Benefit from the AEC

The benefits of being more closely "connected" with other members of ASEAN are many. Consumers, workers and people in general would benefit from improvements in the general economy through greater inflows of foreign direct investment, liberalization of the economy, upgrading of infrastructure (including transportation and info-communications), development of ancillary services and improving ability to create jobs for the populace. The MPAC implementation is now underway, with the ASEAN Infrastructure Fund (AIF) recently established (in May 2012) to support projects for ASEAN's physical connectivity. For Myanmar, cooperation with the other ASEAN member states and development partners to achieve the MPAC commitments will help Myanmar improve its infrastructure and streamline the economic policy processes. All this will lead to a higher standard of living in the country.

The current process in Myanmar to review and reform laws and procedures is encouraging for Myanmar's ASEAN integration efforts. Effective participation in ASEAN processes, especially in AEC, requires policy reforms, consistency in policy and in its application. Important changes will also need to be made to the country's education and labour policies, so that the workforce will be creative, competent and competitive.[7]

This positive future scenario is dependent on whether the current phase of reforms could assist the business community in Myanmar to take full advantage of the opportunities offered under ASEAN economic integration. The main imperative is to "level the playing field" for domestic firms, in order to ensure their competitiveness. Measures to this end would include (a) fair access for all to the country's natural resources; (b) fairness in granting licences and permits to take up business opportunities; (c) equal treatment in applying rules and procedures; (d) getting rid of arbitrary and ever-changing rules and regulations; (e) reducing official corruption; (f) ending payment of arbitrary dues, donations; and (g) transparency and accountability in applying rules and procedures.[8]

Myanmar finally put an end to the confusing and non-productive dual-exchange rate on 1 April 2012 with the unification of the multiple exchange rates and phasing out the Foreign Exchange Certificate (FEC) scheme. However, this is just a first step towards reforming the financial sector, which is an important economic institution. Other concerns to address in ensuring macroeconomic stability include:

(a) fostering greater communication and coordination among the businesspeople and their counterparts in other countries;
(b) improving Myanmar's human resource base to support implementation of the reforms (the country currently has a very limited talent pool of organizational, managerial and marketing skills);
(c) upgrading infrastructure and improving communication systems, including wider, more reliable and cheaper access to internet and mobile phones;
(d) removing barriers to international trade and investment; improving public utilities, electricity, water and energy; and

(e) helping the private sector acquire technology and know-how to interact on an equal basis with counterparts.

After much back-and-forth deliberation between the Hluttaw and the executive branch, Myanmar recently enacted on 2 November 2012 a new Foreign Direct Investment (FDI) Law, to ensure a regulatory framework for attracting much-needed FDI inflows into the country. While responses by Myanmar's business community to the new FDI law has been mostly positive, the prevailing sentiment in the country is that more should be done to support domestic firms in competing with foreign investors.[9] This stems from earlier concerns that Myanmar's business community is not ready to compete effectively in the single market and production base envisaged by 2015 under the AEC.

Myanmar's new FDI law still needs to be tested with regard to intellectual property rights policies and dependable dispute settlement mechanisms for economic agreements and undertakings. A general improvement in the rule of law (and the perception of investors that there is improvement) would facilitate investor attraction and confidence in the country and also support Myanmar's participation in the AEC.

The experience of the Asian "tiger" economies in the 1990s, shows that their policies for economic growth also helped to reduce poverty in these countries. This came about as a result of interaction and collaboration with multinational corporations (MNCs) investing in the countries. It is still too early to judge whether Myanmar can have this opportunity through the framework of the new FDI law. Still, a judicious management of the reforms currently underway in the economic and political spheres should contribute to establishing a welcoming climate for FDI in Myanmar. It is now time for the business community in Myanmar to support this development by improving their domestic competitiveness.

A general improvement in the rule of law and the perception of the investors of this improvement would greatly facilitate Myanmar's participation in the AEC. Equally important is the lifting of sanctions and embargos — particularly the constraints on Myanmar's economic activities — to support Myanmar's opening up. Steps towards the latter have been taken by the U.S. and the European Union starting April 2012. The U.S. matched "action for action" in April 2012 by announcing:

- a fully accredited ambassador;
- an in-country USAID mission and supporting a normal country programme for the UNDP;

- private organizations in the U.S. to pursue range of non-profit activities from democracy building to health and education;
- lifting of visa bans on selected government officials and parliamentarians; and
- start of targeted easing of bans on exports of U.S. financial services and investment.[10]

Also in April, the EU suspended economic sanctions on Myanmar for one year. On 11 July, the U.S. Treasury Department's Office of Foreign Assets Control (OFAC) authorized "certain" U.S. financial services and new U.S. investments in Myanmar.[11] During the high-profile visits by both Thein Sein and Aung San Suu Kyi to the U.S. in October 2012, sanctions banning the import of goods from Myanmar were eased.

Lifting or easing sanctions is seen as necessary to help accelerate economic and political reforms. However, the dismantling of sanctions applied reflexively — especially those enacted into law — will not be as reflexive, nor will the process be as "immediate" as ASEAN members have called for. Additionally, it is difficult to gauge who are the "legitimate economic actors" in Myanmar on whom the sanctions have had a negative impact. Still, it is significant that the countries that led the imposition of the sanctions regime on Myanmar for the past decades are now also at the forefront of easing the sanctions and readily admitting that sanctions alone did not work in moving for change in Myanmar.

IV. Myanmar's Potential

It is mainly due to the Thein Sein administration's reform agenda that Myanmar has attracted the current overwhelming interest by many countries around the world. Much of this interest is related to Myanmar's yet unrealized economic potential.

Energy and mining account for 55 per cent of Myanmar's exports and 86 per cent of FDI. The extractive resource sector has the most significant FDI, especially in natural gas, timber, mining and power generation. These sectors continue to attract the greatest interest today.

Since 1988, Myanmar's economic relations have mainly been with countries in the Southeast and East Asia regions. The largest trading investors are China and Thailand. China is Myanmar's largest investor and second largest foreign creditor. The recent thawing of relations with Japan led to forgiving Myanmar US$3.7 billion of debt.[12] Still, in terms of

FIGURE 10.1
Myanmar: Percent (%) Share of Export Earnings

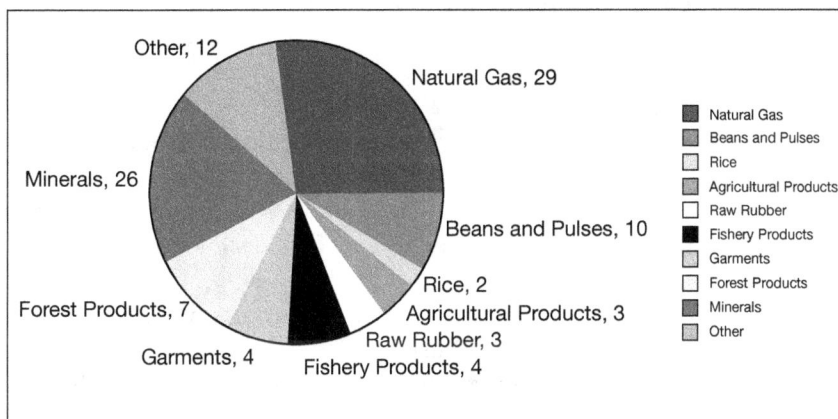

Source: IE Insights Volume 2, July 2012, International Enterprise Singapore, based on figures obtained from Myanmar's Ministry of Commerce.

TABLE 10.1
Myanmar: Foreign Direct Investment (FDI) by Sector

Sector	No. of Permitted Enterprises	Approved Amount (US$ Millions)	Percent Share
Power	4	14,530	40.3
Oil and Gas	104	13,815	38.3
Mining	64	2,794	7.8
Manufacturing	159	1,752	4.9
Hotel and Tourism	45	1,065	2.9
Real Estate	19	1,056	2.9
Livestock and Fisheries	25	324	0.9
Transport and Communications	16	313	0.9
Industrial Estate	3	193	0.5
Agriculture	7	173	0.5
Construction	2	38	0.1
Other Services	6	24	0.1
Total	454	36,078	100.0

Source: IE Insights Volume 2, July 2012, International Enterprise Singapore, based on figures obtained from Myanmar Investment Commission.

trade, Myanmar is largely dependent on her ASEAN neighbours. Intra-ASEAN trade accounts for more than 50 per cent of Myanmar's total trade, even though Myanmar only accounts for 1.1 per cent of trade in the region. If reforms continue and the country opens up to the rest of the world, these figures may change. Figure 10.2 shows the cumulative FDI into Myanmar over 1989–2012.

Myanmar's comparative advantage lies in the potential of its labour-intensive manufacturing sector, which may see a revival with the easing of sanctions. Prior to the U.S. sanctions applied in 2002, Myanmar exported US$860 million worth of garments a year. This declined steadily since 2003 after sanctions took effect.

Other areas with potential to grow are: tourism, infrastructure development, financial and other business services related to liberalization of the economy. Yet, much more needs to be done in terms of providing the

FIGURE 10.2

Cumulative Foreign Direct Investment into Myanmar, 1989–2012
(US$ millions)

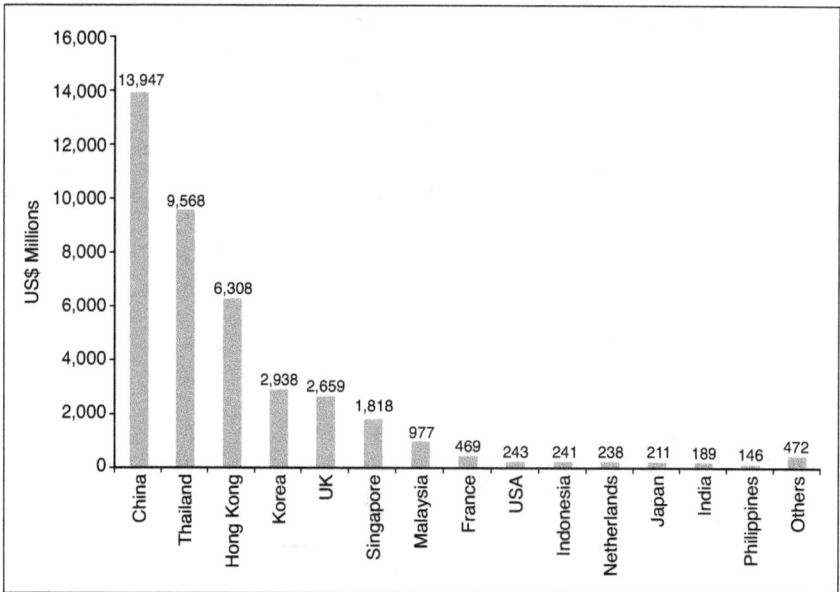

Source: IE Insights Volume 2, July 2012, International Enterprise Singapore, based on figures obtained from the International Monetary Fund (IMF).

supporting infrastructure, communications, and regulatory environment for trade and investment. Capacity-building for the workforce is also necessary to expand the existing limited talent pool.

About 70 per cent of Myanmar's labour force is employed in the agricultural sector which accounts for just over 40 per cent of the country's GDP. There is potential to develop Myanmar's agricultural and fisheries outputs for export. Concerns of the small-hold farmers, whose family farms have produced rice and practically all of Myanmar's important foodstuffs over the past decades, should not be neglected. Aspirations for large-scale plantation-type farming should bear in mind possible fallouts from enactment of the Farmland Law, and the Vacant, Fallow and Virgin Lands Management Law (passed by Parliament in March 2012). Already, there are calls for amendments, as these laws were found to have "mistakes, weaknesses and were incomplete".[13]

V. Myanmar's Readiness for AEC

Myanmar's implementation of ASEAN agreements on trade in goods and services, while largely on track, show some mixed results. There are uneven levels of awareness, understanding and commitment to AEC and its goals and requirements among the business private and government departments. While on track in tariff reduction, Myanmar's score on trade facilitation, compared to other ASEAN Member States, is still low. Table 10.2 shows Myanmar's implementation of tariff reduction under the CEPT scheme.

Myanmar also has some way to go in achieving the commitments under the ASEAN Trade in Goods Agreement (ATIGA), which entered into force on 17 May 2010.[14] Under the ATIGA, ASEAN member states are to eliminate import duties on all products traded between the member states by 2010 for the ASEAN-6 countries, and by 2015 — with flexibility to 2018 — for the CLMV countries.

Free flow of goods entails good logistics capacity. Currently, Myanmar ranks the lowest in logistics performance. Table 10.3 shows the World Bank's comparison of ASEAN member states' logistics performance, against the regional average for East Asia and the Pacific.

The AEC Scorecard[15] shows that Myanmar also scores low in trade facilitation. It lags behind the other member states in customs modernization (Myanmar ranks lowest) and implementation of the National Single Window (second lowest after Laos). Myanmar is second

TABLE 10.2
Myanmar's CEPT Schedule

Category	1998 HS 96	2004 AHTN2002	2005 AHTN2002	2006 AHTN2002	2007 AHTN2002	2008 AHTN2002	2010 AHTN2007
Inclusion List (IL)	2,356 (43,06%)	8,936 (83.60%)	10,461 (97.87%)	10,521 (98.43%)	10,611 (99.27%)	10,615 (99.31%)	8,240 (99.28%)
Temporary Exclusion List (TEL)	2,987 (54.59%)	1,646 (15.40%)	135 (1.26%)	77 (0.72%)	0	0	0
Sensitive List (SL)	21 (0.38%)	36 (0.34%)	34 (0.32 %)	32 (0.30%)	27 (0.25%)	23 (0.22%)	11 (0.13%)
General Exemption List (GEL)	108 (1.97%)	71 (0.66%)	59 (0.55%)	59 (0.55%)	51 (0.48%)	51 (0.48%)	49 (0.59%)
Total	5,472	10,689	10,689	10,689	10,689	10,689	8,300

Legend: HS = Harmonized commodity description and coding system, or HS Code; AHTN = ASEAN Harmonized Tariff Nomenclature.
Source: Ministry of National Planning and Economic Development (2011).

TABLE 10.3

Myanmar's Logistics Performance

Country	LPI	Customs	Infrastructure	International Shipments	Logistics Competence	Tracking and Tracing	Timeliness
Singapore	4.09	4.02	4.22	3.86	4.12	4.15	4.23
Malaysia	3.44	3.11	3.5	3.5	3.34	3.32	3.86
Thailand	3.29	3.02	3.16	3.27	3.16	3.41	3.73
Philippines	3.14	2.67	2.57	3.4	2.95	3.29	3.83
Vietnam	2.96	2.68	2.56	3.04	2.89	3.1	3.44
Indonesia	2.76	2.43	2.54	2.82	2.47	2.77	3.46
East Asia and Pacific (regional average)	2.73	2.41	2.46	2.79	2.58	2.74	3.33
Lao PDR	2.46	2.17	1.95	2.7	2.14	2.45	3.23
Cambodia	2.37	2.28	2.12	2.19	2.29	2.5	2.84
Myanmar	**2.33**	**1.94**	**1.92**	**2.37**	**2.01**	**2.36**	**3.29**

Legend: LPI = Logistic Performance Index rank.
Source: World Bank Logistics Performance Index 2010.

last (after Cambodia) in implementing the ASEAN agreements on trade facilitation.[16] The situation is similar for Myanmar's performance in lowering technical barriers in standards and conformity assessments, and in technical regulations.

Some of the main challenges to overcome are:

(a) *awareness* (and dissemination) of existing, new and revised laws;
(b) *coordination* among line ministries for implementation; and
(c) *capacity* to implement harmonization requirements for the MPAC's institutional connectivity component. (For example, Myanmar is required to implement self-certification for Form D certificates of origin, in customs harmonization.)

These challenges are also true for facilitating implementation and coordination of services liberalization in Myanmar. Services data collection in Myanmar is still difficult, especially in terms of the value of services. This requires inter-departmental coordination.

An encouraging development is the undertaking by the Ministry of Commerce to establish a "good data system".[17] This commitment needs to be translated into action.

VI. Myanmar and ASEAN Connectivity

Discussions on regional connectivity cannot ignore the importance of sea linkages in ASEAN and of building logisitics capacity for these linkages. The Dawei Deep Sea Port project in southern Myanmar (with investment from Thailand and Japan), and the Thilawa Port Project in Yangon (with Japan as the main investor) present considerable potential for the connectivity choices of the Mekong riparian states with ASEAN.

Myanmar is currently one of the least connected countries in ASEAN. The question that arises is whether connectivity via the MPAC with other ASEAN members and large neighbours such as India and China can further enhance economic reforms in the country.

Analysts note that "soft infrastructure" or the widespread capacity to implement the reforms is the most important requirement for speeding up the reforms in line with the MPAC objectives. Yet, investment in "hard infrastructure" is equally necessary to bridge the "missing links" for Myanmar's participation/involvement in infrastructure projects such as the ASEAN Highway Network and the Singapore-Kunming Rail Link, and the gaps in communications and internet technology. Myanmar's strength may lie in boosting capacities to facilitate people-to-people connectivity, particularly in the tourism sector. With the country's opening up, many visitors — business and tourists alike — are flocking to Myanmar to observe the changes at first hand. The country's hospitality industry is currently facing severe constraints in both room and service capacity. At the same time, Myanmar is developing new tourism regulations, in the renewed efforts to develop the tourism sector and attract more visitors. Success stories in the region are being studied with interest, for example, Cambodia's pro-poor, community-based eco-tourism model, and community-involvement in preventing child sex tourism. Nevertheless, considerable challenges remain for Myanmar's tourism and hospitality industry to take off, including lack of human resources and expertise; lack of cross-sectoral strategic planning and coordination as well as with external (intraregional and international) partners; and the need to engender awareness of, and commitment to, enforcement of responsible tourism.

The challenges and concerns highlighted thus far form part of a long laundry list for a country that has remained an agrarian economy since independence in 1948, through the failed years of the "Burmese way to Socialism" and the lost years under military rule. Still, starting from a low base, one can argue that the only direction for Myanmar to go is upwards. Myanmar is confronted with an embarrassment of choices in the array of policy and growth models or the choice of combinations thereof. But Myanmar's ultimate success in securing a progressive and prosperous future for its people will depend on the ability to overcome these key challenges in pursuing economic and social reforms. Myanmar is currently formulating a development policy appropriate for the country's specific situation. An important consideration for the reform process itself is to progress reforms at a pace that the Myanmar people can absorb and adapt to.

Key stakeholders in the economic reforms have observed that public-private partnerships (PPP) would help overcome some of the more challenging bottlenecks. PPP is seen by many as the keystone in speeding up connectivity, but how this will be carried out if the national context continues to be a subject of debate. It is important to ensure that the partnerships are equal, and to ensure the accountability of all concerned.

Myanmar will need to develop a PPP policy framework that clarifies roles and responsibilities, as well as risks.

VII. The Way Forward: Some Recommendations

Thant Myint-U, the well-known historian on Myanmar, in his book "Where China Meets India" presents a potential best case scenario where Myanmar will emerge from her former isolation, with balanced development, cognisant of the need for environmental protection, and social mobility, all of which will assist Myanmar on the road to democratic governance. Assuming this optimum scenario, policy-makers in Myanmar will need to consider the following:

(i)   *Bringing about a more equitable distribution of wealth and social protection.* It is tempting to push this concern to the back seat in the current impetus of generating economic growth. However, Myanmar has been witness to, and now has the opportunity to learn from numerous examples of pursuing growth at all costs around the globe. It is interesting that Myanmar has put poverty alleviation prominently on the national agenda for the first time in decades (poverty was hitherto hidden under the rubric of "border area development"), and as part of economic reform efforts.

(ii) *Balancing economic growth with environmental protection and resource conservation.* This is to ensure sustainability of economic growth and preservation of a conducive living environment for her citizens. Myanmar — with her rich resources — has much to offer to the region and beyond. But exploitation of these resources needs to be properly managed.

(iii) *Finding a useful role for Myanmar in ASEAN,* beyond the responsibilities of hosting and chairing ASEAN Summits. Myanmar is still largely preoccupied with domestic issues and concerns during its transition phase. While in the past, national security concerns overrode proactiveness in relations with neighbours, and the country's position in ASEAN and other regional architecture, Myanmar's foreign policy will now need to integrate economic, environmental and social priorities. Myanmar's assumption of the ASEAN chairmanship in 2014 should thus identify forward-looking priorities for ASEAN community-building to focus on beyond the 2015 goals for regional integration.

Workable options to address these concerns may include:

(a) Establishing a coordinating mechanism for accessing information and coordinating work across the different sectors involved in AEC implementation, as well as developing workable PPP models for priority projects. The Task Force should ideally comprise tripartite representation from government, business and academia. Currently, the Ministry of National Planning and Economic Development (MNPED) involves representatives of the Union of Myanmar Chamber of Commerce and Industry in the various committees and sub-committees monitoring AEC implementation at national level.

(b) Interpreting and contextualizing the ASEAN documents and instruments. This can be done through a series of national workshops, including explanations of implications for businesses and firms. Similarly, awarenesss-raising activities on AEC documents and commitments need to be conducted for all stakeholders, including policy-makers and the media.

VIII. Conclusion

There are certain expectations that fuel the sense of optimism by those participating in the reform process. The first is that the reforms will be successful, with conditions conducive to reforms prevailing. The second is that both President Thein Sein and Daw Aung San Suu Kyi have put into place succession plans to ensure that their successors can continue along the trajectory of change (and are committed to doing so). A third is that the key stakeholders of the reforms — the parliament, the military and the polity — are all supportive of the reforms and play their expected roles.

Underpinning these expectations is the optimism in the measure of Myanmar's governance capacity going forward. According to the WB governance indicators project that monitors governance in countries of the world, Myanmar has consistently ranked in the lowest percentile.[18] Table 10.4 compares the governance indicators from selected years. Although there is slight improvement overall compared to the situation

TABLE 10.4

Myanmar's Performance in the World Governance Index

Governance Indicator	Sources	Year	Percentile Rank (0–100)	Governance Score (–2.5 to +2.5)	Standard Error
Voice and Accountability	9	2011	2.3	–1.86	0.12
	8	2006	0.5	–2.22	0.15
	7	2002	1.0	–2.02	0.17
Political Stability/Absence of Violence	5	2011	13.7	–1.16	0.27
	5	2006	20.2	–0.89	0.28
	4	2002	11.5	–1.49	0.31
Government Effectiveness	6	2011	2.4	–1.64	0.24
	6	2006	3.9	–1.51	0.24
	4	2002	7.3	–1.31	0.20
Regulatory Quality	6	2011	1.4	–2.13	0.21
	6	2006	1.0	–2.23	0.21
	5	2002	0.5	–2.08	0.23
Rule of Law	10	2011	4.2	–1.42	0.17
	9	2006	4.3	–1.47	0.20
	7	2002	2.4	–1.63	0.20
Control of Corruption	6	2011	0.5	–1.69	0.20
	5	2006	0.5	–1.73	0.23
	3	2002	4.4	–1.21	0.20

10th–25th Percentile
0th–10th Percentile

Source: Kaufmann D., A. Kraay, and M. Mastruzzi (2010), "The Worldwide Governance Indicators: Methodology and Analytical Issues".

ten years ago, Myanmar's ranking is still largely confined to the lower percentiles.

Despite the heady atmosphere of change in the country, the present reality is that internal processes of government decision-making remain mostly the same. The institutional framework and regulatory structures are yet to be established in order to entrench the ongoing reforms.

Additionally, the capacity — among the bureaucrats — to manage transition still remains thin, with the bureaucracy riddled by red tape. Additionally, the reforms have a strong urban bias. While this bodes well for developing the major urban agglomerations of Yangon and Mandalay, including their periphery areas and chains of supply from secondary cities and towns, as "engines of development", the socio-economic conditions in the rural areas have remained largely unchanged over the past three decades. Urban development may also bring with it unwelcome challenges such as urban pollution, congestion and housing/settlement issues,[19] as well as the inevitable migration concerns — both internal and cross-border — as people seek to better their living and working conditions.

In the face of these formidable challenges, Myanmar is forging ahead with reforms and democratic transition. Capitalism is inevitable for Myanmar. The question that Myanmar and all those concerned for the country's future should ask is "what kind of capitalism?" Different forms of capitalism impact a country's development in profoundly different ways. Myanmar needs to adapt "best fit"[20] solutions for local conditions in the country today. The national development strategy holistically addresses employment generation, educational standards (including technical education), poverty alleviation and sustainable development. The latter, which requires reconciling economic development with social and environmental needs, challenges not just Myanmar but the world at large. Myanmar, in opening up to the world through her reforms, can possibly add another model of growth and development to the existing array: a compassionate form of capitalism that puts her people at the core.

Myanmar's work has just begun.

NOTES

1. Then ASEAN Secretary-General Dato Ajit Singh had shared this with Myanmar's Ministers for Foreign Affairs and for National Planning and Economic Development during consultations in November 1996.

2. For details see the Strategic Schedule in the ASEAN Economic Community Blueprint, published by the ASEAN Secretariat in 2008, <http://www.asean.org/archive/5187-10.pdf>.

3. Philippine Star, "Myanmar hopes ASEAN master plan reach win-win solution within region", <http://www.philstar.com> (updated 8 August 2010).

4. It also paid tribute to the "sound foundations" laid by the State Peace and Development Council (SPDC), referring to the role of the Tatmadaw "saving the country" from "deteriorating conditions" at several points in the country's history.

5. Hank Lim, "Myanmar Economy in the Context of ASEAN Integration and Regional Change", IDE-Jetro's Policy Review Series on Myanmar Economy, June 2012.

6. The AEC Blueprints identifies four components or pillars, each listing priority measures to be completed by stated deadlines. The pillars are: (a) single market and production base, (b) economic competitiveness, (c) equitable economic development, and (d) integration into the global economy.

7. This section is based on an intervention made by former ASEAN Secretary-General Rodolfo Severino, speaking at a workshop on Myanmar and the AEC, held in Yangon in October 2011.

8. These challenges were highlighted by Dr Myint, the chief presidential economic advisor, and chief of the Myanmar Development Resource Institute (MDRI), in his Keynote address to the above-mentioned workshop.

9. Aye Thidar Kyaw, "Myanmar's Business Community Ponders the Future as Foreign Investment Law Enacted", *Myanmar Times*, 12 November 2012, <http://www.mmtimes.com/index.php/business/3043-business-community-ponders-the-future-as-investment-law-enacted.html>.

10. Statement by U.S. Secretary of State Hillary Clinton, "Recognizing and Supporting Burma's Reforms", 4 April 2012, <http://www.state.gov/secretary/rm/2012/04/187439.htm>.

11. Fried Frank Harris Shriver and Jacobson LLP, Mario Mancuso, J.R. Kraemer and Robert P. Mollen, "U.S. eases economic sanctions against Burma, opens door to U.S. financial services and investment", 13 July 2012, <http://www.lexology.com/library/detail.aspx?g=22c2d87d-9b55-49e3-8417-413aca0c86ac > (accessed 2 August 2012).

12. "Japan to Forgive Myanmar Debt to Support Reforms", Associated Press article in the *New York Times*, 21 April 2012, <http://www.nytimes.com/2012/04/22/world/asia/japan-to-forgive-myanmar-debt-to-speed-development.html?_r=1>.

13. Sandar Lwin, "Farmland law should be amended: committee", *Myanmar Times*, vol. 32, no. 632, 25 June–1 July 2012, <http://www.mmtimes.com/2012/news/632/news63201.html>.

14. It was adopted by the 14th ASEAN Summit on 26 February 2009.
15. AEC Scorecard Phase II Report.
16. The agreements for trade facilitation are: the ASEAN Framework Agreement on Facilitation of Goods in Transit (AFAFGIT), the ASEAN Framework Agreement on Facilitation of Inter-State Transport (AFAFIST) and the ASEAN Framework Agreement on Multimodal Transport (AFAMT).
17. Update provided by Dr Sandar Oo, Head of the Department of Management Studies, Yangon Institute of Economics.
18. See the World Bank's Worldwide Governance Index at <http://info.worldbank.org/governance/wgi/index.asp>. The Index assesses governance capacity of countries through six dimensions of governance: voice and accountability, political stability, government effectiveness, regulatory quality, rule of law and control of corruption. The World Governance Indicators (WGI) project started in 1996 and was recently updated in November 2011. It should be noted that the WGI are a research dataset summarizing the views on the quality of governance provided by a large number of enterprise, citizen and expert survey respondents in industrial and developing countries. These data are gathered from a number of survey institutes, think-tanks, non-governmental organizations, international organizations, and private sector firms. The World Bank has emphasized that the WGI do not reflect the official views of the World Bank, its Executive Directors, or the countries they represent, and that the WGI are not used by the World Bank Group to allocate resources.
19. Myaungmya Aung Myint Myat, "Myanmar's new political and economic contours", *New Mandala*, 2 July 2012, <http://asiapacific.anu.edu.au/newmandala/2012/07/02/myanmar%E2%80%99s-new-political-contours/> (accessed 9 July 2012).
20. U. Soe Thane, the Chairman of the Myanmar Investment Commission and Minister in the President's Office, uses "best fit" instead of "best practice" in describing Myanmar's need to adapt recommendations and solutions of other countries' successes to current realities in Myanmar today.

REFERENCES

"ASEAN Economic Community Blueprint". ASEAN Secretariat 2008. <http://www.asean.org/archive/5187-10.pdf>.
Aye Thidar Kyaw. "Myanmar's Business Community Ponders the Future as Foreign Investment Law Enacted". *Myanmar Times*, 12 November 2012. <http://www.mmtimes.com/index.php/business/3043-business-community-ponders-the-future-as-investment-law-enacted.html>.

Clinton, Hillary. "Recognizing and Supporting Burma's Reforms", 4 April 2012. <http://www.state.gov/secretary/rm/2012/04/187439.htm>.

"Japan to Forgive Myanmar Debt to Support Reforms". Associated Press article in the *New York Times*, 21 April 2012. <http://www.nytimes.com/2012/04/22/world/asia/japan-to-forgive-myanmar-debt-to-speed-development.html?_r=1>.

Lim, Hank. "Myanmar Economy in the Context of ASEAN Integration and Regional Change". IDE-Jetro's Policy Review Series on Myanmar Economy, June 2012.

Lwin, Sandar. "Farmland Law Should Be Amended: Committee". *Myanmar Times*, vol. 32, no. 632 (25 June–1 July 2012). <http://www.mmtimes.com/2012/news/632/news63201.html>.

Myaungmya Aung Myint Myat. "Myanmar's New Political and Economic Contours". *New Mandala*, 2 July 2012. <http://asiapacific.anu.edu.au/newmandala/2012/07/02/myanmar%E2%80%99s-new-political-contours/> (accessed 9 July 2012).

Philippine Star. "Myanmar Hopes ASEAN Master Plan Reach Win-win Solution within Region". <www.philstar.com> (updated 8 August 2010).

Shriver, Fried Frank Harris & Jacobson LLP, Mario Mancuso, J.R. Kraemer, and Robert P. Mollen. "U.S. Eases Economic Sanctions Against Burma, Opens Door to U.S. Financial Services and Investment", 13 July 2012. <http://www.lexology.com/library/detail.aspx?g=22c2d87d-9b55-49e3-8417-413aca0c86ac> (accessed 2 August 2012).

INDEX